THE CRAFT OF POLITICAL RESEARCH

Sixth Edition

W. Phillips Shively

University of Minnesota

PEARSON

Prentice Hall

Upper Saddle River, NJ 07458

Library of Congress Cataloging-in-Publication Data

Shively, W. Phillips
    The craft of political research / W. Phillips Shively.—6th ed.
      p. cm.
    Includes bibliographical references (p.) and index.
    ISBN 0-13-117440-1
    1. Political science—Methodology.   2. Political science—Research.   I. Title.

  JA71.S45   2004
  320'.072—dc22

                                                2004011226

Editorial Director: Charlyce Jones-Owen
Acquisitions Editor: Glenn Johnston
Assistant Editor: John Ragozzine
Editorial Assistant: Suzanne Remore
Production Liaison: Joanne Hakim
Marketing Manager: Kara Kindstrom
Marketing Assistant: Jennifer Lang
Manufacturing Buyer: Sherry Lewis
Cover Art Director: Jayne Conte
Cover Design: Bruce Kenselaar
Composition/Full-Service Project Management: Linda Duarte/Pine Tree Composition
Printer/Binder: The Courier Companies

Pearson Education LTD., London
Pearson Education Singapore, Pte. Ltd
Pearson Education, Canada, Ltd
Pearson Education–Japan
Pearson Education Australia PTY, Limited

Pearson Education North Asia Ltd
Pearson Educación de Mexico, S.A. de C.V.
Pearson Education Malaysia, Pte. Ltd
Pearson Education, Upper Saddle River, New Jersey

10 9 8 7 6 5 4 3 2 1
ISBN 0-13-117440-1

THE CRAFT
OF POLITICAL
RESEARCH

TO BARBARA

Contents

Preface

I wrote this little book in 1970, when I was an assistant professor at Yale University. In teaching a number of sections of Introduction to Research to undergraduates there, I had found that the students benefited from an introduction that emphasized the internal logic of research methods and the collective, cooperative nature of the research process. I could not find a book that presented things in this way at a sufficiently elementary level to be readily accessible by undergraduates. And so I wrote this book.

It has followed me through the rest of my career so far, and has given me enormous pleasure. It has always seemed to me that it fills a needed niche, and it has been a thrill when students have told me that they have benefited from it. I am pleased that it still seems to be working for them.

While the general principles of good argument and investigation don't change, I have made a number of additions and deletions over the last couple of editions to reflect new possibilities in technique. In this sixth edition, most importantly, I have added a new chapter on selecting observations, which deals with sampling, with the problem of censored data, and with the problem of selection on the dependent variable. I have also added a number of new examples, including data from the 2002 election; an example from Przeworski, Alvarez, Cheibub, and Longi, *Democracy and Development*; an example on collective action and burden sharing in defensive alliances; and others. I have spruced up the chapter on the logic of hypothesis testing to make the text clearer, and I have made numerous small revisions throughout.

I must also admit to a change of heart (or, perhaps, a return to old love.) Regular users of this text may recall that a couple of editions ago, under prodding from reviewers, I changed my example of elegant research from Philip Converse's "Of Time and Partisan Stability" to Robert Putnam's *Making Democracy Work*. Putnam's book and the resultant research program on social capital are of course splendid, but I always regretted sacrificing Converse's article. It is still the most beautiful piece of political science research I know. And so I return in this edition to "Of Time and Partisan Stability," and include with it the same explication of Markov chains that I used in those earlier editions.

As you can no doubt tell from the tone of this preface, this is a book for which I have great affection. I hope you will enjoy it as much as I have enjoyed it.

ACKNOWLEDGMENTS

Thanks to the reviewers of this edition, Harvey D. Palmer, University of Mississippi; Nathaniel Beck, New York University; Kristian Skrede Gleditsch, University of California-San Diego; and Ray Christensen, Brigham Young University.

W. Phillips Shively

THE CRAFT
OF POLITICAL
RESEARCH

Chapter 1

Doing Research

Scholarly research is exciting and is fun to do. Some students, caught in the grind of daily and term assignments, may not see it this way. But for people who can carry on research in a more relaxed way, for professors or for students who can involve themselves in a long-range project, research may be a source of fascination and great satisfaction.

> Francis's preoccupation with DNA quickly became full-time. The first afternoon following the discovery that A–T and G–C base pairs had similar shapes, he went back to his thesis measurements, but his effort was ineffectual. Constantly he would pop up from his chair, worriedly look at the cardboard models, fiddle with other combinations, and then, the period of momentary uncertainty over, look satisfied and tell me how important our work was. I enjoyed Francis's words, even though they lacked the casual sense of understatement known to be the correct way to behave in Cambridge. (Watson, 1968, p. 198)*

This is the way James D. Watson describes his and Francis Crick's search for the structure of the DNA molecule. *The Double Helix,* his account of their work, gives a good picture of the excitement of research. It is more gripping than most mystery novels.

Although research can be exciting in this way, the sad fact is that writing papers for courses is too often something of a drag. First of all, course papers are tied to all sorts of rewards and punishments—your future earnings, the approval of others, and so on. All of the anxiety associated with these vulnerabilities comes, indirectly, to lodge on the paper. Yet this is probably the lesser cause for frustration in student

---

*Reprinted with permission from Watson, James D. *The Double Helix* (New York: Atheneum, 1968).

research. After all, each of these anxieties also may be present for professional scholars. A more important reason for the student's lack of enthusiasm is the simple fact that a paper is generally regarded, by both teacher and student, as a practice run, going through the motions of scholarship. Usually, not enough time is allowed for the student to think long and seriously about the subject, especially with other papers competing for attention. And even when adequate time is allowed, there usually is a feeling on both sides that this is "just a student paper"—that it doesn't really matter how good it is, that a student will learn from doing the thing wrong. Students must have the chance to learn from their own mistakes, but this attitude toward the work cheats them of the pleasure and excitement that research can bring, of the feeling of creating something that no one ever saw before.

There is probably no way out of this dilemma. In a book such as this, I cannot give you the drama and excitement of original research. I can only give my own testimony, as one for whom research is very exciting. But I can introduce you to some selected problems you should be aware of if you want to do good research yourself or to evaluate the work of others. I also hope to make you aware of what a challenging game it can be, and of how important inventiveness, originality, and boldness are to good research.

SOCIAL RESEARCH

Social research is an attempt by social scientists to develop and sharpen theories that give us a handle on the universe. Reality unrefined by theory is too chaotic for us to absorb. Some people vote and others do not; in some elections there are major shifts, in others there are not; some bills are passed by Congress, others are not; economic development programs succeed in some countries, but fail in others; sometimes war comes, sometimes it does not. To have any hope of controlling what happens, we must understand why these things happen. And to have any hope of understanding why they happen, we must simplify our perceptions of reality.

Social scientists carry out this simplification by developing theories. A theory takes a set of similar things that happen—say, the development of party systems in democracies—and finds a common pattern among them that allows us to treat each of these different occurrences as a repeated example of the same thing. Instead of having to think about a large number of disparate happenings, we need only think of a single pattern with some variations.

For example, in his book on political parties, Maurice Duverger was concerned with the question of why some countries develop two-party systems and others develop multiparty systems (1963, pp. 206–280). The initial reality was chaotic; scores of countries were involved, with varying numbers and types of parties present at different times in their histories. Duverger devised the theory that (1) if social conflicts overlap, and (2) if the electoral system of the country does not penalize small parties, the country will develop a multiparty system; otherwise, the country will develop a two-party system.

His idea was that where there is more than one sort of political conflict going on simultaneously in a country, and where the groups of people involved in these conflicts overlap, there will be more than two distinct political positions in the country. For example, a conflict between workers and the middle class might occur at the same time as a conflict between Catholics and non-Catholics. Then, if these groups overlapped so that some of the Catholics were workers and some were middle class, while some of the non-Catholics were workers and some were middle class, there would be four distinct political positions in the country: the Catholic worker position, the non-Catholic worker position, the Catholic middle-class position, and the non-Catholic middle-class position. The appropriate number of parties would then tend to arise, with one party corresponding to each distinct position.

However, Duverger thought that this tendency could be short circuited if the electoral system were set up in such a way as to penalize small parties—by requiring that a candidate have a majority, rather than a plurality, of votes in a district, for instance. This requirement would force some of the distinct groups to compromise their positions and merge into larger parties that would have a better chance of winning elections. Such a process of consolidation logically would culminate in a two-party system. To summarize the theory: A country will develop a two-party system (1) if there are only two distinct political positions in the country, or (2) if despite the presence of more than two distinct political positions, the electoral law forces people of diverse positions to consolidate into two large political parties so as to gain an electoral advantage.

Having formulated this theory, Duverger no longer had to concern himself simultaneously with a great number of idiosyncratic party systems. He needed to think only about a single developmental process, of which all those party systems were examples.

Something is always lost when we simplify reality in this way. By restricting his attention to the number of parties competing in the system, for example, Duverger had to forget about many other potentially interesting things, such as whether any one of the parties was revolutionary, or how many of the parties had any chance of getting a majority of the votes.

Note, too, that Duverger restricted himself in more than just his choice of a theme; in addition, he chose deliberately to play down exceptions to his theory, although these exceptions might have provided interesting additional information. Suppose, for instance, that a country for which his theory had predicted a two-party system developed a multiparty system instead. Why was this so? Duverger might have cast around to find an explanation for the exception to his theory, and that explanation could then have been incorporated into the original theory to produce a larger theory. Instead, when faced with exceptions such as these, he chose to accept them as accidents. It was necessary for him to do this in order to keep the theory simple and to the point. Otherwise, it might have grown as complex as the reality that it sought to simplify.

As you can see, there are costs in setting up a theory. Because the theory simplifies reality for us, it also generally requires that we both narrow the range of reality we look at and oversimplify even the portion of reality that falls within that narrowed range. As theorists, we always have to strike a balance between the simplicity of a theory and the number of exceptions we are willing to tolerate. We do not really have any choice. Without theories, we are faced with the unreadable chaos of reality.

Actually, what social scientists do in developing theories is not different from what we normally do every day in *perceiving,* or interpreting, our environment. Social scientists merely interpret reality in a more systematic and explicit way. Without theories, students of society are trapped. They are reduced to merely observing events, without comment. Imagine a physicist—or a fruit picker for that matter— operating in the absence of theory. All she could do if she saw an apple falling from a tree would be to duck, and she would not even know which way to move.

Social theory, then, is the sum total of all those theories developed by social scientists to explain human behavior. Political theory, a subset of social theory, consists of all theories that have been developed to explain *political* behavior.

Types of Political Research

The way a particular political scientist conducts research will depend both on the uses that she visualizes for the project and on the way she marshals evidence. Research may be classified according to these two criteria.

The two main ways by which to distinguish one piece of research from another are:

1. Research may be directed toward providing the answer to a particular problem, or it may be carried on largely for its own sake, to add to our general understanding of politics. This distinction, based on the *uses for which research is designed,* may be thought of as applied versus basic research.
2. Research may also be intended primarily to discover new facts, or it may be intended to provide new ways of looking at old facts. Thus, political research can be characterized by the *extent to which it seeks to provide new factual information* (empirical versus nonempirical).

A glance at Table 1–1 shows us the four types of political research based on different combinations of these two dimensions. *Normative philosophy* consists of argument about *what should be* in politics. Probably the oldest form of political research, it includes among its practitioners Plato, Karl Marx, Ayn Rand, Paul Krugman, George Will, and others. It is applied research; that is, its goal is problem solving. This means that it is not intended so much to develop political theory as to

TABLE 1–1   Types of Political Research

	Applied	Recreational
Nonempirical	Normative philosophy	Formal theory
Empirical	Engineering research	Theory-oriented research

use what political theory tells us about society and politics as a basis for making political decisions. It is also nonempirical in that it does not consist primarily of investigating matters of fact. It typically takes certain political facts as given and combines them with moral arguments to prescribe political action. A good example is John Stuart Mill's argument in "Considerations on Representative Government," in which he urges the adoption of democratic representative government because (1) the chief end of government should be to facilitate the development in each citizen of his full potential (moral argument), and (2) democratic government, by giving the people responsibility, will do this (factual assumption).

Like normative philosophy, *engineering research* is geared to solving problems. However, its stance is empirical; it is concerned with ascertaining the facts needed to solve political problems. Some examples would be measuring the effects of various reapportionment methods, trying to design a diplomatic strategy to effect disarmament procedures, and designing methods of riot control.

These two forms of applied research exist in some estrangement from academic political science. Political engineering is a thriving industry and many courses relevant to it are taught in political science departments, but research in it is often relegated to a separate institute or "school of public policy." Normative philosophy is taught extensively, and research is carried on under that name, but generally this means the *history* of normative philosophy and its development, not the active formulation of normative arguments. For both forms of applied research, we must look largely outside academic life to such sources as the RAND Corporation and the *New York Review of Books.*

At the other end of the continuum from applied research is recreational research. It is usually called "pure" or "basic" research, but this carries the unpleasant implication that applied research is either impure or of limited value. The choice of the term "recreational" to describe this type of research is really not as flippant as it might seem, for this is research carried on for its own sake, to improve political theory. Political scientists pursue this type of research for the twin pleasures of exercising their minds and increasing their understanding of things. In a high sense of the word, it is "recreation."

Formal theory, largely a post–World War II phenomenon, is the most recently introduced form of political research. Like normative philosophers, formal theorists posit certain facts about politics; but in contrast to normative philosophers, they posit facts as empirical conditions rather than as the foundation for moral arguments. And they distinctively operate by deriving further implications of the posited conditions by precise logical and mathematical operations. Their concern is to take the posited facts, or assumptions, and derive theories from them. Their end goal is to develop reasonably broad and general theories based on a small number of agreed-upon assumptions.

A good example of formal theory—indeed, a work by which many would date the emergence of formal theory as a distinct field in political science—is Anthony Downs's *An Economic Theory of Democracy* (1957). Downs builds a wide-ranging theory from a set of assumptions that include, for example: (1) voters and parties behave rationally; (2) political conflict occurs on only one issue at a time; and

(3) political events are not perfectly predictable. Some of the predictions generated from his theory are (1) in a two-party system, parties will tend to agree very closely on issues, whereas in a multiparty system, they will not; (2) it may be rational for the voter to remain uninformed; and (3) democratic governments tend to redistribute income. (Of course, one must recognize that excerpts such as these do even more than the usual violence to a rich net of theories.) It is important to emphasize that this sort of work is almost solely an exercise in deduction. All of the conclusions derive logically from a limited set of explicit assumptions. Downs's purpose in this is simply to see where the assumptions he started with will lead him. Presumably, if the assumptions produced an untenable result, he would go back and reexamine them.

The main use of formal theory, as in the example above, is explanation; the formal theory is used to construct a set of conditions from which the thing we wish to explain would have logically flowed. Such explanatory formal theories are then often tested empirically through theory-oriented research. But because formal theory consists of taking a set of assumptions and working out where they lead—that is, what they logically imply—it is also useful for developing and analyzing strategies for political action. That is, we can use formal theory to construct analyses of the form: If we want to achieve *X,* can we devise a set of reasonably true assumptions and an action which, in the context of those assumptions, will logically lead to *X?* Formal theory is used in this way, for example, to argue for various ways to set up elections; or for various ways to arrange taxes so as to get the outcomes we want. Flat-tax proposals are a good example: They originated in argument of the following form: (a) If we want to maximize investment and economic growth, and (b) if we assume that governmental investment is inefficient and that individual taxpayers act so as to maximize their income, then (c) can we deduce what sort of taxes in the context of the assumptions of (b) would best achieve (a)?

Like normative philosophy, formal theory interacts with empirical research. Formal theorists usually try to start with assumptions that are in accord with existing knowledge about politics, and at the end they may compare their final models with this body of knowledge. But they are not themselves concerned with turning up new factual information.

Good work in formal theory will take a set of seemingly reasonable assumptions and will show by logical deduction that those assumptions lead inescapably to conclusions that surprise the reader. The reader must then either accept the surprising conclusion or reexamine the assumptions that had seemed plausible. Thus, formal theory provides insights by logical argument, not by a direct examination of political facts.

Following from Downs, a great deal of formal theory in political science has based itself on the economists' core assumption of *rational choice:* the assumption that individuals choose their actions in order to maximize some valued object, and minimize the cost expended in achieving it. (In economics the valued object is generally taken to be money; in political science it may be money—as in theories of why and how communities seek pork-barrel spending—but theories may also posit that the valued object is a nonmonetary policy such as abortion, or political power itself. Sometimes the object may even be left unspecified in the theory.)

A good example of formal theory that illustrates the rational choice assumption is Mancur Olson's *The Logic of Collective Action* (1965). The rational choice assumption pointed Olson to a question no one had asked before, and allowed him to stand received wisdom on its head. Olson wrote on the very basic question of political organization in society. Before his book, scholars had assumed that when interests existed in society—racial minorities, businesses, professions, groups with special concerns such as historic preservation—political organizations could be expected to emerge naturally to represent those interests.[1] We should thus expect to see a wide range of parties and interest groups engaged in politics. A whole school of political science, the *pluralist school*, was organized around the expectation that most of the time, most of society's interests would be actively organized.

Based on the rational choice assumption, however, Olson reasoned that there was nothing natural about organization at all. From the standpoint of any individual in a group with a shared object, he concluded, participation in the group is usually nonrational. Remember that the rational choice assumption states that individuals choose their actions in order to maximize a valued object, while minimizing the cost expended in achieving it. If I am a person concerned with historic preservation, I know that unless I have very unusual resources, my individual contribution to an interest group pursuing preservation will not make a measurable difference. Let us say there are 300,000 people around the country who share my interest; if each of us contributes $100 to the cause, the difference if I do or do not contribute is a budget of $29,999,900 versus $30,000,000. To the organization this amount would be trivially small, but to me $100 makes a real difference. If I contribute, I will have expended a significant cost without getting any more of my valued good, which is not rational. What is rational, instead, is to be a *free rider*, and let all those other people make the contributions. However, Olson pointed out, since every potential member of such an organization is in this same situation, the marvel should be that any interest organizations exist at all.

Olson laid out several conditions under which organizations might nonetheless arise. One such condition is that one potential member might have such large resources that she knows no organization is possible without her participation. The largest department store in town, for instance, knows that a Downtown Merchants' Association cannot function if it does not join and contribute. The Bijoux Tee-Shirt Shop on the corner, though, is not in that situation. Under these circumstances, we can count on an organization being set up, because rationally, the large store cannot get its valued good unless it takes the lead in setting up the association.

No theory can ever be all encompassing, and in fact one function of theory may be that it highlights exceptions for closer examination. We know that many people do contribute to political organizations even though, as Olson has proved, it is irrational for them to do so. The virtue of Olson's theory in this case is that instead of viewing such contributions as "natural" and therefore ignoring them, we are forced to treat the contributions as a puzzle requiring further investigation.

---

[1]For example, Duverger (1963) assumed this in the theory I described on pp. 2–3.

However, in a wide array of settings Olson's theory predicts behavior rather well. The excruciating efforts of public television stations to get their viewers to join rather than be free riders ("Please! Only one in ten of our viewers is a member. If you join KXXX-TV today we will send you this beautiful coffee mug!") bears testimony to the power of Olson's logic. In the next chapter you will see that it may also help to explain why small nations typically do not pull their "fair" weight in international alliances.

Although formal theory is the fastest growing type of political research, most research and teaching in political science is still of the fourth type suggested in Table 1–1, *theory-oriented research.* This type of research is concerned with expanding our knowledge of what happens in politics and of why it happens as it does. Like political engineering, it is empirical; it is concerned with discovering facts about politics. But unlike engineering, which deals with facts only for their usefulness in specific political problems, this research deals with them to develop new political theories or to change or confirm old ones. Accordingly, the most important activity in this research is the development of theories linking observed facts about politics. In engineering, facts are sought out if they are needed to solve a problem; here they are sought out if they will be useful in developing theories.

Duverger's study of political parties is an example of theory-oriented research. Another good example is a test by Diehl and Kingston (1987) of the theory that arms buildups lead to military confrontations. They examined changes in military expenditure by major powers from 1816 to 1976 to see whether increases tended to be followed by involvement in war. No matter how they adjusted things—looking for delayed reactions, looking only at "arms races" in which two rivals simultaneously increased their military forces, and so on—they found no relationship. Military engagements were no more or less likely to occur following military buildups than under other circumstances. They concluded by exploring the implications of this finding, one of which is that arms expenditure must therefore be determined more by domestic political considerations than by the international situation.

Research Mix

Practically no research is a *pure* example of any of the types I have presented here. These are abstract distinctions, types of emphasis found in particular pieces of research. Generally, any specific piece of work is a mix of more than one of the types. Although one method will usually predominate, there will almost always be some interaction between the different types in any given work. Two examples may help illustrate this point.

First, let us look a bit more closely at normative philosophy, using Karl Marx's work as an example. Marx's theory of the dialectic is primarily a work in normative philosophy. His argument takes the same general form as that in Mill's essay on representative government: "Because _____ aspects of the human condition today are bad, and because the state and the economy function in _____ ways to produce these bad effects, we should strive to change the state and the economy in _____ ways, which will eliminate the bad effects." But Marx was less willing than Mill simply to *assume* the factual portions of his argument. Instead, he spent years of research trying to work out the precise economic effects of capitalism.

It should be evident that anyone developing normative theories about politics must begin with some factual assumptions. A researcher may be relatively more willing to assume these facts from general experience and/or from the research of others, as Mill was; on the other hand, he may wish, like Marx, to conduct a personal investigation of this factual basis. Such activity will, of course, involve him to some degree in engineering research. It is characteristic of normative philosophy, however, that the researcher need not feel *required* to produce the full factual basis for his argument. In this respect normative philosophy differs from the empirical types of political research.

The distinction is an important one. For one thing, the fact that normative philosophers are not required to provide evidence for all their assumptions leaves them free to devote more energy to other parts of the research task. More important, they often need to assume facts that cannot possibly be tested against reality. The normative philosopher must be free to imagine realities that have never existed before, and these, of course, cannot be "tested." If normative philosophers were held to the same standards of factual evidence as empirical researchers, all utopian dreams would have to be thrown out.

As a second example of the way in which types of research are mixed in any one work, let us look at a case in which researchers working on a primarily engineering project found they had to develop a theory to make sense out of their work. A group of sociologists led by Samuel Stouffer was employed by the Army to study the morale of American soldiers during World War II (Stouffer and others, 1949). Stouffer and his co-workers were puzzled by the fact that often a soldier's morale had little to do with his objective situation.

For instance, MPs were objectively less likely to be promoted than were members of the Army Air Corps. Of Stouffer's sample of MPs, 24 percent were noncommissioned officers, compared with 47 percent of the air corpsmen. Paradoxically, however, the MPs were much more likely than the air corpsmen to think that soldiers with ability had a good chance to advance in the Army. This sort of paradox occurred a number of times in their study, and the researchers felt they had to make some sense of it if their efforts were to help the Army improve morale.

They did this by developing the theory of *relative deprivation* to account for their seemingly contradictory findings. According to this theory, satisfaction with one's condition is not a function of how well-off a person is objectively, but of whether her condition compares favorably or unfavorably with a standard that she perceives as normal.

The fact that so many air corpsmen were NCOs apparently made the corpsmen feel that promotion was the normal thing. Those who were not promoted were disappointed, and those who were promoted did not feel particularly honored. Among the MPs, on the other hand, promotion was sufficiently infrequent that *not* being promoted was seen as the norm. Those who were not promoted were not disappointed, and those who were promoted felt honored. Thus, paradoxically, the air corpsmen, who were more likely to be promoted, felt that chances for promotion in the Army were poor, and the MPs, who were less likely to be promoted, felt that chances for promotion in the Army were good!

I have mentioned these two examples to illustrate my point that most research work involves some mix of the four types of research. Indeed, a mix is so much the usual situation that when I tried to make a rough head count of the frequency of the different types of research in political science journals, I was unable to do so. I was simply unwilling to assign most articles to one or another of the categories. It is just not often the case that a researcher can easily be labeled a normative philosopher, an engineer, a formal theorist, or a theory-oriented empirical researcher. These types interact in the work of every political scientist.

That most research involves a mix of the types does not preclude the importance of the distinctions, however. Generally, one type of research is dominant in any given piece of work, depending on the goals of the researcher. These goals have a lot to do with the way a study should be set up and the criteria according to which it should be judged.

Evaluating Different Types of Research

It is dangerous to set down simple standards for good research. Like any creative work, research should be evaluated subjectively, according to informal and rather flexible criteria. But I will risk suggesting two standards for research that will serve as examples of the way in which the type (or types) of research we are doing dictates the way we should conduct that research.

In the first place, in either form of empirical research, the researcher should be held responsible for *demonstrating the factual basis of his conclusions.* In either form of nonempirical research, this is not necessary, although a normative argument may be made more convincing, or an exercise in formal theory may be made more interesting, by providing evidence for the factual basis on which its assumptions rest.

In the second place, good research of any sort should be *directed to an interesting problem.* But what sort of problem is "interesting" depends largely on the motivation of the study. For either sort of applied research, problems should be chosen which are of real importance for contemporary policy. Today an argument about civil disobedience, for example, makes a more interesting problem in normative theory than an argument about the problem of dynastic succession; a few hundred years ago the reverse would probably have been the case. In other words, applied research should be *relevant,* in the common usage of the word.

Recreational research, on the other hand, requires problems that will have a substantial impact on existing bodies of theory. Many topics that are of considerable importance to an engineer show little promise for theory-oriented research. Similarly, many promising topics for recreational research are not directly relevant. For example, research on the difference between men's and women's voting in Iceland in the 1920s and 1930s would sound absurd from the standpoint of an engineer. But these voting patterns, occurring just after the extension of the vote to women, might be important for theories of how voting patterns become established among new voters. How to choose an interesting problem is one of the most difficult and challenging parts of empirical research. I will discuss this in some detail in Chapter 2.

In general, this book is concerned with empirical research. Within empirical research, I devote somewhat more attention to theory-oriented research than to engineering. There are two reasons for this: (1) It is the more common kind of research in political science, and (2) it poses rather more difficult instructional problems than does engineering.

ETHICS OF POLITICAL RESEARCH

Conducting research is an act by you. You must therefore be concerned about the ethics of your research, just as you are with all of your actions. There are two broad classes of ethical questions regarding our research. First, we must concern ourselves with the *effects on society of what we discover.* For instance, if you study techniques of political persuasion, it is possible that what you learn could be used by a political charlatan to do bad things. A colleague once published a study of the effects of electoral systems on representation, only to learn later that it was used by a military junta in a Latin American country to figure out how to produce a controllable "democracy."

Also, the results of research can be demeaning or dehumanizing. Recent results in psychology suggesting that a wide range of behaviors are genetically controlled go against our prevailing disposition to think of humans as free agents in what they do. Research on racial or ethnic groups is particularly sensitive, as we may fear that innocent research results might reinforce preexisting stereotypes.

Ethical questions of this sort are especially difficult, because the results of our research are so hard to predict. Another colleague, in biology, was upset when he learned that his research on frogs' eyes turned out to have applications in the design of guidance systems for missiles! In the case of demeaning or dehumanizing research, a further problem arises, in that what seems "dehumanizing" to a person depends on what the person thinks "human" means—that is, it is very much a matter of personal beliefs and cultural context. The psychological research noted above may seem wholly appropriate, for instance, depending on one's view of humanness. As another example, the theory of evolution appears dehumanizing to many fundamentalist Christians but does not appear so to many other people.

One response to such difficulties might be to take a "pure science" approach, arguing that because it is so hard to judge the results of knowledge anyway, we should let the chips fall where they may. We should simply seek truth and not worry about its effects. As we will see throughout this book, however, the social scientist rarely deals in unquestioned truths. We work under sufficient difficulties, especially the fact that we usually cannot operate by experimentation (see pp. 86–88), that our results are to some extent a subjective interpretation of reality. We operate within rules of evidence in interpreting reality, so we are constrained in what we can assert and cannot simply pull findings out of a hat; but still our results involve individual choices and judgment by us. We are not simply neutral agents of truth; we must take personal responsibility for the results of our research, difficult though these ethical questions may be.

A second class of questions, more specific than the ones described earlier but not necessarily easier to answer, deals with *our treatment of the people we are studying.* We are responsible to treat the subjects of our study fairly and decently. Particular problems arise in the following ways:

1. *Harm to subjects.* You generally should avoid harming the subjects of your study, either by doing harmful things to them or by withholding good things from them. Is it ethically right, for example, in evaluating the effects of a program to get people off the welfare rolls and into jobs, to withhold the program from some deserving people while administering it to others, in order to see how effective it is?
2. *Embarrassment or psychological stress.* You should avoid shaming people into participating in your study, submitting them to embarrassing situations, and so on.
3. *Imposition.* You are asking your subjects to help you. Don't demand more of them than is reasonable. Public officials may get a hundred questionnaires a year; keep yours short. Dinnertime is a good time to reach people by phone, but it is also an annoying time if you have 15 minutes' worth of questions to ask.
4. *Confidentiality.* Generally, the subjects of your study will wish to have their privacy protected. It is not enough just to withhold publishing their names. Relevant details you include in your report might make it easy to identify the subject (a member of Congress, female, from the South, the senior member of her committee). You should take care to truly mask the subjects who have helped you.
5. *Fooling or misleading the subjects.* As an overall rule, you should make certain that your subjects know exactly what they will be doing and what use you will make of them. As you will see in Chapter 6, the results of your study might well be more valid if the people you study are unaware that they are being studied. However, everyone has the right not to be fooled and not to be used without his or her consent.

The problems I have noted here pose difficult ethical questions of the "ends and means" sort. If research will benefit society but can be conducted only by mistreating subjects, should it be done? There is no clear answer. If the costs to subjects are slight (inconvenience, pain of which they are informed in advance) and the social benefits great, we would generally say yes, it should be done. But what if it puts subjects in danger of death, as may be true of political research that delves into racketeering or corruption?

The one firm rule, for me at least, is that people should never be coerced or tricked into participation and should always be fully informed before they agree to participate. The most horrible historic example of science gone bad is that of the Nazi doctors who killed prisoners by immersing them in ice water to see how long people could survive in freezing water. A painful ethical question today is whether even to use the results of that research, which was purchased at great human pain, but which may potentially help in saving lives and—we hope—will never be available again from any source. Does using the results of the research justify it? If so, perhaps we should destroy the results. But might that not lead to greater human pain for victims of freezing and exposure whom we might have helped?

Chapter 2

Political Theories and Research Topics

In this chapter we look more closely at the nature of political theories and at the factors that enter into deciding to do research on a particular theory. Along the way I will discuss some standards to use in deciding whether a theory is weak or strong.

Although this chapter deals with political theories, you should not assume that it is important only for what I have called theory-oriented research. Indeed, as I pointed out in Chapter 1, the key to solving many engineering problems may be a political theory of some sort. To effect a change in some given phenomenon, you may need to develop a theory that accounts for several factors and allows you to manipulate them to produce the desired change. Much applied research on the problem of enriching the education of underprivileged children, for example, has had to concern itself with developing theories to explain why one child learns things more quickly than another. The Stouffer study, cited in Chapter 1, is another example of an engineering study in which it was necessary to develop a theory. In that case, Stouffer and his collaborators had to explain why MPs had higher morale than air corpsmen. This was necessary if they were to devise ways to raise the morale of Army personnel in general.

On the other hand, many engineering studies do not require that a theory be developed; they simply involve measuring things that need to be measured. Taking the U.S. census is one example of such engineering research. Others include the Gallup Poll, studies measuring the malapportionment of state legislatures, and comparisons of the relative military strength of various countries.

In sum, engineering research may or may not involve the development of political theories; theory-oriented research always does. Theory is a tool in the one type of research; it is an end in itself in the other. But no matter which type of research one is currently engaged in, it is worth taking a closer look at the nature of theory.

CAUSALITY AND POLITICAL THEORY

In the social sciences, theories generally are stated in a causal mode: "If *X* happens, then *Y* will follow as a result." The examples we looked at in Chapter 1 were all of this form. In the Duverger example, *if* a certain configuration of political conflicts exists, and *if* the country adopts a certain electoral law, *then* the number of political parties in the country can be expected to grow or shrink to a certain number. In the Diehl and Kingston study, the authors tested a theory that *if* the country increases its military expenditure, *then* it might be expected to go to war.

A causal theory always includes some phenomenon that is to be explained or accounted for. This is the *dependent variable*. In Duverger's theory, the dependent variable was the number of parties. A causal theory also includes one or more factors that are thought to affect the dependent variable. These are called the *independent variables*. Duverger used two independent variables in his theory: the nature of social conflicts in a country and the country's electoral system.

All of these factors are called "variables" simply because it is the variation of each that makes it of interest to us. If party systems had not varied—that is, if each country had had exactly the same number of parties—there would have been nothing for Duverger to explain. If one or the other of his independent variables had not varied, that factor would have been useless in explaining the dependent variable. For instance, if all countries had had the same electoral system, the variations in party systems that puzzled him could not have been due to differences in the countries' electoral systems, inasmuch as there were no differences.

The dependent variable is so named because *in terms of the particular theory used* it is thought to be the result of other factors (the independent variables). The shape it takes "depends" on the configuration of the other factors. Similarly, the independent variables are thus designated because *in terms of the particular theory,* they are not taken as determined by anything in particular.

The same variable may be an independent variable in one theory and a dependent variable in another. For instance, one theory might use the social status of a person's father (the independent variable) to explain the person's social status (the dependent variable). Another theory might use the person's social status as an *independent* variable to explain something else, perhaps the way the person votes.

Thus, no variable is innately either independent or dependent. Independence and dependence are the two roles a variable may play in a causal theory, not something about the variable itself. It all depends on the theory:

Theory 1:   Democracies do not tend to initiate wars.
Theory 2:   Countries with high per capita incomes are more likely to be democracies than poor countries are.

In theory 1, *democracy* functions as an independent variable; the tendency to wage war depends on whether or not a country is a democracy. In theory 2, *democracy* functions as a dependent variable; whether or not a country is likely to be a democracy depends on its per capita income.

WHAT DOES GOOD THEORY LOOK LIKE?

Three things are important if we are to develop good, effective theories:

1. *Simplicity.* A theory should give us as *simple* a handle on the universe as possible. It should use no more than a few independent variables. It would not be very useful to develop a theory that used 30 variables, in intricate combinations, to explain why people vote the way they do. Such a theory would be about as chaotic and as difficult to absorb as the reality it sought to simplify.
2. *Predictive accuracy.* A theory should make *accurate predictions.* It does not help to have a simple, broad theory which gives predictions that are not much better than one could get by guessing.
3. *Importance.* A theory should be *important.* However, what makes a theory important is different in engineering research than in theory-oriented research, so we shall consider them separately.

In *engineering* research, a theory should address a problem that is currently pressing. This is a subjective judgment, of course, but before you begin your research, you should try to justify your choice of topic, not only to yourself but also to your audience. Your research report should include some discussion of the importance of the problem and of possible applications for your findings. It may seem unnecessary to point this out, but it is an important part of the engineering research project, one that is often carried out sloppily and in an incomplete way. Students have been known, for example, simply to turn in a computer printout as a paper, because "the applications are obvious." True, the *obvious* applications are obvious, but an imaginative researcher who sits down and thinks about it for awhile may be able to point up additional, more varied ways in which the results can be used.

In *theory-oriented* research, the theory should give a handle on as big a portion of the universe as possible; that is, it should apply broadly and generally. It is easy to develop a trivial theory. A theory of the organization of borough presidencies in New York City, for example, might predict quite accurately for that specific situation. But inasmuch as the borough presidents have little power, it would not help us very much to reduce the chaos of New York City politics, let alone the chaos of politics in general.

When we say that a theory should apply "broadly" and "generally," we are referring not only to how large a selection of items from reality the theory deals with, but also to how great a variety of preexisting theories are affected by the new theory. A theory can attain great generality rather economically if it helps to recast older theories, each of which involves its own portion of reality. Thus, a theory of electoral change might take on importance partly from the phenomena it explained directly—changes in people's votes; but it would be a more valuable tool if it could be shown to have significant implications for other areas of social theory—democratic theory, general theories of attitude change, or whatever. In effect, it would perform two simplifying functions: It would not only give us a handle on the rather limited portion of our environment that it sought to explain directly, but it would also shed light on the wider universe dealt with by the other theories.

In the example just cited, a theory to explain the organization of borough presidencies in New York, the theory accrues so little importance directly as to look absurd. But it might be possible, if the borough presidents were taken as examples of some broader concept in urban politics, that the study would borrow importance from this underlying phenomenon. The borough presidencies might, for example, serve as a useful microcosm for studying the workings of patronage.

If a theory can succeed reasonably well at meeting these three criteria—importance, simplicity, and predictive accuracy—it will be useful as a tool for simplifying reality. Such a theory is sometimes described as *elegant*.[1] One difficulty in creating elegant theory is that trying to meet any one of the three basic criteria tends to make it harder to meet the other two. In the example of Duverger's theory, we saw that he might have improved the accuracy of his theory's predictions by bringing in additional explanatory variables; but this would have reduced the simplicity of the theory. Similarly, an attempt to make a theory more general often will cost us something in either the simplicity of the theory or the accuracy of its predictions.

Aside from its utility and simplicity, there is also an element of "beautiful surprise" to elegant research. A piece of research that goes against our expectations, that makes us rethink our world, gives us a special kind of pleasure. Political scientists often jokingly refer to this element as the "interocular subjectivity test" of research—Does it hit us between the eyes?

A good example of research with beautiful surprise is a study of the impact of "get tough" policies against illegal immigration across the United States–Mexican border. In the late 1980s and early 1990s, the U.S. Immigration and Naturalization Service added extra guards and imposed punishments on employers found to be hiring illegal immigrants. One thousand extra border patrol officers were then added each year for several years afterward. Douglas S. Massey and Kristin E. Espinosa (1997) found that since the border crossing had been made tougher, illegal immigrants who originally would have come to the United States for only a few months of seasonal labor now stayed year-round because they knew it would be hard to get back into the United States if they went home to Mexico. The end result was that the number of illegal immigrants present at any given time was increased, not decreased, by the stepped-up enforcement.

It appears to be particularly hard to achieve elegant research in the social sciences, compared with other scientific areas. Human behavior is more complex than the behavior of physical objects—in fact, some think it may perhaps be largely beyond explanation. On the other hand, it may be that human behavior can be understood, but that we have not yet come up with a social theory that could show the true potential of our field. At any rate, it is rare for theory in the social sciences to achieve elegance. If a theory's predictions are reasonably accurate, it is usually because the scope of the theory is restricted or because many of the exceptions to the theory have been absorbed into it as additional variables, making it very complex.[2]

---

[1]The choice of this word typifies the esthetic pleasure—and the vanity—with which researchers approach their work.

[2]Another reason for the difficulty of attaining elegance in social research, of course, is simply that most social science terms are imprecise and ambiguous. This problem is addressed in Chapter 3.

The fact that most social science theory is not very elegant does not mean that it is not good. The real test of a theory's value is whether its subject matter is important and how close it has come to elegance, *given* that subject matter. If it is important to understand humankind's behavior, it is important to try to develop theories about it, even if things do not fall as neatly into place as we would like.

I am always amused when people say of a question that is being made to look more difficult than it really is, "This shouldn't be that hard; what the heck, it's not rocket science"—implying that rocket science is the essence of difficulty and complexity. Not to take away from the difficulty of rocket science, but plotting the trajectory of an object in a vacuum is far simpler than understanding the motivation of a human being. Perhaps one day the old saw will become, "This shouldn't be that hard; what the heck, it's not social science."

Example of Elegant Research: Philip Converse

In his article "Of Time and Partisan Stability" (1969), Philip Converse comes about as close to developing an "elegant" theory as one can commonly do in the social sciences. His study is worth looking at in some detail.

Converse took as his dependent variable the strength of the "party identification" of individuals—their sense that they are supporters of one or another of the political parties. In an earlier study, he and Georges Dupeux had found that, whereas about 75 percent of Americans who were polled identified with some political party, a similar poll conducted in France showed that less than 45 percent of the respondents did so (Converse & Dupeux, 1962). Other studies had shown high levels of party identification in Britain and Norway, and lower levels of party identification in Germany and Italy. Because the overall extent to which citizens of a particular country felt bound to the existing parties seemed likely to have something to do with how stable politics in that country would be, Converse wanted to know why the level of party identification varied as it did from country to country.

At the time of their earlier study, he and Dupeux had found that the difference in percentage of party identifiers between France and the United States seemed to be explained almost wholly by the fact that more Americans than French had some idea of what party their fathers had identified with. As we can see in Table 2–1, within each row there was practically no difference between the French and American levels of party identification. In both countries about 50 percent of those who did not know their father's party expressed identification with some party themselves. About 80 percent of those who *did* know their father's party were political party adherents. Thus, the difference between the two countries was apparently a result of the fact that the Americans knew their father's party so much more frequently than the French did.

TABLE 2–1   Percent Having Same Sort of Party Identification

	France	USA
Know Father's Party	79.4	81.6
Do Not Know Father's Party	47.7	50.7

At the time, Converse and Dupeux accepted this as an interesting finding and did not elaborate on it. But in "Of Time and Partisan Stability," Converse used the earlier finding to suggest a general theory of the process by which countries developed stable patterns of party preference.

In doing so he brought two strands of theory together. First, he reasoned that the difference between France and the United States could be explained easily if the previous generation in France had indeed included very few voters who identified with a party. It could have been, of course, that the difference was due to the fact that the French did not talk to their children about politics as much as the Americans did. But for the purposes of argument, Converse chose to assume that this was not the case. He then showed that if his assumption about the previous generation's low level of party identification were true, one could expect the next generation in France to be much more like the Americans. Also, if the assumption were true, France must be moving toward the level of party identification found in the United States, Britain, and Norway. (This development can be seen in the box, "Markov chains," on p. 19.)

Converse further reasoned that the 80 percent and 50 percent figures might be universally true. (He *knew* only that they held for France and the United States.) If this were so, then both France and the United States might simply be examples of a general process that all countries undergo when their citizens are first given the vote. In the first election, scarcely any voters in a given country would identify with a party, but 50 percent of second generation voters would express identification. Thus, gradually party adherence would reach a stable level. According to this scheme, the relatively low level of party identification in France must have resulted because the vote was extended later and less completely there than in America. (French women, for one thing, were first given the vote in 1945.) Thus, France must be at an earlier stage of the process than America.

The second strand of theory came into play when Converse tied his theory of national development to some older findings on individual voters in the American electorate. Voting studies commonly had shown that within an individual's life span, the older he was the more likely he was to identify strongly with a party. Moreover, this had been shown to be a result of how long he had been exposed to the party by being able to vote for it, rather than of his age itself (see, for example, Campbell et al., 1960, pp. 161–64).

Working from these two angles, Converse developed a simple theory that predicts the strength of a voter's party identification from just two things: (1) the number of years the person has been eligible to vote (which is a dual function of age and how long elections have been held in his/her country); and (2) the likelihood that the individual's father had identified with a party (which in turn depends on what portion of the father's adult life elections were held in which he was eligible to vote). The first of these derived from the earlier research on individual development, the second from his and Dupeux's comparative study of France and the United States. Thus, essentially, party identification is predicted from the individual's age and the length of time that the country has been holding elections.

Markov Chains

Converse's reasoning is based on some cute, simple mathematics that you can play with for yourself. If the rates of transferring identifications are in fact the same in two countries, then even though the countries differ greatly in the level of identification at present, we would expect them to converge rapidly. For example, Converse and Dupeux estimated for France and the United States that about 80 percent of those whose fathers had identified with a party developed an identification of their own, and that, of those whose fathers had not identified with a party, about 50 percent developed an identification of their own. Given these figures, and assuming that party identifiers have the same number of children as nonidentifiers, then if 30 percent of the population of country A presently identify with a party, and 90 percent of the population of country B presently identify with a party, in the next generation we would expect to see

$$(0.8 \times 30\%) + (0.5 \times 70\%) = 59\%$$

of country A having an identification, and

$$(0.8 \times 90\%) + (0.5 \times 10\%) = 77\%$$

of country B having an identification. In the next generation after that, we would expect to see

$$(0.8 \times 59\%) + (0.5 \times 41\%) = 67.7\%$$

of country A having an identification, and

$$(0.8 \times 77\%) + (0.5 \times 23\%) = 73.1\%$$

of country B having an identification. Thus, in two generations the two countries, which had started out being quite different, would have moved to similar levels of party identification. The process involved here, called a "Markov chain," is described in J. Kemeny, J. Snell, and G. Thompson, *Introduction to Finite Mathematics* (Englewood Cliffs, N.J.: Prentice-Hall, Inc., 1957), pp. 171–78.

A few examples of predictions from his theory are (1) at the time elections are first held in a country, the pattern we typically observe in Europe and America (the young being weakly identified, the old strongly) should not hold; all should identify at the same low levels; (2) if elections were interrupted in a country (as in Germany from 1933 to 1945), levels of party identification should decline at a predictable rate; (3) *if* the transition rates for all countries were roughly the same as for France and the United States, then party identification levels in all electoral democracies should converge over the next few generations toward a single value of about 72 percent.

Thus, although Converse's theory was quite simple, it was applicable to a wide variety of questions. It simultaneously explained individual behavior and characteristics of political systems. It implied a more or less universal form of political development at the mass level—with a prediction of initial, but rapidly decreasing, potential for electoral instability in a new electorate. And it included the startling suggestion of a convergence of "mature" electorates to a common level of party identification approximately equal to that of Britain, Norway, or the United States.

The theory was simple, and it was broadly applicable. What was more, it seemed to predict fairly accurately, thus fulfilling the third criterion for "elegance." Using data from Britain, Germany, Italy, the United States, and Mexico to test the theory, Converse found that the theory predicted quite well for all five countries.

Over the years after it appeared, the Converse article stimulated a great deal of further research, which is what one would expect of elegant work. His findings served as assumptions for formal theoretic work (Przeworski, 1975). They also stimulated researchers to investigate whether in fact the transition probabilities on which the Markov chain is based are the same in all industrialized countries (Butler & Stokes, 1969, p. 53), and to test whether new electorates actually behave as Converse's theory predicts they would (Shively, 1972). It is in this way that a good piece of theoretical work feeds, and becomes enmeshed in, the whole body of theoretical exploration.

To Quantify or Not

A side issue in the question of how to develop elegant theory is the old chestnut: Should political science be "quantitative" or not? There has been much rhetoric spilled over this. As long ago as 1956, James Prothro called the dispute "the nonsense fight over scientific method," but it has not cooled sufficiently in the intervening years.

It is a bit hard to pin down what the term *quantitative* means, but generally, research that pays a good deal of attention to *numerical* measures of things, and tends to make *mathematical* statements about them, is considered quantitative. Research that is less concerned with measuring things numerically, and tends to make *verbal* statements about them, is considered relatively less quantitative.

Anything in political science can be stated with varying degrees of quantification. To give a crude example: "The length of service of members of the U.S. House increased from 1880 to 1965 on the average by 0.78 years every decade; the rate of increase was 0.68 years per decade before 1922, and 0.86 years per decade after 1922," says approximately the same thing as "From 1880 to 1965, representatives served a steadily increasing length of time in the House; the change proceeded a bit more rapidly in the latter half of that period." The first form of the statement gives more precise information, but the sense of the two statements is the same.

Each approach involves costs and benefits for research. Most people would agree that precise information is more useful than imprecise information, all other things being equal. But it may be that the time and attention spent in gathering precise data make it difficult for the researcher to appreciate the larger aspects of a theory. Also, because some kinds of data by their very nature are more amenable to precise formulation, there is danger that overconcern with precision may restrict our choice of research to those variables we can more easily quantify. It is striking, for instance, how little the U.S. presidency is studied by political scientists. This oversight may well be due to the difficulty of getting "hard" data on what goes on in that office.

I deal with the issue of proper levels of precision in Chapter 5. For our purposes here, the important thing is to see what relationship degrees of quantification bear to elegance in research.

First of all, the particular subject we are studying affects the extent to which it is possible for us to quantify. In election studies, there is considerable scope for quantification. Records from earlier elections are usually kept in fairly good order; the results of many attitude surveys are also available, and most voters do not regard their actions as something about which they need to maintain secrecy. Thus, the quantitative researcher is able to do a great deal. On the other hand, in Chinese studies, or in studies dealing with the U.S. presidency, sources of quantitative data are quite restricted, and most research must be relatively nonquantitative.

In virtually every field of political research, however, work can be conducted in either a primarily quantitative or a primarily nonquantitative mode. It is probably best that studies with *varying degrees of quantification* be carried on in any given field of political research, for the different levels of quantification complement each other. Typically, less quantitative research provides greater breadth, greater openness to totally new theories, and a greater awareness of the complexity of social phenomena. Studies employing more quantitative data, however, are more likely to produce simple, usable theories; and they are certainly more likely to give us a clear idea of how accurate a theory's predictions are. Thus, each approach has its own costs and benefits, and it is well to remember that no particular degree of quantification has a corner on elegance.

CHOICE OF A TOPIC

The choice of a research topic is intimately bound up with the elegance of what comes out of the research effort. In selecting a topic, of course, the first step is to choose a general area that is interesting and significant for you. By choosing to study political science you have already begun to narrow the field, and you certainly will narrow things more before you are ready to begin. There is no difficulty in this; you simply follow your interests.

But once you have chosen a general area to work in, picking a particular topic to research is difficult. This is the critical decision in doing research. It is also the most difficult aspect of research to teach anyone. It is at this step—seeing that a problem exists and that there is a good chance you can provide new insight into it—that originality and talent are most critical.

The important thing in choosing a topic is to pick one that shows promise of giving you new and elegant results. This implies two things: (1) You want to formulate your topic question so that your results will be likely to alter existing opinion on a subject, and (2) you want your results, as much as possible, to attain the three criteria for elegance: simplicity, predictive accuracy, and importance.

Engineering Research

Choosing a topic is somewhat simpler in engineering research than it is in theory-oriented research. Here, it is primarily a question of using your time and talents efficiently. To yield elegant results, the topic should be one that deals with a pressing problem and one on which you think you are likely to come up with findings that are both accurate and simple enough to be useful. At the same time, you will want to state your thesis so that your results will not duplicate an earlier study, or at least point up where that work produced mistaken results. There is no sense in wasting your time running over ground that has already been worked unless you think you are likely to discover discrepancies.

One difficulty in choosing the topic is that you probably will have to compromise among your goals. You may decide that for the problem nearest your heart, there simply is not enough material available to let you study it satisfactorily. Many topics relating to defense or to the executive are of this sort. Or it may be that a topic interests you not because it deals with the most pressing problem you can think of, but because you have seen some research on it that you think would be rather easy to correct.

The main thing to do in looking for a topic is to read. You should read so that you are certain you are picking an important problem, and you should read to find out how likely it is that your topic will yield useful results. Finally, you should read to see what other work has been done on the problem, or on similar problems, so that you will see where you are most likely to produce results that are new.

Theory-Oriented Research

Choosing a topic that will produce important results for theory is undoubtedly more difficult than formulating a question that may yield important practical applications. You will recall that if theory-oriented research is to be important, it should have a broad and general effect on theory. This effect can be achieved either directly through the phenomena it explains, or indirectly through the variety of other theories it affects. Similarly, to be "new," the research results must either produce totally new theories or lead to some change in the status of older theories.

This means that in framing any topic for research, you are involved at once in the full body of political science theory, for a single piece of research may simultaneously affect many different theories. Research on how a congressional committee reaches its decisions, for example, can affect theories about power in Congress, general theories about committees and organizations, theories about executive–congressional relations, theories about elite political behavior, and so on.

Thus, what the researcher in this area must do is to decide which research topic is going to produce the greatest change in the status of existing theories. This task requires not only that she be familiar with as broad a range of existing theories as possible, but that she also have some idea of where an existing body of research is weakest and most needs to be supported or changed.

Deciding where you are likely to produce theoretical results that are simple and predict accurately requires the same sort of guessing as in engineering research, but in theory-oriented research it is harder to decide how important the results of a study are likely to be. You must juggle all of these decisions around so as to get the best mix—a topic that will produce results that are as new and as elegant as possible. This is something for which no rules can be laid down. It is an art.

DEVELOPMENT OF A RESEARCH DESIGN

It may be true, as I say, that choosing a topic is not something for which rules can be laid down. But it is certainly something for which rules *have* been laid down. Because of an exaggerated fear of *ex post facto* argument, some social scientists have developed a very restrictive procedure to serve as a standard in carrying on research.[3] According to this procedure, the researcher should first frame a theory, stating it in the form of a set of hypotheses to be tested. These hypotheses presumably are based on work others have done in the past. The researcher should then gather fresh data with which to test the theory. Finally, having tested the theory, the researcher should either reject it or enshrine it, *solely on the basis of those new data.* It is true that this procedure erects formidable barriers to protect us from *ex post facto* argument, but it has a number of serious drawbacks.

In the first place, it lends an exaggerated significance to the results of the new study. Even in cases where a variety of previously existing evidence favors a particular theory, that evidence presumably is to be ignored if the new test gives contradictory results. Second and more important, the usual procedure deters researchers from casting about creatively for research topics and theories. Because it requires that hypotheses be fixed firmly at the beginning of the research process, it effectively reduces the research task to a selection of obvious hypotheses. It offers researchers no encouragement to think about their theories once research has begun. Researchers are not supposed to remold theory as they go along, learning more about the subject. They are merely supposed to react to old theories and concepts rather than to think up entirely new problems for explanation. In short, this approach encourages the researcher to function as a clerk.

---

[3]*Ex post facto* argument results when an investigator forms a theory on the basis of certain evidence, then uses that evidence to affirm the theory. If a political scientist formed a theory of congressional committees on the basis of intimate experience with the House Appropriations Committee, for example, and then carried out a study of the House Appropriations Committee to test the theory, this would be *ex post facto* argument. The danger in this is that any given situation has certain unique aspects, and these are likely to be included in any theory based on it. If the same situation is then used to test the theory, it will look as if the unique aspects are indeed general, whereas if a different test situation had been used, those parts of the theory would have been found wanting.

The epitome of this type of thinking is the *research design*—a common student exercise in which students are instructed to frame some hypotheses (presumably based on their reading) and show how they might gather data to test those hypotheses. A doctoral candidate whom I once talked with seemed to me the perfect example of repeated exposure to exercises such as these. He needed to find a topic for his dissertation and he thought that a good way to do this would be to look through Lane's *Political Life,* pick a few of Lane's propositions about voting behavior, and test them with some data.

This is how we train people to do research, but most of us have better sense than to follow our own precepts. A search of articles in political science journals will turn up only a few that report research that follows the rules. One of the better-kept secrets in political science is that good political scientists generally do not draw up research designs before they start to work on a topic. Nor do they usually "frame hypotheses" in any formal sense before they start to work, although they usually have some operational hunches about what they expect to find. And they most certainly do not ignore older evidence, even the evidence that suggested a theory to them in the first place.

Their procedure is much less formal than the one they prescribe for students. They play with data, immerse themselves in what other people have written, argue with colleagues, and think. In doing so, they grope for interesting theories, theories that are elegant and give a new slant to things.

Although I have condemned the formal procedure for designing research, I hasten to add that it should not be rejected completely. One of its advantages is safeguarding against *ex post facto* argument. Furthermore, even though the research design undoubtedly stifles initiative and creativity, it is more methodical and easier to apply for the beginning researcher. Because students usually operate under stricter deadlines than other researchers, it may make sense for them to work with specific goals in mind so that they can estimate accurately at the beginning of a project when it will be completed. Also, it is hard to teach someone to grope for interesting topics and theories. Perhaps a good way to learn is by starting with the more clear and obvious procedures, then gradually loosening up as experience is gained.

Observations, Puzzles, and the Construction of Theories

One way to look at choosing topics and developing theories is to realize that they are at heart very commonsensical processes, based on our daily experiences. This is often lost in the forest of scholarship, in which scholars frequently deal with abstractions (and with each other's rival abstractions). But at heart all theory-oriented research in the social sciences is of the following sort:

1. Something in our lives puzzles us, and we try to think of an explanation to account for it.
2. To account for it, we put it in a broader, general category of causal relationships (that is, a theory).
3. To test whether the broader theory is valid as an explanation, we draw other specific predictions from the theory and test these to see whether the theory's predictions are generally true. If they are, the theory qualifies as a plausible explanation of the thing we are trying to explain.

TABLE 2–2   U.S. Defense Spending, Compared with the Seven Smallest
Members of NATO

	Gross National Product, 2002 (billions of $)	Defense Spending as Percentage of Gross National Product, 2002
United States	10,400	3.4
Belgium	277	1.3
Norway	192	1.9
Turkey	182	5.1
Denmark	172	1.6
Greece	149	4.4
Portugal	137	2.3
Luxembourg	24	0.9

Source: International Institute for Strategic Studies (2003).

As an example, consider the puzzle that the United States has always contributed proportionally more than almost all other members of the NATO military alliance, especially as compared with the smaller members of the alliance, as seen in Table 2–2.

Only Greece and Turkey, which arm heavily because of their conflicts with each other, contribute as high a percentage of their gross national product to the common alliance as the United States does. The other small allies all appear to varying degrees to ride on the coattails of the United States. One way to explain this would be to treat it as a specific instance of a more general relationship—that in any voluntary cooperative group the member with the greatest resources always tends to make disproportionate contributions. That is, a member who sees that the group would fail without his contribution will come through strongly; a relatively insignificant member will see that the group would do about equally well whether or not he contributes, and will tend to sit back and be a free rider. In the NATO example, if the United States does not contribute vigorously, the alliance languishes, but little Denmark hardly makes a difference one way or another.

A lot of the political scientist's creativity will then come into play in devising other, testable predictions from the theory to see whether it is generally valid. In this example we might examine chambers of commerce to see whether the biggest merchants in town usually carry most of the freight. Or we might look at trade union–supported political parties such as the Labour Party of Great Britain to see whether the largest unions carry a disproportionate share of the burden. If the theory holds up well across a variety of such tests, it will be a plausible potential explanation for the "Denmark problem."[4]

[4]The theory used in this example derives from the broader theoretical structure of Mancur Olson's *The Logic of Collective Action* (1965), which was discussed in pp. 7–8. The structure of argument discussed in this section—see a puzzle, frame an explanation based on a more general principle, devise other unrelated predictions from the general principle in order to test it—is presented skillfully by Charles A. Lave and James G. March in *Introduction to Models in the Social Sciences* (1975), especially in the first three chapters.

Lest working out a theory or a puzzle should seem too easy or too pat from these examples, let me review for you a puzzle currently in real play, to show the uncertainty and the progression of steps by which scientific discussion of a puzzle usually proceeds in real life.[5] A great deal of attention has been directed over the past decade to the so-called democratic peace—the observation that no democracy has ever been observed to initiate war with another democracy. It is extremely rare in the social sciences for any relationship to be as invariant as this one, and the relationship is also of great importance in the assessment of democracy, so it is not surprising that this has attracted the attention of some very good minds.

First of all, a number of scholars have questioned whether the observation is as infallible as it is claimed to be. Both "democracy" and "war" are subject to a certain amount of interpretation. Since no country is a pure democracy, how much democracy is enough to have the country count as democratic? When the NATO alliance attacked the Yugoslavian government of Slobodan Milosevic in 1998 (a government which had been elected, but in an election without much real competition), was that a case of democracies attacking another democracy? Similarly, "war" is not always a black-and-white concept. When the U.S. Central Intelligence Agency gave covert support to a military coup against democratically elected President Allende of Chile, was that war?

Granting the gray areas of definition, however, most political scientists consider the democratic peace to be an enduring relationship of quite unusual regularity. This observation, then, poses the puzzle: Why is it that democracies do not attack one another?

There have been two primary explanations offered. First, many scholars argue that democracies share a number of values in common, such as respect for individual liberties and a high value on competition. They also share an international norm of compromise and bounded resolutions to conflicts. These characteristics, it is said, make democracies unlikely to wage war on those with whom they agree in so many areas.

Alternatively, a number of scholars point to the institutional structure of democracies as the explanation. People generally do not want to fight wars, and in democracies the wishes of the broad populace count for more than in nondemocracies. Accordingly, the chance that two countries will enter a war, if in both of them the people's concerns count for a good deal, is low.

Bueno de Mesquita, Morrow, Siverson and Smith (1999) point out, however, that both of these explanations are hard to reconcile with the fairly strong willingness of democracies to initiate wars of conquest or empire. In the late nineteenth century, for instance, democratic France and Great Britain frequently sent armed forces to help acquire additions to their empires. And in the early twentieth century the democratic United States enthusiastically engaged Spain in a war intended to lift some parts of the Spanish Empire such as Puerto Rico and the Philippines. These were not wars waged on democracies, but it was certainly the case that democratic values, and the influence of "the people" in these democracies, did not prevent these countries from entering into warfare rather happily.

---

[5]The discussion that follows draws heavily on the useful review of the democratic peace literature in Bueno de Mesquita, Morrow, Siverson, and Smith (1999).

Bueno de Mesquita and his co-authors propose instead a slightly complicated explanation based on rational choice theory.

1. In a democracy, a leader must satisfy a fairly large number of people in order to stay in power; in an autocracy, leaders typically need only satisfy a small number—the army, for instance—or a single party.
2. A war involves costs, but also benefits if won. A democratic leader needs a higher ratio of potential benefits to costs to justify going to war than an autocrat does, because the democratic leader has to reward more people. (See [1.] above.) Therefore, the stakes are higher for democratic leaders. An autocrat might lose a war yet stay in power (Saddam Hussein of Iraq was an example, continuing in office after he lost the first Gulf War in 1991; he was ousted only later by direct action of American troops in 2003.) It is hard to imagine a democratic leader losing a war and not being voted out of office.
3. Since the stakes are higher for democratic leaders, they will be more careful about entering wars than will autocrats; and once involved in wars, democratic leaders will fight them more determinedly.
4. Given reasonably good information about each other, it is unlikely that either of two democrats involved in a conflict will think that he or she has a preponderant chance of winning a war; and each will know that the other (because it is a democracy) will fight very determinedly if there is a war. Therefore, they can be expected to try to negotiate their disputes rather than go to war over them.

This is a good explanation, but it will certainly not represent the last word in political scientists' collective effort to work out an explanation of the puzzle. (A good exercise for you would be to frame rebuttals of the rational choice explanation from the standpoint of the first two explanations—the "shared values" explanation and the "institutional role of the people" explanation.)

Note that throughout this discussion of puzzles and explanations, I have said that what is produced is a *plausible potential explanation*. It typically is the case that more than one plausible potential explanation can be produced for anything needing explanation. It then becomes the task of the scholar to decide among them on the basis of how broadly they apply, how simple they are (remember, a theory that is as complicated as the reality it is meant to explain has not gotten you very far), how accurately it predicts, and so on. But the basic building blocks of political explanation are plausible potential explanations, derived in just the way that I have outlined here.

MACHIAVELLIAN GUIDE TO DEVELOPING RESEARCH TOPICS

There are really no guidelines that I can give you to developing a research topic other than to remind you once again that you are working toward results that are both *new* and *elegant*. Perhaps if we view the development task from the perspective of political research in general, however, we will gain some clue as to its place in the entire scheme.

Implicit in this chapter is that scholarly research represents a loose cooperative effort among many people. I mentioned earlier the pleasure that researchers feel in creating something that no one has seen before. This is mixed, however, with a sense of pride in being part of an ongoing tradition. One's work is something brand new, but it also draws on Karl Marx, or Emile Durkheim, or Robert Putnam, and *modifies the meaning of their work.* Scholars involved in developing theory form a kind of priesthood—admittedly sometimes run less on faith and more according to the laws of laissez-faire and caveat emptor—focused on the common goal of perfecting elegant theories. As we have seen, the celebrants carry on this process by developing new theories and adapting old ones, fitting these theories to the real world to see how accurately they predict things, and feeding the results of such research back into the body of theory.[6]

From this description of the process of research, we can derive a set of rules to guide the individual researcher. If empirical research is motivated by a desire to affect the state of theories, either by confirming them or by working changes in them, you will be doing your best job when you maximize your effect on theory with a given investment of time and money. To do this, you must:

1. Maximize the generality of the theory you intend to examine.   This is basically a restatement of the first criterion for elegant research. Note, though, that this rule is not something absolute, for any phenomenon can be examined at different levels of generality. One man may be hit on the head by an apple and form a theory of falling apples; another may have the same experience and form a theory of universal gravitation. The physical activity of the "study" is the same in both cases; the difference lies solely in the level at which the researcher works.

As an example from political science research, consider the variety of studies done on the presidency. The narrowest range of theory is found in biographies of particular presidents. The researcher in such a biography generally is concerned only with explaining what happened during a particular president's life, especially during his term in office. A broader range of theory is aimed at in studies of the U.S. presidency, which may analyze the nature of the office, the sources of executive power, the way in which presidents' personalities can influence their behavior in office, and so on.[7] A still broader range of theory is seen in studies that use the U.S. presidency as an example of sovereigns in general and seek to explain the sources and limitations of sovereign power. Richard Neustadt's *Presidential Power and the Modern Presidents* (1991), for instance, often operates at this level of generality.

2. Pick a weak theory to work on.   The weaker the previous confirmations of a theory have been, the greater the likelihood that the theory will be refuted by your findings.

---

[6]Needless to say, it is not quite as neat as this. For one thing, a given person usually does not handle all these aspects of a particular problem. One person may work simply at clarifying theories, another may do a descriptive study of a particular case, and a third may relate the new evidence to the body of older theory. Most researchers can expect to carry on any or all activities at any time.

[7]For example, a study of the nature of the presidential office (such as Koenig, 1968), a study of presidents' political personalities (Barber, 1972), or an analysis of presidents' leadership (Greenstein, 2000).

If, however, your research does confirm the theory, your work will again be more significant than if the theory already had a good deal of confirming evidence.

Perhaps the best way to use the strategy of picking a weak theory is to state a new, original theory yourself. In this case, your hypotheses are necessarily in need of proof, and any evidence you can buttress them with will be important. Remember, though, that "new, original theories" that are also elegant are hard to come up with.

Another way to follow this strategy is to pick an anomaly—that is, a question on which previous research has been contradictory. A good example of research stimulated by an anomaly is the study by Sidney Tarrow (1971) of the political participation of French peasants. Tarrow was struck by the fact that although French peasants regularly responded to surveys by stating that they were not very interested in politics, they also regularly turned out to vote in greater numbers than did the urban French.

This anomaly led Tarrow to probe more deeply into what political involvement means to the French, so as to resolve the apparent contradiction. His conclusions led to the rejection of the traditional "interest in politics" measure. They also shed new light on the nature of French voters' attachment to political parties. On this hinged the apparent contradiction, since French peasants were fiercely independent, and understood "interest in politics" to imply some sort of approval of the existing parties. Though they were in fact interested in politics, they denied this because of their antipathy to the parties. Anomalies such as this are hard to come by, because earlier investigators generally have noticed them already and have tried to resolve them. If you can find an anomaly having to do with a significant area of political theory, however, you can be certain that any plausible efforts at resolution will be interesting.

Another example of a nice anomaly just waiting to be analyzed is the fact that in the 2000 election, the higher voters' incomes were, the more likely they were to vote for George W. Bush. But if you look at the "red states"—the states he carried—they are on the whole poor states with low average incomes. What sort of theory might you devise to explain this?

Besides anomalies, you might choose a problem you believe has just not been sufficiently researched, perhaps one in which all variables have not been covered. Thus, you might replicate a study in a different context from the original one. Arthur A. Goldsmith (1987) noted that Mancur Olson's (1982) well-known theory, that prolonged political stability produces rigid social and economic structures that retard economic growth, was based mostly on the experiences of the West and Japan. Less-developed countries of the Third World would provide a laboratory of countries with a wider range of cultures and economic circumstances. In fact, Goldsmith found that examination of these countries did not support Olson's theory, though he hastened to add that his measure of "instability" was questionable and might have been a source of the disparity. The most likely reason, at least to my taste, is that the context is different. Olson's theory relies on the negative economic effects of organized interest groups. Such groups are strong and active in the countries Olson studied, but not in the Third World context that Goldsmith studied. Goldsmith's negative results may thus point up the importance of organized interest groups in Olson's theory.

3. Make the connection between the general theory and your specific operations as clear as possible. This really just boils down to making sure you say what you think you are saying. It involves such things as the accuracy of your deductions from the theory to the specific situation, the accuracy with which you have measured things, and so on. Much of the rest of this book focuses on such problems.

You may have noticed that these three rules resemble the criteria for elegance fairly closely. You also may have noticed that the basic philosophy behind them— "Do research that makes as big a splash as possible"—reads like a guide for ruthless and hungry assistant professors. But each of the rules, derived from my underlying Machiavellian outlook, also has a beneficial effect on the field as a whole. If individuals choose those problems of theory that have so far had the weakest verification, for example, the entire field will benefit from an examination of those theories most in need of investigation.

Needless to say, these guidelines should remain flexible enough to allow different mixes of research strategy. There is no one "scientific method" involved here. One person may find a tool that measures a variable better than had been done before and then simply apply it to sharpen previously examined relationships. Another may note an anomaly in a theory and organize an experiment to resolve the problem. A third may look over previous research findings and place a new, broader, or simpler interpretation on them. All are following the rule of maximizing their impact on theory.

4. Present your theory as clearly and vividly as possible. A Machiavellian researcher wants to influence as many people as possible, so it makes sense to make your reader's life easier and your message more compelling. This means, write well and present any graphic information well. People often think *how* you say something is separable from *what* you say, but that is simply not true. If the purpose of theory is to change people's understanding of the world, then the way the theory is communicated to them is an integral part of the development of the theory.

How to write well and design graphic displays well are beyond the scope of this book; each really requires a book in its own right. Fortunately, I can suggest two truly good books that will help you. For writing, I recommend William Knowlton Zinsser's *On Writing Well: The Classic Guide to Writing Nonfiction* (New York: HarperCollins, 1998). An excellent introduction to good graphic presentation is Edward R. Tufte's *The Visual Display of Quantitative Information* (Cheshire, Conn.: Graphics Press, 1983).

FURTHER DISCUSSION

An intriguing book relevant to this chapter is Arthur Koestler's *The Act of Creation* (1969). An article that presents some interesting, rather controversial ideas about appropriate ways to build and test theory is Ronald Brunner's "An 'Intentional' Alternative in Public Opinion Research" (1977). Another perspective is offered persuasively by J. Donald Moon (1975). An excellent introduction to building elegant theories is found in the first three chapters of Lave and March (1975). Some questions you might consider are:

1. Presumably, work in normative philosophy or in formal theory could be evaluated in terms of elegance, just as empirical research is. What changes would this require in the definition of elegance?
2. This chapter has implied that the usual way to come up with a theory is to focus on a body of observations and look for regular patterns in them. Although this is the usual procedure, it is not the only nor necessarily the best approach. What drawbacks might it involve? In what alternative ways might one develop a theory?
3. I stated in this chapter that most social science theories are causal. What would a non-causal theory look like? Under what circumstances would it be likely to be used? (*Hint:* Consider Einstein's famous theory, $E = mc^2$.)

Chapter 3

Importance
of Dimensional
Thinking

In Chapter 2 I argued that flexibility and originality—in a word, freedom—are important in doing good research. In this chapter I shall stress the need to state theories in a clear, unambiguous way—a form of self-discipline that must accompany such freedom.

In particular, we shall be concerned with framing theories in terms of concepts that cannot easily be subdivided into further distinct meanings, either denotative or connotative. In other words, very simple concepts whose meaning is unequivocal. I shall call such simple concepts *unidimensional,* in contrast to concepts whose meaning may vary from reader to reader and even from time to time, that is, *multidimensional* concepts.

Consider the following example: As a description of climates, "temperature" is a unidimensional concept. Temperature can vary along only one dimension, from hot to cold. Therefore, if a theory states that a temperature below x degrees causes the spotted ibex to stop breeding, that statement will mean the same thing to every reader. "Good weather," on the other hand, is a multidimensional concept that involves among other things temperature, wind velocity, humidity, amount of precipitation, and degree of cloud cover. If there is a variation along any one of these separate dimensions, the "goodness" of weather varies. If the aforementioned theory stated that "bad weather" caused the spotted ibex to stop breeding, the meaning of that theory would be left to the reader's judgment. Is it rain that discourages the ibex's ardor? Or do high winds make him think of other things? Is it the heat? The humidity?

As we can see from this example, it is preferable to frame theories in terms of unidimensional rather than multidimensional concepts. The English language does not always make this easy, however. In this chapter we shall look at the English language in general and at the varied theories that may be hidden in ordinary language.

ENGLISH AS A LANGUAGE FOR RESEARCH

I have assumed so far that if political research is to be useful, a minimal requirement is that its results should mean the same thing to any two different readers. Unfortunately, the English language is badly designed to function as a medium for stating research results clearly and without ambiguity. Most English words can take on a variety of meanings, depending on the context and on the mood of the reader. To use an everyday example, the statement, "The welfare bill failed in the House because the administration did not fight for it," might mean:

1. A welfare bill was passed, but not the one the writer wanted.
2. No welfare bill passed at all.

Whichever of these is the case, the failure could have resulted from any number of other events, for example:

3. The administration privately passed the word to its supporters to undercut the bill.
4. The administration wanted the bill, but did not campaign as hard as it usually does for bills it wants.
5. The administration campaigned as hard as it usually does for bills it wants, but not as hard as the writer would have done had he been in the administration.
6. The administration went all-out for the bill, but failed to get it passed—and the writer is in the opposing party.

Note that in these statements there are many additional phrases that are ambiguous: "pass the word," "undercut the bill," "want the bill," "campaign for the bill," "go all-out."

As another example of a multidimensional concept, consider *political party.* This concept can be broken down into at least six component dimensions: those people who vote for the party in a given election, those people who are registered with the party, those people who identify themselves in their minds with the party, those people who do voluntary work for the party at some given time, the officers of the party, those who are running or elected as candidates under the party label. When researchers write about "the political party," they may be referring to any or all of these various dimensions of the term. Thus, unless political scientists specify which dimensions apply, they may merely succeed in creating confusion. A few further examples of multidimensional terms are: *power, enjoyment, conservative, economic development, intelligent,* and *love.*

Debates in political science sometimes resolve themselves into the fact that participants are using the same term in different ways. The word *liberal,* for instance, has many dimensions, some of which are probably even inconsistent. Just to look at one of its dimensions, it often connotes "free-spending," although in its original usage, which is still fairly current in Europe, it means "favoring a limited role for government." Since *liberal* has generally unpopular connotations in the United States and is multidimensional in complex ways, it is natural to use this flexible word as a club in describing candidates. In the election of 1996, for instance, the late Senator Paul Wellstone of Minnesota was described by his opponent as "embarrassingly liberal" for his vote against a welfare reform bill. He responded that his vote was actually "deeply conservative" because it reflected the moral values of Minnesotans. Was Wellstone's vote "liberal" or "conservative"? The argument proceeded almost irrespective of its merits.

The strategy I am introducing here, framing theories in terms of unidimensional concepts, can help us to keep clear the meanings of the words we use and to avoid this kind of confusion.

Ordinary Language

As we have just seen, many English words involve more than one dimension, and these component dimensions are rarely specified in ordinary language. Multidimensional concepts are valuable and useful in ordinary language, as is indicated by their popularity. The connotations accruing to a word that means many different things simultaneously add richness to our language. Art and rhetoric could not be restricted to unidimensional vocabularies.

But in the social sciences, we pay a high price for this benefit. Rich connotations, which are so important to art, get in the way of analytic thinking. A poet is pleased if she chooses a word whose meanings give the reader pause for thought; it is the poet's job to create a rich confusion of varied nuances. The job of the social analyst, however, is to bring order out of social chaos by means of simple theories.

Multidimensional words hamper social scientists in at least three ways:

1. *Poor communication.* Because a reader can never be certain what meaning an author intended, multidimensional words in effect hamper communication.
2. *Difficulty with measurement.* Whenever social scientists want to measure a variable, they confront an impossible task unless they have defined the variable in such a way that it consists of a single dimension. For example, consider a political scientist who wanted to measure the "amount of interaction" between various nations. Now, "interaction" involves a number of dimensions: alliances, volume of trade, tourism, exchanges of mail, and so on. Suppose that this political scientist discovered the following things about countries A, B, and C:

Between Countries	Volume Trade/Year	Items of Mail/Year	Alliance
A and B	$1 billion	2 million	Yes
B and C	$½ billion	3 million	Yes
A and C	$2 billion	1 million	No

Between which two countries is there greater interaction? A and C trade together a great deal but are not allies; B and C exchange a great deal of mail but do not trade together as much as A and B. Clearly, "amount of interaction" is not a unidimensional variable. Had the investigator chosen three separate measures—trade, mail flow, and alliance—there would have been no problem in comparing the countries. We can confidently state, for instance, that A and C share the greatest trade, followed by A and B and by B and C. We return to such problems of measurement in Chapter 4.

3. *Ambiguous associations.* From the standpoint of the social scientist, another fault in multidimensional words is that each such word is itself a theory of sorts. By associating several distinct things under a single term, a multidimensional word implies the theory that these things go together. *But unless its component dimensions are made explicit, it is a poorly articulated and poorly controlled theory.*

For example, the word *wise* has long connoted (1) broad practical knowledge, (2) a highly developed understanding of relationships, (3) a contemplative bent, and (4) a long background of practical experience. Among other things, it has implied the theory that the older (and thus the more experienced) one got, the better one understood things. So, if I use the word "wise" rather than "intelligent," my reader picks up this little theory subliminally embedded in my statement.

Theories such as this, embedded in multidimensional words, change as common usage reflects changed moods and new experiences. But the process by which they change is not a very satisfactory one; it is a process that gives us little confidence in the new theories that are produced. It may be an unarticulated dislike for the theory implied by the word *wise,* for example, which has led to diminished use of the word in egalitarian America, and its degradation in such slang as "Don't get wise with me!" and "wise guy." It is in just such a way that word usage gradually changes, reflecting different views of the world. The polite substitution of the term *developing nations* for *underdeveloped countries* in the 1950s and 1960s is another example. This change in usage reflected the changed status of the Third World and at least some hopeful thinking about what was happening there.[1]

This process of theory development is uncontrolled. In a sense it is very democratic—probably more democratic than we would like. Everyone who uses a particular word takes part in the process, and a person's influence is more or less proportional to the number of people who hear her use the word. There is no provision made for greater influence on the process by those who know more about the subject. Dictionaries, by codifying word usage, serve to slow down the process of change, but they do not affect the *quality* of the change.

Another problem with the process is that these changes often proceed at a snail's pace. Thus, theories that are embedded in multidimensional words survive practical refutation much longer than if they were made explicit. The words *liberal* and *conservative* are a case in point. Because such attitudes as a desire for economic activism on the part of government, concern for the legal rights of individuals, pacifism, and internationalism often seemed to go together when one looked at the political elite in the United States, the term *liberal* came to denote their presence and

---

[1]Today, of course, reality has caught up with rhetoric in the explosive economic growth of countries such as China, India, and South Korea.

conservative their absence. (The words were borrowed from a European context, but their meanings were considerably changed, which only added to the subsequent confusion.) The implied theory—that these attitudes tended to coincide—was never very accurate as a description of the elite and it has proved to be quite inaccurate in describing people in general.[2] It turns out, for example, that people who are liberal on individuals' rights are often conservative on economic issues. All this went unnoticed until at least the late 1940s, so that even today there are still many people who use the words *liberal* and *conservative* in this way, as if they had general validity.

Thus, while changes in usage do produce changes in the theories implied by multidimensional words, the process by which these changes are made is capricious; this is presumably not the way we want to develop social theory. Social scientists should be uncomfortable if hidden away in their statement of a theory are additional little theories that are implicit and uncontrolled.

Let me sum up the argument thus far: Social scientists should use unidimensional language for three reasons:

1. The meaning of a theory is not unambiguously clear if it is couched in multidimensional words.
2. Variables cannot be measured unambiguously if they have been defined in a multidimensional way.
3. Inclusion of multidimensional words in a theory confuses that theory with additional theories that are implied by the existence of the multidimensional words themselves.

Despite our prescription, however, we must acknowledge the fact that the English language contains many words that hold a rich variety of meanings and connotations. These are to be valued in their own right, yet social scientists often must create their own vocabulary. If ordinary language does not provide unidimensional words for the things social scientists want to say, they must invent the words themselves. This is one reason that social science writing so often strikes readers as flat and cold. What most people mean by "social science jargon" is the unidimensional vocabulary invented by social scientists for their use in analytic research.

Writing from which the richness of varied connotations has been removed is flat. This is simply one of the costs we must pay to write analytically. Of course, this is not meant to excuse poor writing in the social sciences or anywhere else. Unidimensional language is a minor handicap under which social scientists operate, but it need not prevent them from writing clear and graceful prose.

Actually, writers in any analytic field suffer the same handicap. Natural scientists must create their own vocabularies, too. But somehow the loss of richness seems more painful in the social sciences than in other fields. The physicist may describe a body's motion in terms of "mass," "velocity," and "acceleration" rather than saying that it "hurtles through space," and the mind does not rebel. But when the political scientist describes politics as consisting of "system inputs," "system outputs," and "feedback loops," the mind does rebel. This is because the social scientist deals with *people*, the thing we care most passionately about. It does not bother us when a

---

[2]A good demonstration of this—there are dozens—was found in Converse (1964).

physicist tries to reduce the complex motion of a particle to unidimensional concepts, but when social scientists try to simplify the complex reality of politics, the family, or of protests, we are disturbed.

PROPER USE OF MULTIDIMENSIONAL WORDS

I have argued that we should try to use only indivisible dimensions as concepts in political science. But there is another side to the question, which leads me to temper that stance somewhat. Although it is always necessary to think and work with unidimensional concepts in the social sciences, it may be convenient to put separate dimensions together in *explicit* multidimensional combinations.

"National integration" may provide an example of such a concept. There are many dimensions implied in the term: political consensus within the nation; widespread communication and personal interchanges within the nation; a feeling, among the nation's people, that they all belong together; legal integration; and so on. It would be possible to do without the term *national integration,* and work directly with these dimensions, but it would be awkward. There are a great number of dimensions involved, and they may combine in odd ways. At the same time, there *is* a widespread feeling among political scientists that these things tend to go together to constitute a general process. This process might not be at all easy to discern if we were forced to work simultaneously with the large number of unidimensional concepts involved in it. Accordingly, political scientists over the last few decades have explicitly developed the term *national integration,* composed of these various dimensions, to refer to the general process. The result has not been fully satisfactory, but there does appear to be a need for such a summary term.

The use of an explicit combination of separate dimensions such as this has some of the advantages of both "ordinary language" and unidimensional language, and some of the disadvantages of each. Such summary constructs may add grace and interest to the presentation of your results and ideas. They may add clarity, too, if you are working with so many dimensions simultaneously that readers would have difficulty keeping track of them. And they help to keep your theory parsimonious.

Such explicit combinations of dimensions have the advantage, as compared with ordinary language, that you have built your own juxtaposition of dimensions into the word. However, these contrived concepts retain many of the disadvantages of ordinary language. A reader cannot tell, for example, when faced with a high score on a variable that combines dimensions A, B, and C, whether this means that A and B were high and C low, or that B was high and A and C were low, or whatever. Although explicit multidimensional words are more useful than ordinary language, you should not use them casually.

I have used as my "bad" examples words from ordinary language rather than words specifically designed for use by scholars. In general, as I have indicated, when scholars design terminology it is a good deal tighter than ordinary language. However, even scholarly vocabulary is often not as tight as it could be. It may happen, for instance, that several scholars working independently of each other devise related unidimensional words, each set up for one particular research use. When these related words are taken as a group, they may produce confusion as great as that resulting from ordinary language. In one study, Kroeber and Kluckhohn (1952) counted several hundred different ways in which the word *culture* was used by anthropologists.

Accordingly, explicit dimensional analysis of a body of scholarly work, even if it is already at a quite abstract level, can help us to clarify the meaning of the whole body of work and may point up new directions for theoretical development. Conceptual analysis of this sort is terribly important to research. Perhaps the most frequent failing in research is that this part of the work is done casually and sloppily. The following analysis of different ways of using the concept *power* is an extended example of how such dimensional analysis might proceed.

Example of Dimensional Analysis

The basic building block of all political science analysis is the concept of power. (In the 1970s, when there was a spate of bumper stickers of the form "fashion designers do it with style" or "anthropologists do it with culture," I waited in vain to see a car with "political scientists do it with power.") But this concept is multidimensional and notoriously difficult to pin down. Major debates of the last few decades can be clarified by dimensional analysis.

Robert Dahl led off the modern debate over the nature of power with a study of power in local politics in New Haven, Connecticut (Dahl, 1961). He noted that on different issues, different sorts of people were involved, so he concluded that local political power was not concentrated in an elite but was widely distributed. Bachrach and Baratz (1962) responded that the true essence of power lay not in participation in decisions but in being able to lay out the agenda for what questions were to be discussed. Despite the fact that a wide range of people had participated in New Haven discussions, it might be that a small group of powerful figures had determined what issues would be open for discussion. The question of the city government taking over the public utilities had not been on the table, for instance; nor at that time had there been any interest in the relative situation of women vis-à-vis men.

In 1974, Steven Lukes added a further complication. True power lay not in the mechanics of decision making, either in the decision itself *or* in setting the agenda. Rather, true power lay in the ability to define for people what their interests were. If one could convince white workers in New Haven that the most important thing to them was education for their children rather than defending whites' prerogatives against blacks—or if you did the reverse of this—you would have already pretty well determined the political outcomes.

As a final hook, Peter Digeser (1992) drew on the work of Michel Foucault to suggest that *real* power consists not of determining what people will see as in their interests but rather in determining what leads them to define their very identity. If the New Haven workers can be led to identify themselves as whites rather than as workers, that determines all that follows.

Although the scholars involved in these arguments have generally viewed their own version of power as ruling out one or more of the others, dimensional analysis can show how they all work together. Each of these conceptualizations actually emphasizes a different dimension of power: Dahl emphasizes *whether one has participated in a decision;* Bachrach and Baratz *whether one has helped set the agenda for public decisions;* Lukes *whether one has influenced people's understanding of their interests;* and Digeser *whether one has influenced people's political identities.*

Figure 3–1 lays these out as four dimensions of power. The power any person holds in a particular political decision may be analyzed in terms of her position on the four dimensions. On a question of park policy, for instance, a newspaper editor may have been involved in the setting of identities, in influencing people's understanding of their interests, and in determining the agenda of issues facing the city but may not have been involved in the actual decisions. A member of the city park board may have been involved in the decision but may not have exercised power in any of its other dimensions. An elementary school teacher may have been involved in the

Figure 3–1   Four Dimensions of Power

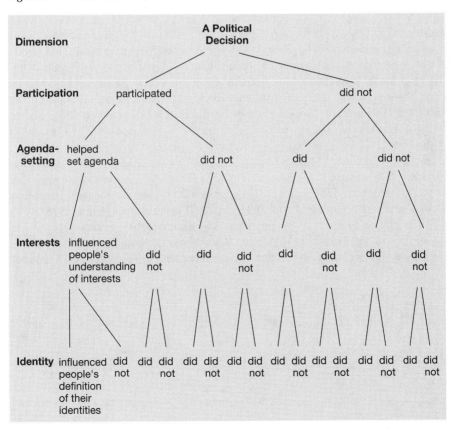

process of forming identities but may not have exercised power in its other dimensions; another school teacher, interested and active on park questions, may have been involved in the process of forming identities, and may have participated in the decisions, but not have exercised power in the other two dimensions.

Dimensional analysis of this sort allows us to see the interrelations of various approaches to a question and can also give us a rich framework with which to apply a multidimensional concept. It also allows us to compare the importance of the dimensions. Implicit in each later scholar in the discussion sketched above was the idea that his notion of power was deeper and more basic than those that went before. A dimensional analysis gives us a structure within which we can address this question.

FURTHER DISCUSSION

An excellent formal treatment of dimensional analysis is Allan H. Barton, "The Concept of Property-Space in Social Research" (1955). Philip E. Jacob's "A Multidimensional Classification of Atrocity Stories" (1955) furnishes a good example of dimensional analysis in practice.

Some examples from political science are Chapter 11 of Robert Dahl's *Political Oppositions in Western Democracies* (1966), a first-rate analysis of the relevant dimensions for classifying "opposition"; Harry Eckstein's *Pressure Group Politics* (1960), especially pages 15–40, in which he classifies pressure group activities; and the third chapter of his *Division and Cohesion in Democracy* (1966), an excellent dimensional analysis of "political division"; Hanna Pitkin's *Representation* (1969), a collection of various writings on the concept of representation, among which Pitkin's own essay is particularly insightful; also Pitkin's *The Concept of Representation* (1967); and Giovanni Sartori's *Parties and Party Systems* (1976).

One branch of political philosophy is the "analytic political philosophy" approach, which seeks to study political ideas by a close examination of the meaning of concepts used to describe politics. This approach is reviewed in Richard Bernstein's *Restructuring of Social and Political Theory* (1978) and in Oppenheim (1975).

Finally, as an exercise, you might consider the conceptual problems involved in the well-worn aphorism of Lord Acton: "Power tends to corrupt and absolute power corrupts absolutely." How would you analyze this conceptually? *Can* it be analyzed?

Chapter 4

Problems
of Measurement

Accuracy

In this chapter I explore problems of accurate measurement. These are problems that arise when we try to relate the actual operations in a piece of research—that is, measures of things—to the concepts that form the basis of our underlying theory. Concepts, of course, exist only in the mind. One necessary assumption, if we are to claim that a piece of research has tested a given theory, is that the things measured in the research correspond to the things in the theorist's mind.

This is often a difficult assumption to make. In the preceding chapter, you saw one kind of problem that can stand in the way of it. The political scientist who wanted to measure the amount of interaction between nations found that there was no single satisfactory indicator of "interaction." A number of things—trade, mail exchanges, alliance, and so on—partook of "interaction," but no one of them alone was synonymous with the mental construct.

In the social sciences, only rarely are we able to measure our concepts directly. Consider, for example, the concepts "social class," "respect for the presidency," and "power in the community." Any variables we would choose to measure these concepts correspond only indirectly or in part to our mental constructs. This is the basic problem of measurement in the social sciences.

Consider the concept "social status." Among social scientists there are two popular versions of this concept: "subjective social status," the class that individuals consider themselves as belonging to; and "objective social status," an individual's rank with regard to prestige along social hierarchies such as education, income, and occupation. Neither version of the concept can be measured directly.

In the case of "subjective social status," we cannot measure directly what individuals feel about their status. We know what they report, but their replies to our inquiries may not be what we are looking for. They may not know what they "really" feel, for instance; or they may misunderstand the question and give a misleading answer.

Then again, a person may feel differently from one day to the next, in which case the measure of his status will depend on our rather arbitrary choice of day.

In the case of "objective social status," again we cannot measure the variable directly. "Objective status" has something to do with income, something to do with education, something to do with occupation, and something to do with various other hierarchies, some of which we may not know about. None of these provides a sufficient measure in itself. For example, if we tried to use occupation alone as a measure of social status, we would be faced with the difficult question of whether a plumber who made $40,000 a year was really of lower social status than a bank teller who made $25,000 a year. Similarly, if we tried to use income alone as a measure, we would be faced with the problem of what to do with a retired teacher, whose income might be below the poverty level. "Social status" in this case is a concept that is related to a number of measurable things but is related only imperfectly to each of them. The best we can do in measuring it is to combine the various measurable indicators into a pooled measure that is roughly related to the concept "objective social status."

We encounter similar problems in measuring the other concepts I have cited as examples. Like many other variables in political science, these concepts are of considerable interest and use in theories but are by their nature impossible to measure directly. The general problem posed by such variables is presented schematically in Figure 4–1.

As you saw in Chapter 2, in political research we are commonly interested in relating concepts through a theory. This is always true in theory-oriented research, and it is often true in engineering research as well. If we cannot measure directly the concepts we wish to use, we find ourselves in the position depicted in Figure 4–1. We want to say, "Concept A bears a relationship of thus-and-so form to concept B." But all that we can observe is the relationship between measure A and measure B. Whether what we say about the measures is an accurate statement of the relationship

Figure 4–1   The Problem of Measurement

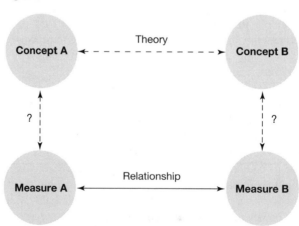

between the concepts depends on the unobserved relationships between concept A and measure A and between concept B and measure B. We can only assume what these relationships are. Like the theory itself, the relationships cannot be observed.

As an example, suppose you want to assess the simple theory that countries that are increasing their armaments tend to engage in aggressive international policies. You might be faced with the following relationships:

1. *Relationship between the concept "increasing armaments" and the measure of "increasing armaments."* You clearly cannot measure increases in a nation's armaments directly; only a national intelligence apparatus has the facilities to do that, and even then, the result is imperfect. Therefore, you might take as your measure the country's reported expenditures on armaments. Now, a country that is not preparing to launch an aggressive military venture would have less reason to lie about an arms buildup than would a country (such as Germany in 1933) that was consciously preparing for aggression. Therefore, the relationship between concept and measure in this case might be: When a country is not building up its armaments, or when it is building them up in order to launch an aggressive action, its reported expenditures on arms will not increase.
2. *Relationship between the concept "increasing armaments" and the concept "aggressive international policies."* Let us assume, for this example, that countries that are increasing their armaments do tend to engage in aggressive international policies.
3. *Relationship between the concept "aggressive international policies" and the measure of "aggressive international policies."* Let us assume, for this example, that we are able to develop a measure that corresponds almost perfectly to the concept "aggressive international policies." (In practice, of course, this would be a difficult variable to measure, and it certainly would be necessary first to analyze the varied dimensions involved in "aggression" and "policies" in order to state more clearly just what was meant by the concept.)

We now find ourselves in the position depicted in Figure 4–2. Here, because of peculiarities in the relationships between the concepts and the measures of these concepts, the relationship you can observe between the measures turns out to be the opposite of the true relationship between the concepts. Worse yet, inasmuch as the two measures and the connection between them are all that you can observe, you would have no way of knowing that this was happening. This is why I have called indirect measurement of concepts *the* problem of measurement.

One solution to the problem might be to measure variables only directly. Some concepts are directly measurable. A few examples are people's votes if an election is nonsecret and you tabulate the result yourself; statements you hear made on the Senate floor; a bomb you see dropped or thrown.[1]

The difficulty with such a solution is that concepts that can be measured directly are usually trivial in and of themselves. They are too idiosyncratic to use in general, interesting theories. I would hate to say that particular statements by U.S. senators lead nowhere, but as far as political theory is concerned, it is true. Any given

---

[1]It is reasonable, also, to include here reliable observers' accounts of such events. Even though the measurement of these things is technically indirect if you accept another observer's account of them, you should be able to achieve a very tight fit between the concept "event happens" and the measure "reliable observer says that event happens."

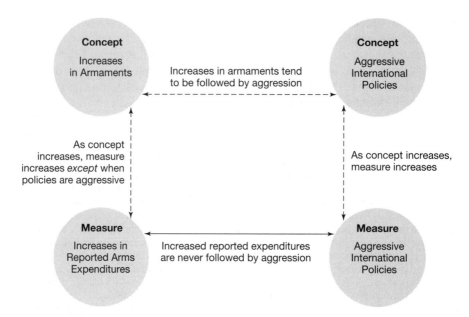

Figure 4–2   Example of the Problem of Measurement

statement can apply only to itself. It takes on a general meaning only if it is placed in a category, so that it can be compared with other statements. For instance, Senator _____'s statement, "The president's policies are bankrupting the people of my state," is not intrinsically of theoretical interest. It can be placed in various categories, however: "statements of opposition to the president," "statements of concern for constituents' needs," "bombastic statements." Placing it in one of these categories allows us to compare it with other senatorial statements and to develop theories about the causes and effects of such statements.

Note, though, that by placing it into a category we have used the statement as an indirect measure of the concept which the category represents. No given statement is a perfect case of the "bombastic statement" or of the "statement of opposition to the president." Rather, a number of statements *approximate* each category, and we choose to use these statements as indirect measures of the abstract concept we cannot measure.

To sum up the argument thus far: For a concept to be useful in building theories, it usually must be an abstraction, which cannot be measured directly. Further, of those interesting concepts that *are* in principle directly measurable (how individuals vote in an election, for example), many cannot be measured directly for practical reasons (the elections are held with a secret ballot). Therefore, most of the time we must work with variables that are indirect measures of the concepts in which we are interested. This means that there are interposed, between our operations and the theory we want to work on, the relationships between our concepts and their measures. This is the situation illustrated graphically in Figures 4–1 and 4–2. *The chief problem of measurement is to ensure, as much as possible, that the relationships between concepts and measures are such that the relationship between the measures mirrors the relationship between the concepts.*

Problems we may encounter in trying to achieve this correspondence between measures and concepts fall under two headings: problems of measure *reliability* and problems of measure *validity*.

RELIABILITY

A measure is reliable to the extent that it gives the same result again and again if the measurement is repeated. For example, if people are asked several days in a row whether they are married, and their answers vary from one day to the next, the measure of their marital state is unreliable. If their answers are stable from one time to the next, the measure is reliable.

The analogy of measuring with a yardstick may help make the meaning of reliability clear. If an object is measured a number of times with an ordinary wooden yardstick, it will give approximately the same length each time. If the yardstick were made of an elastic material, its results would not be so reliable. It might say that a chair was 20 inches high one day, 16 the next. Similarly, if it were made of a material that expanded or contracted greatly with changes in temperature, its results would not be reliable. On hot days it would say that the chair was shorter than on cold days. In fact, the choice of wood as a material for yardsticks is in part a response to the problem of reliability in measurement, a problem certainly not confined to the social sciences. Wood is cheap, rigid, and relatively unresponsive to changes in temperature.

There are many sources of unreliability in social science data. The sources vary, depending on what kinds of data are used. Official statistics, for example, may be unreliable because of an unusual number of clerical errors or because of variability in how categories are defined from one time to the next. ("Votes cast in an election," for instance, may mean "all votes, including spoiled ballots" at one time, "all valid votes" at another.) Attitude measures may be unreliable because a question is hard for respondents to understand, and they interpret it one way at one time, another way the next. Or the people entering their responses into the computer may make mistakes.

As an illustration, let us list the various sources of unreliability that might be involved in our example of tabulating responses to a simple question about marital status:

1. The question might be phrased badly, so that respondents sometimes interpreted it to mean "Are you now married?" and sometimes "Have you ever been married?" It might not be clear how people who were separated from their spouses, but not divorced, should answer.
2. Respondents might be playing games with the interviewer, answering questions randomly.
3. Dishonest interviewers might be playing games with the researcher by filling out the forms themselves instead of going to the trouble of getting the respondents to answer them.

4. Respondents' answers might depend on their mood. Perhaps they would answer "yes" when they had had a good day, or "no" when they had had a bad day.
5. Respondents' answers might depend on the context of the interview. A person might say "no" to an attractive interviewer, or "yes" to everyone else.
6. There might be simple clerical errors in copying down the answers, either by the interviewer on the spot or by the person who transcribes the interviewers' copy into a computer.

Admittedly, many of these possibilities are farfetched. The example itself is a bit strained, inasmuch as straightforward informational items like this one can usually be measured with reasonable reliability. But the same sorts of conditions affect the reliability of less straightforward survey questions, such as "What do you like about candidate *X*?" "What social class do you consider yourself to be a member of?" and "Do you feel people generally can be trusted?"

A few examples will help give you a sense of the magnitude of this problem, at least in American survey research.[2] Even on attributes that should be relatively easy to measure reliably, such as gender and race, some errors appeared when the same respondents were interviewed at two-year intervals by a well-administered survey. On the average, the reported gender of respondents changed 0.5 percent of the time from one interview to the next, whereas race did not change at all. Characteristics on which it is somewhat easier to be vague or mistaken showed substantial unreliability. For example, the report of respondents' educational background showed *lower* education two years later (which is logically impossible) an average of 13 percent of the time. Presumably, questions that permit a considerable degree of interpretation, such as attitudinal questions, would show even more unreliability.

Reliability as a Characteristic of Concepts

Thus far I have treated the unreliability of a measure as if it were a result of unpredictability in the relationship between the concept and its measure. An additional source of unreliability in the measure is variability in the "true value" of the concept. In our previous example, perhaps some people got married, or divorced, from one time to the next. This source of unreliability would be easily distinguishable from others, however, because it would show up as a recognizable pattern of stable answers up to a certain point, followed by changed, but once again stable, answers.

A more interesting case is presented when the true value itself varies randomly. This situation sometimes provides the basis for interesting theories. In one study, Converse (1964) noted that on many standard questions of political policy, people's attitudes appeared to vary randomly across time. He concluded that on certain issues, the mass public simply did not form stable opinions; and he went on to draw interesting comparisons between elite and mass opinion, based on that conclusion.

Note that to reach this conclusion, Converse had to assume that he had effectively eliminated other sources of unreliability, such as interviewer error and confusion about

[2]These are drawn from Asher (1974).

the meaning of questions. Having first eliminated these sources of unpredictability in the relationship between concept and measure, he could then treat the unreliability in his measure as a reflection of unreliability in the concept. Christopher Achen (1975) later challenged Converse's conclusions on just these grounds.

Testing the Reliability of a Measure

Although unreliability may sometimes spur on further theoretical research, as it did in this case, it is usually a barrier we want to eliminate. Careful work is the best way to achieve reasonable reliability—double-checking all clerical work, trying out the questionnaire on a small pilot study in order to catch and correct unclear questions, and so on.

We often wish to know how successfully we have reduced unreliability. A number of tests have been developed to help researchers check the reliability of a measure. I shall describe two of them briefly.

The *test-retest check for reliability* simply consists of repeating the measurement a second time, allowing for a suitable interval of time between the two measurements. If the second measure strongly resembles the first—that is, if the measure is stable over the elapsed time—it is considered relatively reliable. One problem with this test, of course, is that there is no way to distinguish instability that stems from "real" unreliability in the concept being measured from instability due to problems in the measurement process.

Another test, the *split-half check for reliability,* avoids this problem. It is particularly useful whenever a measure is multidimensional—for instance, a measure of "social status," which is made by combining such items as an individual's income, occupation, education, house size, and neighborhood into a single summary measure; or a measure of "welfare policy expenditures," comprising such disparate items as welfare payments, unemployment relief, hospital subsidies, and school lunch programs.

In the split-half test, the researcher randomly divides these assorted items into two groups and then composes a summary "measure" out of each of the groups. Because all of the items are taken to be measures of the same thing, the two summary measures should tend to be the same. A measure of how close they are to each other provides a check on how reliable the total summary measure is.

As an example, consider a state-by-state measure of "welfare policy expenditures." It might be that one particular item—disaster relief, for instance—varies greatly from state to state and from one year to the next in any one state. In one year there might be no natural disasters; in another there might be floods or a hurricane. That particular item would be a source of unreliability in the overall measure. It also should cause the split-half test to show a relatively low reliability, for its erratic variation would make the score based on the group in which it was included less likely to equal the score based on the group that did not include it.

These two checks for reliability complement each other. The test-retest check is appropriate for any sort of measure that can be replicated. It checks for *all* sources of unreliability, but this often includes changes in the true value of the concept rather than only the instability that is due to the measurement process.

The split-half check is appropriate for measures comprising a group of subitems. It checks only for those sources of unreliability that do not operate over time, inasmuch as all of the subitems presumably are measured at the same time. Accordingly, it can miss some sources of instability in the measurement process, such as the effect of the length of time since payday or of changes in the weather, on respondents' answers to an interview question. But this is actually an important benefit: If we are able to screen out true change over time in the concept, we will have a much better idea of any instability due to the measurement process.

VALIDITY

Reliability has to do with how dependably a measure mirrors its concept. In thinking about reliability, we assumed implicitly that the measure tended to mirror the concept faithfully and that the problem of reliability was simply that this tendency may be a rather loose one. We assumed, in other words, that if the concept were measured a large number of times, the average of those measures would reflect our "ideal" concept. The problem in reliability is that since the measures vary, any one of them could be rather far from the true value of the concept.

A more serious failing of our measurements, however, could result if they lack *validity*. A measure is valid if it actually measures what it purports to measure. That is, if there is in principle a *relationship of equivalence* between a measure and its concept, the measure is valid. A measure cannot be valid and yet not be reliable. But it can be reliable and yet not be valid. If it gives the same result repeatedly, the measure is reliable, but it could distort the concept in the same way each of these times, so that it does not tend to mirror it faithfully. In effect, it is "reliably invalid."

The relationship between the measure "increases in reported arms expenditures" and the concept "increases in armaments" in Figure 4–2 is an example of invalid measurement. The relationship between the concept and the measure is such that when "increases in armaments" are high, "increases in reported arms expenditures" may be either high or low, depending on the reason for the arms buildup. The measure might be reliable (a country that reported low increases in one year, for instance, should be likely to report low increases the next year also), but it would still be invalid, because the measure does not mirror the concept accurately.

The relationship between validity and reliability can be clarified by introducing the notion of *random error* and *nonrandom error,* which will also be important when we look at measuring the strength of relationships in Chapter 8. Random error is the sort of error we have addressed in discussing reliability. If in the long run, on the average, the measures of a concept tend to be true, we can assume that any error in the measure is random. In measuring education, for example (see p. 46), we encountered a good deal of random error; people tended to report their level of education differently from one time to the next. There was no reason to expect that people were deliberately misrepresenting their educational level, however, so we would expect that in the long run, accidental reporting errors would cancel each other out and the average of many such reports would give a true measure of the concept for a particular group of people.

By contrast, nonrandom error is systematic error that tends in the long run, on the average, to distort a given measure of a concept. Thus, if we asked people whether they had a prison record, it is likely that there would be a good deal of non-random error in the measure, as people systematically tried to suppress their prison records. Even in the long run, on the average, this measure would not give an accurate estimate of the true value.

Quite simply, a measure is valid to the extent that it is free of both sorts of error. A measure is reliable to the extent that it is free of random error alone. Thus, reliability is a necessary but not a sufficient condition of validity.

The two sorts of error are presented visually in Figure 4–3. Think of an archer who is trying to produce "valid" shots, that is, shots at the center of a target. The shooting may suffer from either random error (the archer is erratic), or non-random error (the archer has some systematic problem—perhaps there is a wind from the left, and the archer has not yet learned to correct for it), or both. These two sorts of error result in the four possible combinations shown in Figure 4–3. The archer achieves "reliability" on both targets B and D but achieves "validity" only on target D.

Figure 4–3   Random and Nonrandom Error

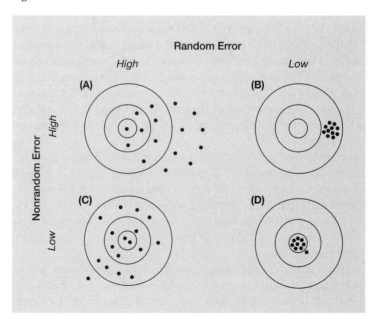

Some Examples

A few examples are in order. There are many ways that a measure can be invalid. We have already discussed several instances of random error, so we will confine ourselves here to examples of nonrandom error.

One common source of invalid measures is extrapolation from a sample to a population that is not really represented by that sample. Using letters to the editor as an indicator of public opinion would be unwise, for instance, because the people who write such letters are not an accurate cross section of the public as a whole. Their opinions would not be a valid measure of "public opinion."

A comic case of sampling problems from the early days of opinion polls is the *Literary Digest* poll. The *Literary Digest* was a giant magazine in the United States in the early part of the twentieth century. Starting in 1924, the *Digest* ran an ambitious poll in presidential election years. Virtually everyone who owned a car or a telephone was reached by the poll, which was sent out to a mailing list obtained from telephone directories and state automobile registration lists. Only about 20 percent of the sample ballots mailed out were returned, but even at that, the *Digest* had over 2 million responses each time.

The *Digest* sample distorted the U.S. population in two ways. First, it essentially sampled only the upper and middle classes, inasmuch as those who did not have a car or a telephone—at a time when cars and telephones were far less universally owned than today—did not get onto the mailing list. Also, it sampled only those who were interested enough and energetic enough to return the sample ballot. Because only 20 percent of those who received the ballot returned it, this seems to have been a rather select sample.

In 1924, 1928, and again in 1932, the *Digest* poll was very successful, coming within a few percentage points of the actual outcome in each of those elections. By 1932 the poll had become an institution; it was attacked in the *Congressional Record* and featured in *New Yorker* cartoons. Thus it was a shock when the poll's prediction of a landslide victory for Landon in 1936 was gainsaid by FDR's decisive victory. When the *Literary Digest* went out of business the next year, it was thought that the shock and loss of reputation from having called the election so badly was a factor in the magazine's demise.

Apparently, the interested, middle-class sample the *Digest* drew upon did not vote much differently from the rest of the country from 1924 through 1932. Accordingly, its sympathies were a valid measure of the way the country was going to vote in those elections. Between 1932 and 1936, however, Roosevelt initiated the New Deal, which broadened his support among the poor and drove the middle class to the Republicans. After 1936, the sympathies of the middle class were no longer a valid measure of the way the country would vote.

A questionnaire item may also result in an invalid measure when respondents attach a significantly different meaning to the question than was intended by the researcher. It had always been thought, for example, that French farmers were essentially apolitical. When asked in surveys "How interested are you in politics?" they had generally responded, "Not at all." At the same time, it was striking that voting participation was higher among farmers than among most groups in the French population. If they were not interested in politics, why did they vote?

In a study designed to explore this paradox (see p. 29), Sidney Tarrow discovered that the innocent question about political interest had been spreading confusion. French farmers apparently interpreted "interest in politics" to mean commitment to some particular party, which many of them vehemently rejected. Thus, many farmers who were interested in politics but considered themselves independents responded "Not at all" to this invalid measure of "interest in politics."

Checks for Validity

Taking precautions.   Our problem in checking the validity of a measure is similar to the general problem of measurement, depicted in Figure 4–1. We say that a measure is valid if it is a true measure of its concept. *But the general problem of measurement is precisely the fact that usually all we can observe is the measures.* We cannot know what the relationship between a concept and its measure is. How, then, can we assess the validity of the measure?

The answer, of course, is that there is no pat way to do so. Part of the "craft" in the craft of political research is cleverness and care in developing measures that appear likely to be valid. Some techniques are available to help in developing valid measures.

These deceptively simple strategies consist of taking various precautions against invalidity during the construction of a measure. The most important thing is to think through the measurement process carefully and to be on guard against any way in which the relationship between concept and measure might be distorted.

For example, we now know that drawing a sample in certain ways (drawing a random sample, for instance) guards against a fiasco like that which destroyed the *Literary Digest* poll. Also, in determining the final form of a questionnaire that you hope to use in a study, you should ask a few people to answer your questions and then to relate their understanding of the questions themselves. This may alert you to questions that mean something different to your respondents than they mean to you. Such preliminary testing of one's measures is called a "pilot study." Similarly, in using official documents, you should go thoroughly into the background of the things reported there—how they were developed, what the terms mean, how broadly they are intended to apply, and so on.

These techniques simply require that the investigator think ahead to problems that could occur in the relationship between concept and measure and either act to prevent these or to check to see whether they are present. At the most general level, the strategy I have suggested here requires only that the investigator consider carefully how plausible it is that the measure mirrors the concept.

Test of validity.   Thus far our strategies have not actually provided a test of the validity of the measure. Such a test can be made, although it is necessarily subjective and open to varying interpretations. Let us say that we want to decide whether measure α is a valid measure of concept A. If there is some measure β that we are certain is strongly related to concept A, we can check to see whether measure β is related to measure α. If it is not, and our assumption of a relationship between β and A is true, then α must not be a valid measure of A.

The study by Tarrow cited earlier provides an example of this logic. Tarrow's initial conclusion that the usual question "How interested are you in politics?" was providing an invalid measure of "political interest" among French farmers came from his observation that farmers had in fact one of the highest levels of electoral participation among French citizens. Because he could not conceive of high electoral participation occurring in the absence of high political interest, he concluded that the conventional measures, which had showed low political interest coinciding with high participation, must not have been measuring political interest validly.[3]

As another example of this kind of test, consider a measure of nations' hostility to each other—based on content analysis of the nations' newspapers (α) If we found that two of the nations went to war against each other (β) yet the measure did not show an accompanying increase in feelings of hostility between the two, we would be suspicious of the validity of the measures.

Such an indirect test of validity is possible only when a researcher is quite certain that β must go along with A. That kind of certainty is uncommon and may not be shared equally by every observer. Thus, this test is not always, or even usually, possible; and it is always rather subjective. But assessing the validity of measures is so important that an indirect test, when it can be used, will greatly strengthen your findings.

The most general test of validity is what is called *face validity*. This is just a fancy term for whether a measure looks right to you. Is it valid "on its face"? After all, you have considerable experience with politics and must judge for yourself whether the measure does what you want it to do. If you think it does (and people who read your work agree with you), it has face validity.

IMPACT OF RANDOM AND NONRANDOM ERRORS

It should be obvious that the only good measure is one that is valid, that is, one that has in it neither random nor nonrandom error. Because social scientists often operate with measures that suffer from one or the other sort of error, however, it is worth considering what happens under those circumstances. As it happens, the two sorts of error have rather different effects on the development of theory.

The effect of nonrandom error is simple and severe. If a measure is systematically invalid, there is no reason for us to expect any correspondence between the

---

[3]In this example, "political interest" corresponds to A, farmers' responses to the question on political interest correspond to α, and farmers' electoral participation corresponds to β.

relationship we actually observe from our measures and the idealized relationship we wish to investigate.

The effect of unreliability (if the measures are otherwise valid) is more subtle. To the extent that measures are unreliable, the relationship at the measure level will tend to be looser and weaker than the true relationship. It will parallel the true relationship but will appear weaker than is actually the case. If the measures are sufficiently unreliable, the basic relationship can be so weakened that it will appear, from what we can observe, as if there is no relationship at all.

This is illustrated in Table 4–1. Each set of two columns tabulates the closeness of elections in ten congressional districts, as well as their representatives' seniority. It is apparent from the figures in the first set of columns (True Values) that there is a relationship between the two, inasmuch as representatives from safe districts tend to have greater seniority than those from marginal districts. The relationship is also quite strong; seniority increases without exception as the representatives' margins of victory increase.

In the third and fourth columns, random error, such as might occur from clerical errors or other sources of unreliability, has been added to the original measures, making them less reliable. In the fifth and sixth columns, an even greater degree of random error has been added. Note that the relationship becomes weaker in the second set of data (there are more exceptions to the general tendency) and virtually disappears in the last. If we were to test the relationship between safe districts and seniority and had only the data from the last two columns in hand, we would probably conclude that there was no relationship.

TABLE 4–1   Safe Districts Related to Seniority, Using Simulated Data

True Values		Less Reliable Measures		Very Unreliable Measures	
Seniority	*Margin of Victory (%)*	*Seniority*	*Margin of Victory (%)*	*Seniority*	*Margin of Victory (%)*
32	18	32.0	21.6	12.8	9.0
24	12	19.2	12.0	12.0	12.6
23	11	11.5	12.1	30.2	8.8
20	11	22.0	4.4	22.4	6.6
14	8	14.0	5.6	21.2	12.0
11	6	11.0	6.0	13.1	3.6
10	6	9.0	10.8	2.5	0.1
6	4	3.6	4.0	13.8	2.8
5	3	4.5	3.6	21.3	1.5
2	1	2.4	0.5	0.2	12.9

IMPORTANCE OF ACCURACY

Accuracy in measurement is a critical problem whose potential for mischief does not yet seem well enough understood by political scientists. Because the variables we work with are difficult to measure, we have in many cases come to accept measures that we know full well are inadequate. Much of survey research tends to fall into this category. The loose acceptance of cross-national indicators (for instance, using "newspapers read per 1,000 population" as a measure of the political awareness of various electorates) is another example of this problem.

To the extent that our measures are not valid, what we do with them is irrelevant. This simple fact has tended to be forgotten in a general ethos of "making do" with poor measures. Fortunately, political scientists are now becoming more aware of the problem of measurement, but its importance must be constantly underscored.

Let me reemphasize the important pitfalls to be careful of in measurement:

1. Be sure that the measures you choose fit the relationship among concepts that you wish to examine. Often, an interesting question is lost through mistakes in setting up empirical operations to parallel the theoretical question.

Stephen Ansolabehere, Alan Gerber, and James M. Snyder, Jr. (2000) demonstrated this problem well in a paper showing that three decades of research on whether electoral reapportionment affected public policy had been subtly misdirected and had, as a result, reached exactly the wrong conclusion. In the wake of the *Baker v. Carr* decision, scholars had looked to see whether taking away the unfair overrepresentation of rural counties had led to an expansion of state spending. The implicit assumption was that rural areas would have preferred to keep spending down, so if they lost influence on policy, spending should have risen.[4] When they found that spending levels after reapportionment were no higher than they had been before reapportionment, scholars concluded that changing the electoral rules had had no impact on public policy. The reason was pretty clear: Under the bad, old system both Republican suburbs and Democratic cities had been disenfranchised, while rural areas, which had benefited, were not all that clearly either Democratic or Republican. So redressing the imbalances was approximately a wash in terms of party strength.

Ansolabehere and his co-authors pointed out, though, that the true test of whether electoral institutions affected policy was not the effect on the two parties, or on the overall spending level of the state, but whether counties that gained fair representation thereafter got a more equal share of state expenditures. In other words, the true test of whether equality of representation affected policy was not whether the level of spending

---

[4]*Baker v. Carr* 369 US 186 (1962). In this decision the Supreme Court ruled that it was unconstitutional to have state legislative districts with widely varying populations. Prior to the decision many states had done no legislative redistricting for half a century, so backward rural areas that had not experienced much growth in their populations were hugely advantaged relative to rapidly growing cities and suburbs. For instance, in Florida, before the Court's decision, Jefferson County, with a population of 9,543, had had one seat in the state senate and one seat in the state house of representatives. Miami's Dade County, population 935,047, had had one seat in the state senate and three seats in the state house of representatives.

rose—it was pretty obvious why it did not—but whether it was distributed more equally as a result of more equal representation. When Ansolabehere and his co-authors tested the effect in this way, they found dramatic policy effects from reapportionment. Three decades of research and commentary had missed the point.

2. Test your measures for possible inadequacies. Even when a measurement problem is not so central as to nullify the results of a study, recurrent nagging inadequacies in the chosen measures may debilitate a theory so that it becomes almost a trivial exercise. Consider a test for the simple theory: "To the extent that they understand politics, if people's need for public services is relatively great, they will be more liberal." It might well be that a political scientist would operationalize the three variables of this theory in a way such as the following:

1. "Understanding of politics" indicated by *years of education.* This would seem reasonable; at least, understanding should be fairly closely related to education.
2. "Need for public services" indicated by the *size of the person's family.* Again, although this is a rough measure, it would seem that the more dependents a person had, the more that person would depend on a variety of public services.
3. "Liberalism" indicated by *voting Democratic.*

Now, the empirical analog of the theory becomes: "The more educated a person is, the stronger the relationship between the size of that person's family and the probability that the person will vote Democratic." This statement is ridiculous. I have exaggerated here slightly, but only slightly, the extent to which unimaginative scholars will allow moderate errors of measurement to accumulate in a statement until the statement loses much of its meaning. The cure for this problem is simply to use care and imagination in developing measures.

In this chapter I have discussed problems in the accuracy of measurement. These problems turn out to be of two basic types, depending on whether they stem from flux in the measure (the problem of reliability) or from a basic lack of correspondence between measure and concept (the problem of nonrandom error). In the next chapter we look at another aspect of measurement, the question of how precisely a measure should be calibrated. In Chapter 8 we will return to tackle the problem of measuring relationships when random or nonrandom error is present.

FURTHER DISCUSSION

A delightful book with a unique approach to handling certain problems of validity is *Unobtrusive Measures,* by Eugene J. Webb, Donald T. Campbell, Richard D. Schwartz, and Lee Sechrist (1966). The ideas presented in the book are both creative and sound, and the text itself is filled with interesting and highly unusual examples. Frederick Mosteller's article "Errors," in the *International Encyclopedia of the Social Sciences* (1968), is well worth reading. Mosteller details a variety of possible sources of invalidity and unreliability. Herbert Asher (1974) presents some good examples of reliability problems, with a rather technical discussion of ways to handle them. See also Kirk and Miller, *Reliability and Validity in Qualitative Research* (1985).

Several good examples of specific measurement problems are Niemi and Krehbiel (1984), "The Quality of Surveying Responses About Parents and the Family"; Hammond and Fraser (1984), "Studying Presidential Performance in Congress"; Feldman (1983), "The Measurement and Meaning of Trust in Government"; and Converse and Pierce (1985), "Measuring Partisanship."

A useful exercise would be to list as many factors as you can that would lead to random or nonrandom error for each of the following measures: intended vote (in surveys); strength of armed forces; agreement with the president (in congressional voting); tribalism; unemployment; hierarchical control in an agency; and personal income.

Chapter 5

Problems
of Measurement

Precision

The preceding chapter dealt with problems of the reliability and validity of measures. Those problems concerned the relationship between a measure and the concept that measure is intended to mirror. In this chapter we deal with the "quality" of the measure itself—how precise it should be, or how finely calibrated, if it is to be useful.

In his study of Norwegian politics, Harry Eckstein felt that it was necessary to apologize for the fact that some measures he would use were subjective intangibles ("warmth in social relations," for instance, and "sense of community") rather than precise numerical quantities.

> [M]any of the indicators used in the text may not be readily recognized as such by contemporary social scientists. By an indicator we usually mean nowadays a precisely ascertainable quantity that stands for some imprecise quantity (as GNP may indicate level of economic development, or as the number of casualties in revolutionary violence may indicate its intensity). I do use such quantities in what follows. More often, however, readily observable "qualities" are used as indicators of not-so-readily observable qualities. This strikes me as both defensible and desirable, for quantitative indicators are not always as "indicative" of what one wants to know as other observations, nor always obtainable. In overemphasizing quantities we sometimes miss the most telling data—in any case, data that may be reliable in their own right or used as checks on the inferences drawn from quantitative data. I conceive of all social behavior as a vast "data bank," only some of which is quantitatively aggregated in yearbooks and the like, and much of the rest of which may speak volumes to our purposes, if used circumspectly. (Eckstein, 1966, footnote pp. 79–80)*

*From Eckstein, Harry. *Division and Cohesion in Democracy: A Study of Norway* (© 1966 by Princeton University Press). Reprinted by permission of Princeton University Press.

It is wrong that Eckstein should have felt the need to apologize. This should have been an unnecessary justification, but unfortunately, precise measurement has become enough of a fetish in political science that it is no doubt always possible to find someone who will dismiss a piece of work because it is not "quantitative." In this chapter I sort out just what kinds of precise quantification are helpful in political research.

The Cardinal Rule of Precision might read: *Use measurements that are as precise as possible, given the subject you are studying; do not waste information by imprecise measurement.* One theme of this chapter will be that this rule is as susceptible to violation by "quantifiers" as by "nonquantifiers." To discuss it further, I must first distinguish between two kinds of precision with which we shall be concerned. I call the first of these *precision in measures*, and the second, *precision in measurement*.

PRECISION IN MEASURES

Precision in measures corresponds roughly to our colloquial use of the word *precision*—that is, keeping the units of measurement relatively fine. For example, reporting a person's income in dollars is more precise than rounding it off to the nearest thousand dollars, and rounding income off to the nearest ten thousand dollars is still less precise. Similarly, reporting a person's religion as "Presbyterian," "Reformed Jewish," "Greek Orthodox," and so on, is more precise than reporting it as "Protestant," "Catholic," and "other."

Although as a general rule precision in measures is obviously a good thing, its importance can be overrated. First, the degree of precision we need is determined by what we wish to do with the data. If we were registering voters, for instance, any precision in measuring age that went beyond labeling people "under 18" and "over 18" would be unnecessary and possibly a nuisance as well. Generally, though, in theory-oriented research, we are not able to limit the necessary level of precision in this way. Instead, we are interested in looking at the entire range of variation and have no particular cutoff point in mind.

Sometimes, even in theory-oriented research, too much precision in measures can be a nuisance. Consider Figure 5–1, which shows the relationship between age and participation in the 2002 congressional election. The figure is so chaotic that it is hard to decipher a relationship.

Given the limited number of individuals (about 1,300) consulted in the poll, there is only a small number of respondents for each particular age. This means that the percent voting fluctuates a good deal from one age group to the next. (See the box "Law of Large Numbers," page 61.) Thus, in the ensuing, largely random fluctuation of percent voting, it is difficult to pick out a systematic pattern in the relationship between age and participation in elections, although we can see that participation generally rises with age.

One way to handle this problem, of course, would be to expand the study by considering more individuals in each category. But this usually is neither practical

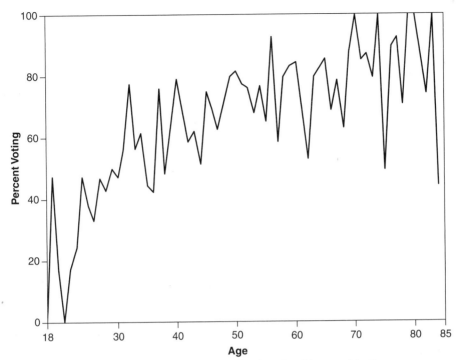

Figure 5–1   Age and Participation in 2002 Election: Age Measured by Years

Source: *2002 Congressional Election Survey, National Election Study.* Data provided by the Interuniversity Consortium for Political and Social Research.

nor in many cases possible. If we study U.S. presidents, for example, we are limited to a population of 43.

Another way to handle the problem is to decrease the precision of the measure, creating a smaller number of categories with a larger number of cases in each.[1] This has been done in Figure 5–2, with age measured to the nearest half-decade rather than to the nearest year. With the larger number of cases in each age class, the measures of percent voting fluctuate less and the form of the relationship between age and participation becomes clearer.

If it is true that sometimes we may be better off with less precision in our measures, then it appears likely that this sort of precision is not so important that research should be judged solely, or even largely, on how precise its measures are. On the other hand, although there are situations in which we may want to back off from

---

[1]Reducing precision in this way to eliminate random noise in the data is appropriate only for chart-making and visual presentation. Data analysis techniques such as regression analysis handle random noise in their own way. Reducing precision in measures is thus unnecessary when one is *analyzing* data, and it may cause such techniques to give systematically inaccurate results. (See Chapter 7 for a description of regression analysis.)

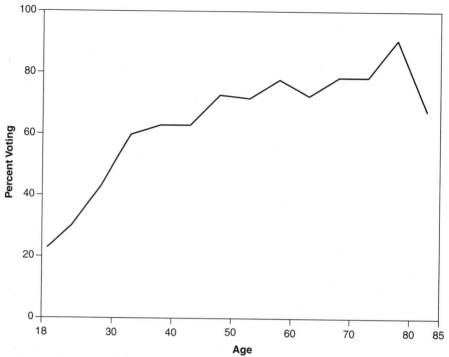

Figure 5–2   Age and Participation in 2002 Election: Age Measured by Half-Decades

precise measures, one should not conclude that precision is not helpful or important. To continue with the example of age and participation, if age were measured still less precisely than in Figure 5–2, we could again lose some of the pattern that appeared there. If age were measured in units of 33 years, for example, we would find that 54 percent of those in the first unit (18–50) voted, and that 77 percent of those in the second unit (51–84) voted. Although we would still see a strong relationship in these figures, much of the interesting detail of Figure 5–2 would be lost.

The time to ensure that your measures will be as precise as you want is when you are gathering data. A number of precautions are in order. First, make sure that you include as large a number of cases as is practical, so that you will not have to re-duce the precision more than you would like. For example, if your study concerns a specific group within the population, it makes sense to get an adequate number of the group into your study, even if the resultant data are not "typical" of the entire popu-lation. This sort of selection is known as drawing a *stratified sample*. Thus, if you wanted to study the effects of different kinds of discrimination, you might draw up a sample consisting of equal numbers of WASP, white ethnics, blacks, Puerto Ricans, and Chicanos. Had you simply drawn a random sample of the population, you prob-ably would have drawn too few Puerto Ricans and Chicanos, and you would have had to lump them together with either the blacks or the white ethnics.

Law of Large Numbers

The fact that the smaller the group of individuals sampled, the more any measure based on that group will deviate from its norm, is one part of the Law of Large Numbers. (This law forms the basis for a great deal of statistics.) The fact is intuitively obvious. If a research team selected groups of 1,000 people randomly and calculated the percent male, they would expect to get very nearly the national figure in all of them. With groups of 100, they would get increasingly erratic measurement. (It would not be un-likely for there to be 60 males in a hundred people, for example.) With groups of 10, there would be wild fluctuation; and with groups of 1 (the smallest possible "group") all groups would be either 0 or 100 percent male.

Another pitfall to avoid at the data-gathering stage is casually throwing away precision that might later prove useful. When asking people their age, record the number of years old, not "under 30," "30–40," and the like. You can always group the data later if you want to; at this point you should save all the information you get. If you ask people their religion, write down "Presbyterian," "Roman Catholic," and so on—not "Protestant," "Catholic," or "Jewish." In short, do not group the information you have until you have finished gathering it. You will have a better idea then of how fine a grouping you want to end up with.

If it is true, as the Cardinal Rule states, that it is important to be as precise as possible and not to waste information, these suggestions will help meet that rule. But the rule also states that we should be as precise as we can, *given the subject we are studying*. Because of the limitations imposed by a specific research topic, we must be careful not to overemphasize the importance of precision in measures. Many questions in political science simply do not admit of great precision of this type. Eckstein's study, which he defended in the quotation given at the start of this chap-ter, is a case in point. He wanted to study the degree of "community" in Norway. That concept does not lend itself to finely calibrated measures.

It would be foolish to give up such studies on this account. Precision in measures is important, but not indispensable. No one should stop studying the presidency because the number of cases is limited; or stop studying past historical periods because data are limited and many kinds are "pregrouped" in inconvenient ways; or stop studying political corruption because many facts are hidden or grouped together.

PRECISION IN MEASUREMENT

The sort of precision discussed in the preceding section, precision in measures, can be overemphasized. But the next sort, precision in measurement, cannot. "Precision in measures" referred to keeping distinctions as fine as was possible and practical. But we also find varying levels of information in the process of measurement itself.

There are basically three different ways to measure, each of which is qualitatively different from the others, in that it contains information not included in the others.

The most primitive way to measure a variable is simply to assign the individuals being studied to categories of that variable. This is called *nominal* measurement. For example, to measure religion, we may label people "Catholic," "Protestant," "Jew," "other." To measure nationality, we may label them "British," "German," "Russian," and so on. Nominal measurement places individuals into distinct categories of a variable, but it does not tell us anything about how the categories relate to each other.

If, in addition to assigning categories, we can rank the categories according to "how much" of the variable they embody, we have achieved *ordinal* measurement. In such measurement, we have some idea of a scale that might ideally represent the variable, and the scores we assign to individuals show whether they fall higher or lower than others on such a scale. Examples are (1) social status, measured in some way, such as "lower/working/middle/upper"; and (2) party identification, measured as "strong Democrat/weak Democrat/independent/weak Republican/strong Republican."

Further precision in measurement is possible if in addition to ranking the scores according to "how much" of the variable they represent, we can say how great the differences between the scores are. To do this, we must have some common unit of measurement for our scale. Note that such a unit was lacking in the two examples of ordinal measurement. We could not say whether the difference in status between "working" and "middle" was greater than that between "lower" and "working," nor could we say whether the difference between "weak Republican" and "strong Republican" was greater than that between "independent" and "weak Republican."

If units exist by which we can measure the intervals between scores like these, we have achieved *interval* measurement. Some variables commonly measured in intervals are income (with the unit expressed in dollars), percent voting by districts (with the unit expressed in percentage points), governmental expenditure on a program (with the unit expressed either in dollars or in percentage points if measured as a percentage of the budget), air power (with the unit expressed in kilotons of bombing coverage, number of planes, or whatever), body counts (with the unit expressed in number of dead people), and so on.

It is clear that these levels of precision comprise a nesting progression, as shown in Figure 5–3. All interval measurements are also ordinal measurements and nominal measurements, and all ordinal measurements are also nominal measurements. That is, if we had an interval measure but chose to ignore our knowledge of the distances involved between scores, we would still have scores on an ordinal measure. And if we had scores on an ordinal measure but chose to ignore our knowledge of the relative ranking on the variable, we would still have a nominal measure, a set of distinct classes to which individuals were assigned.[2]

---

[2]A further refinement in precision is possible if in addition to measuring the length of intervals along a scale, we can assign a score of zero to some point on the scale. We are then said to have "ratio" measurement (because we can take one score as a multiple of another score, which is not possible if there is no zero point). I have not included ratio measurement in my discussion here because it has not, as yet, figured importantly in data analysis in the social sciences. All of the interval scales I noted above could in fact be treated as ratio scales. Generally, however, this is ignored and they are treated simply as interval scales.

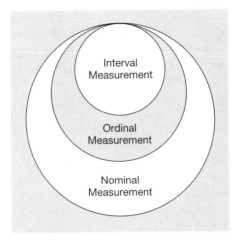

Figure 5–3   Levels of Precision

To put it a little differently, if two individuals have different scores on a variable, then (1) if the variable is measured nominally, we know that the two differ on the variable; (2) if the variable is measured ordinally, we know that the two differ on the variable *and* which one has the higher score; and (3) if the variable is measured intervally, we know that the two differ on the variable, which one has the higher score, *and* how much higher that score is than the other person's.

The three major levels of measurement, then, are nominal, ordinal, and interval measurement. As a definition of "precision in measurement," we can say that measurement is relatively precise insofar as it operates at a level that is relatively informative. Interval measurement is more precise than ordinal measurement, which is in turn more precise than nominal measurement.

Innate Nature of Levels of Measurement

Obviously, the level at which we measure things is not just a choice we make; if it were, we would simply measure everything at the interval level. Some measures are *continuous*; that is, they consist of gradations which, in principle, can be subdivided infinitely. An example is income, which can be expressed in thousands of dollars but which could be subdivided to hundreds of dollars, to dollars, to cents, to tenths of a cent, and so on. All continuous measures lend themselves naturally to interval measurement because their infinite divisibility requires that there be some unit of measurement that can be divided.

Measures that are not continuous are called *discrete*. These consist naturally of separate points that cannot be further divided. There are a few discrete measures that are interval. Elections, for example, are periodic events that cannot be subdivided. We could use the number of elections that a person had experienced as a measure of his political exposure, which would produce an interval measure, with "five elections" being two units higher than "three elections." The measure would be interval but would not be continuous; we could not subdivide elections into half-elections, or anything like that. For most discrete variables, however, such as "race," "religion," "region," or "social class," no unit presents itself by which categories (such as "African-American" and "white") can be compared. Thus, with a few exceptions, such as "elections," discrete variables are by their nature either ordinal (if they have an ordering to them) or nominal.

We see, then, that all continuous measures can be expressed as interval measures, whereas almost all discrete variables are naturally either ordinal or nominal. As a result, the level of measurement we use is generally not a personal choice but inheres in the thing we are measuring. There are two caveats to this statement, however: (1) We could always ignore information we have about a measure, and treat it as a lower-level measure (the next section, "The Sin of Wasting Information," argues against this); and (2) *sometimes* we can add other information or theory to a naturally nominal or ordinal measure and enrich it to a higher level than its natural level: this is discussed in the section after next, "Enriching the Level of Precision in Measurement."

The Sin of Wasting Information

Time and again data collected at a higher level of precision are collapsed to a lower level to simplify handling the data, writing reports, and so on. Age is often grouped into categories such as "youngest," "younger middle-aged," "older middle-aged," and "oldest"—an ordinal measure. Or income is grouped into "low," "middle," and "high."

Esthetically, of course, it would seem better to know more about a subject rather than less. This alone should be enough to justify our Cardinal Rule: "Use measurements that are as precise as possible, given the subject you are studying; do not waste information by imprecise measurement." This esthetic consideration applies both to precision in measures and to precision in measurement. But inasmuch as I argued earlier that for practical purposes precision in measures might sometimes be sacrificed, it appears that by itself the esthetic consideration is not compelling.

A more important reason for following the Cardinal Rule, one that applies only to precision in measurement, arises if we are interested in using the measures to study a relationship between two or more variables. In this case, we can do qualitatively different things with data measured at different levels of precision. With more precise measurement we can do a greater variety of things with our data and thus have more of an opportunity to develop interesting theories. It is for this reason that precision in measurement is more important than precision in measures. Let me provide an example.

In Figure 5–4, the relationship between age and percent voting, which we looked at earlier, is presented in three forms, according as (A) age is collapsed to a nominal measure and all knowledge of ranking and unit distance in it is lost; (B) age is collapsed to an ordinal measure and the knowledge of unit distance in it is lost; and (C) age is maintained at an interval level of measurement.

In the first case, with age measured nominally, we can see that there is a relationship between age and participation in elections. This is indicated by the fact that

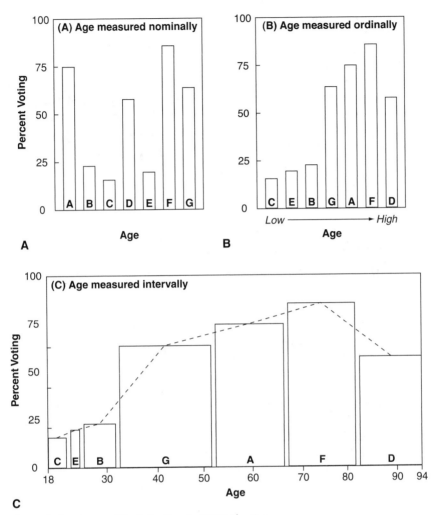

Figure 5–4 Age and Participation in 2002 Election

different age groups participate at different rates. Only 16 percent of the individuals in category C vote, for instance, as compared with 86 percent of those in category F. If age and participation were not related, we would expect about the same percentage of individuals in each category to vote. With nominal measurement, this is all we can say—*that the variables are or are not related.*

In the second case, with ordinal measurement, we can say a good deal more. We now know the ranking of the different categories of age: C is youngest, E the next to youngest, and then come B, G, A, F, and D. In addition to seeing whether or not the variables are related, we can see *the pattern of the relationship.* In this case, that pattern is one of increasing participation with increasing age up to some point, and then a reversal, with participation decreasing as age increases.

If age were measured intervally, we could say still more about the relationship. Interval measurement adds information about the magnitude of differences in age expressed by the categories. If age were measured intervally, we could see whether or not there was a relationship, we could see the pattern of the relationship, and we also could see *the rate at which one variable changed in response to changes in the other variable.*

In Figure 5–4C, the bars in the graph have been stretched to take into account the added information that the categories represent the following age groups, measured in a common unit, years:

C 18–20
E 21–23
B 24–30
G 31–50
A 51–64
F 65–80
D 81–91

We can now see that the initial increase in participation, between the ages of 20 and 30, is slow; that there is a big jump over about the next ten years; and that participation peaks around age 70, after which there is a decline. The dashed line tracing the path of the bars approximates the pattern we have already seen in Figure 5–2. This suggests an interesting combination of processes: Learning and acquiring the habit of voting during the first years of eligibility causes participation to rise rapidly at first after an initial pause; as this increase levels off, it is followed by a decline, perhaps due to enfeeblement. This is a richer description of the relationship than we could have gotten using the ordinal measurement.

Notice that in part C of Figure 5–4, greater precision in *measures* also would have been useful, especially a finer breakdown of ages above 40. With the greater precision in measures of Figure 5–2, we can see that the peak occurs in the late 70s.

However, the information lost through the low precision in measures in part C is slight compared with the information lost by lowering the precision in measurement in parts A and B. *Preserving a high level of precision in measurement deserves a strong priority in research.*

Enrichment of the Level of Precision in Measurement

So far I have argued that we should try not to drop data carelessly to a lower level of measurement. By a similar argument, we should always try to *raise* data to a higher level when this is possible. Given a certain amount of boldness and ingenuity, we may sometimes be able to do this.

Often, we can enrich our data in this way if we know something more about the data than is reflected in our measurement—in other words, if we have information about the data that would otherwise be wasted. This information may not be enough to provide neat, clean measurement at the higher level. If it were, we probably would have measured at the higher level in the first place. Generally, though, untidy measurement at a higher level is better than neat measurement at a lower level. A few examples may be the best way to show how measurement can be "enriched" in this way, by raising the level of measurement.

Examples of Enrichment

*1. **Example 1.*** You are studying the relationship between the colonial experience of new nations and the stability of democratic institutions in those nations. That is, you want to compare the stability of democratic institutions in former French, British, Dutch, and American colonies, for example. One way to do this would be simply to treat the problem as one of a relationship involving nominal measurement.

But it is likely that you have in mind some underlying scale along which the colonial experience varied, depending on which country had done the colonizing, and that you are really interested in the relationship between this scale and the stability of democratic institutions. If you can array the different mother countries along this scale, you can use them as an ordinal or interval measure of the scale.

You might, for example, be interested in whether or not the colonizing country tried to assimilate the native population to its own culture and the effect this had on the stability of the resulting institutions. On the scale "level of assimilation," the British colonial experience would rank low and the French quite high. The Dutch and American experiences would fall somewhere between these, with the United States possibly lower than the Dutch. For this particular purpose, then, the colonizing countries comprise at least an ordinal measure of the level of assimilation. If you could make a reasonably informed guess at the relative differences (such as Dutch rather close to the French; large gap between British and American), you might even be able to bring your data up to the level of rough interval measurement.

Further, you well might want to use a given nominal measurement twice or more in the same analysis, as a measure of different underlying scales. Thus you might be interested in predicting the stability of democratic institutions from two variables simultaneously: (1) the level of assimilation at which the colonizer aimed, and (2) the extent of oppression and violence during the colonial period. The colonizers would be arrayed differently along these two scales, and thus each would represent a different mix of the two variables. The United States, for example, probably would fall above the middle in assimilation, but low in oppression; France, high in assimilation and toward the middle in oppression; Belgium, low on assimilation but high on oppression; and so on.[3]

---

[3]Notice that the manner in which measurement of nominal variables has been enriched in these examples parallels the "dimensional analysis" that I urged in Chapter 3. Like vague, multidimensional concepts, nominal classifications involve an infinite number of dimensions. The various types of colonial experience we cited vary on degree of assimilation, extent of oppression, speed of economic development, geopolitical position, or what have you. Abstracting the appropriate ordered variable(s) from a nominally measured variable is much the same as abstracting the appropriate dimension(s) from a set of multidimensional concepts.

2. Example 2. You are studying the relationship between religion and political alienation. Religion could simply be measured nominally (Jewish, old-Reformation Protestant, Roman Catholic, and so on). Perhaps, however, you have in mind an underlying dimension that causes you to expect a relationship between the two variables. You might be thinking in terms of the extent to which one's religion promotes an apocalyptic view of the universe. If so, then as in Example 1, you could take the different religions ranked by their apocalyptic content as an ordinal or interval measure of this scale. Jews would fall near the bottom of such a scale and fundamental Protestants, near the top.

Alternatively, your theory might be that religious groups, simply as social organizations, build involvement among their members. In this case you could array the different religions in terms of the size and "closeness" of their congregations, how democratic their legal structure is, or whatever. Note that the "right" ordinal or interval arrangement of the nominal categories depends on which underlying scale you want to tap. Thus, Jews would fall low on the "apocalyptic" scale but high on the "closeness" scale.

In working with ordinal variables (either "enriched" nominal variables or variables which obviously are ordered from the outset), a common unit may appear immediately, and you can treat the variables readily and directly as interval measures. For instance, abstracting the degree of "closeness" from religious affiliation suggests one ready interval measure—average size of congregations—although this admittedly would be only a rough measure whose validity would be questionable. Often, to enrich ordinal data, we must use a good deal of ingenuity, as in the next example.

3. Example 3. You want to measure the extent to which different educational programs tend to encourage pro- or anti-military attitudes. You can distinguish three types of educational programs: military academy; general university, with participation in ROTC; general university, without participation in ROTC. These form an ordinal measure of "militariness" readily enough, with the military academy highest and the non-ROTC program lowest. Can you make an interval measure out of this ranking?

Fortunately, you might have some additional information on the subject. In a 1971 study of Annapolis midshipmen, ROTC, and non-ROTC students, for instance, it was found that 39 percent of the midshipmen thought the American military budget was too small; 10 percent of the ROTC students agreed, as did 4 percent of the non-ROTC students (Karsten and others, 1971). If you were willing to assume that at that time the Naval Academy was typical of the military academies and that there was a linear relationship between the pro-military orientation of an educational program and the percentage of its students who believed that the military budget was too small, this information would have allowed you to reconstruct the interval measure implicit in the ordered variable. (For a more detailed explanation of "linear relationship," see the box on p. 70.)

If the degree of pro-military orientation in ROTC programs increased support of higher budgets by 6 percentage points over non-ROTC students, but the Naval Academy increased budget support by 29 percentage points over ROTC students, then (given your assumptions) the interval between military academies and ROTC must have been 4.83 times as great as the interval between ROTC and non-ROTC. This is demonstrated geometrically in Figure 5–5.

Here I have drawn two of the many possible linear relationships between the "military content" of education and support for the defense budget. It should be clear that the same principle would hold for any linear relationship. Because you know the scores on budget support for non-ROTC, ROTC, and the Naval Academy, you can project across the graph to see where they should fall on the line showing the relationship. Non-ROTC falls at A, ROTC at B, and the Naval Academy at C. Now look

Figure 5–5 Enriching the Measure of Military Content

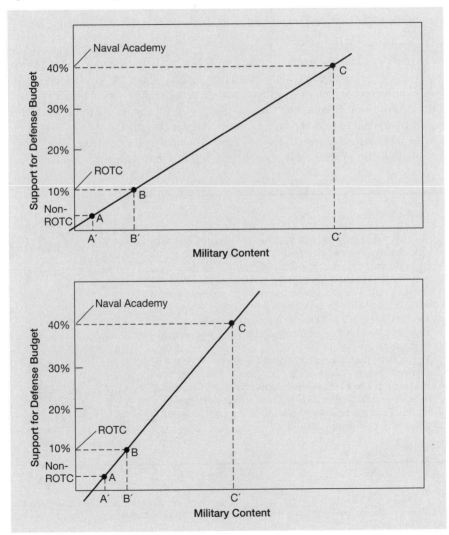

down the graph, to see what scores on "military content" must be associated with positions A, B, and C on the line. These scores are A′ B, and C′. Of course, you do not have units in advance by which to measure military content, but it is apparent that whatever units you conceive of, and whatever linear relationship between the two variables exists, the distance from B′ to C′ must be approximately five times the distance from A′ to B. (To be exact, the ratio of the distances is 4.83.)

This gives you all you need to construct an interval measure—that is, an estimate of the relative differences (intervals) between scores of the measure. Because an interval measure does not assume that a zero point is known, you can arbitrarily pick the unit in which to express your measure. You might assign 1.0 to non-ROTC and 2.0 to ROTC, in which case Naval Academy would have to be 6.83. You might assign 4.0 to non-ROTC and 8.0 to ROTC; Naval Academy would then have to be 27.32. Most simply, the scores assigned might be non-ROTC, 4; ROTC, 10; and academy, 39.

4. Example 4.   In Example 3, a rather precise piece of outside information was used to tell how long the intervals should be. Often such a precise guide is simply unavailable, but you still could know more than nothing about the length of the intervals. Consider a problem in which you want to measure the national power of Costa Rica, Spain, Great Britain, and Russia.[4] The *order* is clear, and a timid researcher would be content to treat this as an ordinal variable. On the other hand, you know that the intervals are not equal, and you know which intervals are greater than others. You could create an acceptable, though quite rough, interval measure of the national

---

Linear Relationship

A relationship between two variables is *linear* if one variable changes by a constant amount with a change of one unit in the second variable, regardless of the value of the second variable. The relationship in graph A is linear; *y* increases by one-half unit when *x* changes by one unit, no matter what value *x* starts with. The relationship in graph B is nonlinear. Here, if *x* is high, a unit change in *x* produces relatively little change in *y*; if *x* is low, a unit change in *x* produces relatively great change in *y*.

Thus, the relationship in graph A can be expressed by a straight line, inasmuch as the relationship is the same at all values of *x*. The relationship in graph B must be expressed by a curve which tilts differently at different values of *x*, inasmuch as the relationship between the two variables is different for different values of *x*.

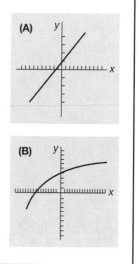

---

[4]Although I have dubbed the variable "national power," for most purposes this would be broken down more profitably into component dimensions, such as "diplomatic influence," "economic power," and "military power."

power of the various countries simply by assigning arbitrary interval lengths in accordance with your general idea of the magnitudes involved. You might choose, for example, Costa Rica, 1; Spain, 7; Great Britain, 10; and Russia, 40. The measure is rough and subjective, but it could be refined by bringing to bear the impressions of more knowledgeable observers with regard to relative national power. Most important, measuring in this way does not ignore the valuable collection of outside information—most of it admittedly undigested—that you already possess.

The interval measures you derive in Examples 3 and 4 may not leave you fully satisfied. Because of the indirect chain of reasoning in Example 3, and the assumptions required for it, and because of the arbitrary decisions to be made in Example 4, there is plenty of room for errors to occur. The question remains: Are you better off with such rough interval measures, or should you opt to ignore the size of intervals and treat the variables as ordinal measures? Given the wider range of theoretical concerns that one can cover using interval data, I think the answer is obvious. It makes sense to use all the information we have about a question, even if we must supplement that information with assumptions and hunches. The alternative is to ignore a portion of what we know. Taking the "safer" course allows us to state our results with more confidence but reduces the importance of what we have to say.

Enriching measurement in this way is a research technique for which the researcher's creativity and ingenuity are critical. One mark of a good researcher is that she boldly seeks out all chances—not just the obvious or safe ones—to raise the level of measurement in her work.

Quantifiers and Nonquantifiers Again

This discussion of precision in measures and precision in measurement has centered on the work of "quantifiers" (those who work by preference with objective data, especially with numerical data), simply because it was more convenient to introduce it in that way. But the same general conclusions hold for "nonquantifiers" as well.[5] To return to the quotation from Eckstein with which I introduced this chapter, it is clear that he was interested in doing the same things as quantifiers do, but in a different way. He wanted to measure variables and to assess relationships between those variables. His subject matter, however, rarely allowed him to use objective or numerical measures. For many variables in which he was interested, he could use only vague descriptions, such as "rather strong sense of community," "highly developed team spirit," and so on. Most of these descriptions had to depend on his subjective judgment rather than on impersonal outside indicators.

Can this sort of work be described in terms of precision in measures and precision in measurement? Do the rules I have prescribed in this chapter hold for this sort of work as they do for more quantitative studies? First, we may note that measuring

---

[5]Let me repeat my earlier admonition. Being a "quantifier" or "nonquantifier" is not an either/or question. The extent to which a researcher uses objective data is generally not a matter of personality but rather of the subject he is studying and the data available for that subject.

variables nonquantitatively requires the same sort of boldness that I urged in enriching data to a higher level of measurement. More important, we can see that this is primarily a problem of precision in measures, not of precision in measurement. A nonquantifier can measure things only approximately, but there is no particular reason why such research cannot approximate interval measurement.

For example, a student of Chinese politics might suggest that the higher a Chinese politician rises in the hierarchy, the less likely he is to press for the interests of his region. This statement approximates a relationship between two variables measured at the ordinal level ("height in the hierarchy" and "likelihood of lobbying"). Working more boldly and imaginatively, another student might approximate interval measurement. She might state, for example, that the higher a Chinese politician rises in the hierarchy, the less likely he is to press for the interest of his region; that this shift occurs very sharply as he moves from some particular level of the hierarchy to another; that the shift continues from there on up the hierarchy at a diminished rate; and finally, that near the top of the hierarchy, the process reverses itself, with the men at the top feeling secure enough to concern themselves more than those immediately below them with the interests of their regions.[6] This is certainly a richer statement than the earlier version, but it is no more "quantified" than the other. It is still based on subjective descriptions, made in the absence of objective indicators. The only difference is that in the second case the researcher enriches the level of measurement at which she is working.

FURTHER DISCUSSION

A readable presentation along the lines developed in this chapter is Edward R. Tufte's "Improving Data Analysis in Political Science" (1968–1969). You should note that in this chapter I have presented a fairly radical position in favor of upgrading levels of measurement, a position that would not be accepted by all social scientists. To the extent that one is worried about measurement error, either random or nonrandom, one should be concerned about the possibility that "enriching" a level of measurement may insert either sort of error into the new measure. Personally, I think the risk is often justified; however, many scholars believe that the costs in carrying out such "enrichment" are greater than the benefits. A fairly technical paper that urges researchers to take seriously the risk of inserting measurement error by treating ordinal variables as if they were interval (an extrapolation similar to enrichment but riskier and less well thought out) is that by Wilson (1971). Another excellent article, a bit technical, is by Carter (1971).

---

[6] I have no idea whether this is a reasonable theory. I have constructed it merely as an example of the wide applicability of pseudo-interval measurement.

Two questions you might consider are:

1. Why would the technique in Example 3 not be appropriate if the relationship between "military content" and "support for defense budget" were nonlinear? What might you do in this case?
2. "Ratio" measurement is interval measurement for which, in addition to being able to measure the relative interval between different values of the measure, it is possible to assign the value zero to some point on the measure (see footnote 2). One difference between interval and ratio measurement is that whereas it is possible to add and subtract interval measures, it is possible to add and subtract, *multiply*, and *divide* ratio measures. It is possible to say that a given score is twice as great as another score, given ratio measurements; this is not possible with simple interval measurement. Fahrenheit temperature is an example of an interval measure that is *not* a true ratio measure, even though "zero" is arbitrarily assigned to one point on the scale. It is not true, for example, that a temperature of +20°F is half as "hot" as +40°F. In this chapter I pointed out that the different levels of measurement were important because it was possible to make a greater variety of statements about relationships between variables that were measured in "advanced" ways. What statements might be made about relationships between ratio-measured variables that could not be made about relationships between interval-measured variables?

Chapter 6

Causal Thinking and Design of Research

Thus far everything we have looked at in this book has been justified in terms of how useful it is in establishing relationships between variables. It is time now to look more closely at what a "relationship" is, and how we interpret it.

Two variables are related if certain values of one variable tend to coincide with certain values of the other variable. Thus, social class and party vote are related in the United States, because those who vote Republican tend to be from the middle and upper classes. We have seen many such examples of relationships in earlier chapters.

If, in addition, we consider that the values of one variable *produce* the values of the other variable, the relationship is a *causal relationship*. The example of class and voting, noted above, is an example of a causal relationship. We feel that there is something about a person's social class that makes that person more likely to vote in a certain way. Therefore, we say that social class is a "cause" of party vote. It is not merely true that the two variables tend to coincide; they tend to coincide *because values of the one tend to produce distinct values of the other.*

Empirical, theory-oriented political research is almost exclusively concerned with *causal* relationships. As I pointed out earlier, a theory in its simplest form usually consists of three things: independent variables (those we think of as doing the "producing"), dependent variables (those we think of as being "produced"), and causal statements linking the two (refer again to p. 14).

In this chapter we first discuss the idea of causation, and then follow this up with some ideas on research design. Research design—the way in which we structure the gathering of data—strongly affects the confidence with which we can put a causal interpretation on the results of research.

CAUSALITY: AN INTERPRETATION

The most important thing to note about causal thinking is that it is an interpretation of reality. In this regard, the assertion of a *causal relationship* differs from the mere assertion of a *relationship,* which is a rather objective statement. In the example of social class and the vote, for instance, there is objective evidence for the existence of a relationship, but a causal interpretation of this relationship is much more subjective. It might be argued, for instance, that class does not produce the vote, but that both are produced by something else—the ethnic, religious, and racial conflicts that have surfaced often in American politics. Thus someone could argue—and it would not be an unreasonable argument—that class is not a cause of the vote. Rather, someone might say, certain ethnic groups tend to vote for the Democrats; and these same groups, simply by accident, also tend to be working class. Therefore, the coincidence of class and party votes is just that—a coincidence. Distinguishing between this version of the relationship and the more common version is at least partly a matter of judgment.

Almost every situation in which we wish to make causal statements is similar to this example. The question of whether or not there is a relationship is objectively testable. The question of whether the relationship is a causal one, and of which variable causes which, requires an interpretation. Generally speaking, all that we know directly from our data is that two variables tend to occur together. To read causality into such co-occurrence, we must add something more, although as you will see, it is possible to design the research in ways that can help us significantly in doing this.

Consider two further examples: If we see that people who smoke regularly have a greater incidence of heart disease than nonsmokers, we might conclude that smoking causes heart disease. If we see that those U.S. senators who conform to the informal rules of the Senate tend to be the ones whose bills get passed, we might conclude that conformity is rewarded in the Senate. In both cases, we observe that two phenomena tend to occur together (smoking and heart disease, conformity and success). Our interpretation of this is that one of the phenomena causes the other. This interpretation is a subjective one.

We cannot always make a causal interpretation when two phenomena tend to coincide. The notion of cause involves more than that. Winter does not cause spring, although the one follows the other regularly. Similarly, hair color does not cause political party preference, although it is probably true in the United States that blonds, who are relatively likely to be white and Protestant, are more apt than brunettes to be Republicans. To qualify as a "causal" relationship, the coincidence of two phenomena must include the idea that one of them *produces* the other.

A good example of the difficulty of ascribing causal direction is the relationship between central bank independence and inflation. In general, economists think that if central banks (such as the Federal Reserve in the United States) are relatively independent of political control, they will use monetary policy more aggressively to fight inflation. Certainly, where central banks are independent, inflation is low. In a 1993 study, the three countries with the most politicized banks had averaged almost 8 percent inflation from 1955 to 1985; the three countries whose central banks were most independent had averaged only about 3.75 percent inflation.[1]

We see, then, that there is a relationship between the two; but is it true, as the economists believe, that bank independence causes low inflation? Batalla (1993) suggests that the opposite causal interpretation may be true. Reviewing the history of the 1920s and 1930s in Latin America, he notes that many countries had established autonomous central banks by the late 1920s, but that when high rates of inflation hit in the mid-1930s, most of them took away that autonomy. That is, low inflation rates allowed governments to tolerate independent central banks, while high inflation rates led the governments to pull the banks under their control. So, which causes which? Do independent central banks give us low inflation, or does low inflation give us independent central banks?

If ascribing *cause* to the coincidence of two things is so tricky, why do we bother with the notion of causation in our theories? What difference does it make whether class causes voting for a certain party, or whether the coincidence of class and party is due to something else that causes both of them? Remember that the ultimate purpose of theories is to give us levers on reality, some basis for choosing how to act. If A and B coincide but A does not cause B, changing A will not change B. A coincidence without cause gives you no lever.

ELIMINATION OF ALTERNATIVE CAUSAL INTERPRETATIONS

A causal interpretation is something that cannot come solely from our observations. But by setting up a study in certain ways and by manipulating the data appropriately, we can settle *some* of the problems in making causal interpretations. In our previous example of hair color, for instance, we might have looked only at WASPS, and compared blonds and brunettes. If we then found that blond WASPS did not tend more often than brunette WASPS to be Republican, we could infer that hair color did not cause party preference.

In general, where we think that a third variable is causing two other variables to coincide accidentally, as in this hair color example, we can use our data to test the relationship. By *holding constant* the third variable, we can see whether it has led the original two variables to coincide in such a way as to resemble a causal relationship. Thus, if we artificially hold social position constant by looking only at WASPS, and now blonds and brunettes no longer differ in their politics, we can infer that the difference in voting was due not to the difference in hair color (which was merely a

---

[1]*The Economist*, November 20, 1993, p. 94.

coincident variable) but to the difference in socioethnic background. We can then conclude that hair color does not cause political preference.[2]

Thus there are techniques by which we can manipulate our data to eliminate *some* of the alternative causal interpretations of a relationship. But there is always one question about causation that remains purely subjective and that cannot be resolved completely by any techniques of data handling. Given that two variables are causally related, which of the variables causes which?

Suppose that two phenomena coincide and that there appears to be a causal relationship between them. Only you can decide which is the cause and which the result. One useful convention in Western culture—but it is only a convention, even though it is so well established that it seems "natural" to us—is that causation works forward in time.[3] Accordingly, if we can establish that change in one of the variables precedes change in the other, then if we are sure that there is causation between the two, it is clear which variable must be the cause. For example, we assume that pulling a trigger causes the shot that follows that action, rather than vice versa.

Although this convention frequently simplifies things for the researcher, there are many instances in which it cannot be used. Survey research, in which variables usually are measured just once and in a single interview, is a case in point. If voters who like the Republican party also tend to oppose welfare programs, which causes which? We might think that voters choose the party that offers the policies they prefer, but it might also be that voters choose the Republican party for other reasons, such as foreign policy, and then are influenced by the party's leaders to adopt its position on welfare programs as their own.

As another example, consider the fact that many important social variables are environmental "givens," such that one can never be said to precede another in a person's life. Race, gender, social class, and other factors are intermingled; how can we sort out causal relationships involving them? Is the "gender gap" by which women are less likely than men to support the Republican party due to the two parties' differing positions on feminist issues, or is it due to the fact that women are also more likely than men to live in poverty and thus support the party of the have-nots?

Summary

Let me pull together the argument to this point. It generally is not enough for us to note that two phenomena coincide. We generally also want to interpret *why* they coincide. There are three interpretations available to us, and our choice from among them is ultimately subjective.

---

[2]The technique of holding constant is discussed in greater detail at the conclusion of the chapter.

[3]An example of a cultural tradition in which causation does not necessarily work forward in time is that of the Old Testament, whose writers believed that some people could prophesy what was to come in the future. In effect, the future event caused the prior prophecy to occur.

1. Causation is not involved at all.   The phenomena coincide because of logical necessity; that is, their coincidence is tautologically determined. Thus, by definition, spring follows winter, yet we do not think of winter as producing spring. A slight variation of this often occurs in the social sciences. It often happens that two slightly different measures of the same concept coincide. We would expect them to coincide, simply because they measure the same thing; we do not think of either of them as causing the other. For example, members of Congress who vote to increase aid to education tend also to support increases in welfare spending. This is not because their votes on one issue *cause* them to vote the way they do on the other. Rather, both votes are an expression of their general disposition to spend money on social programs. We must decide from outside the data at hand whether a coincidence of two phenomena is of this type or whether it involves causation.

2. Causation is involved somewhere.   This may mean one of two things: either (A) *the relationship we observe is a result of outside factors that cause the two phenomena at hand, and thus neither of these phenomena causes the other;* or (B) *one of the phenomena causes the other.*

The study of hair color and party preference was an example of possibility A. By setting up the study appropriately, we can control for various outside factors in order to concentrate on the relationship in question. In the hair color example, such a control was used. To this extent, we can see *from the data* whether the coincidence of the phenomena is of this sort. But we are still not exempt from making assumptions, for we must first have assumed the outside factor(s) causally prior to the two coincident phenomena. This is not always an easy decision to make. If it is possible to set up a true experiment (described in the next section), we can eliminate this possibility. But this is rare in "field" social sciences such as political science or sociology.

In possibility B, we have a true causal statement. We are still not finished making assumptions, of course, for we must decide which of the phenomena is the cause and which the effect. That is ultimately a subjective decision, though often we are aided in making it by the convention that causation must run forward in time.

As I have said so often in this book, one of the pleasures of research is that nothing in it is automatic. Even the most "quantitative" techniques do not take away our obligation and our right to be creative and imaginative. The fact that causal analysis is ultimately subjective may trouble us—objectivity always seems more comforting than the responsibility imposed by subjective judgment—but in a way it is also a great comfort, inasmuch as it keeps us, and what we do with our minds, at the heart of our research.

A FEW BASICS OF RESEARCH DESIGN

It should be evident from the discussion so far that the basic problem in causal analysis is that of eliminating alternative causal interpretations. Whenever two variables vary together (are related, coincide), there is a variety of causal sequences that might account for their doing so. A might cause B, B might cause A, both A and B might be caused by something else, or there might be no causation involved. Our task is to eliminate all but one of these, thus leaving an observed relationship, together with a single causal interpretation of it. Some of these alternatives can be eliminated only if we make assumptions from outside the actual study. But we also can design the study in such a way that certain alternatives are impossible. This will leave an interpretation that is dependent on fewer subjective assumptions and can thus lend a greater measure of certainty to the results.

Consider these examples:

1. Agency study. An organizational analysis of a government agency is made in which each worker keeps track of his output for a week. The organization is then re-structured to decentralize decision making. After the reform, another week's tabulation shows increased output. Conclusion: Decentralized decision making increases output.

2. The Spock revolution. During the 1950s, American child-rearing practices became more "permissive," under the influence of Dr. Benjamin Spock's *Baby and Child Care*. In the 1960s, American youth became more radical. Conclusion: Permissive child-rearing produces radical youth.

3. Organizing the poor. In anticipation of a major campaign to organize the poor of a city, a survey is taken among them to measure their interest in politics. At the end of the organizing campaign, the same people are asked the same questions a second time. It turns out that those who were contacted by the campaign workers have indeed acquired an increased interest in politics, compared with those who were not. Conclusion: The campaign has increased the political awareness of the poor.

4. Tax-reform mail. The *Congressional Quarterly* reports the proportion of each senator's mail which favored tax reform. Comparing these figures with the senators' votes on a tax-reform bill, we see that senators who had received relatively favorable mail tended to vote for the bill, whereas those who had received relatively unfavorable mail tended to vote against it. Conclusion: How favorable a senator's mail was on tax reform affected whether or not she voted for it.

5. Presidential lobbying. In an attempt to measure his influence over Congress, the president randomly selects half the members of the House. He conducts a straw vote to find out how all the members of the House intend to vote on a bill important to him. He then lobbies intensively among the half he has randomly selected. In the final vote in the House, the group that he had lobbied shifted in his favor compared with what he could have expected from the earlier straw vote; the other half voted as predicted from the straw vote. Conclusion: His lobbying helped the bill.

Let us look at the design of these studies to see how many alternative causal interpretations each can eliminate.

Designs Without a Control Group

In the first two examples, the design is of the form:

1. Measure the dependent variable.
2. Observe that the independent variable occurs.

3. Measure the dependent variable again.
4. If the dependent variable has changed, ascribe that to the occurrence of the independent variable.

Thus, in "Agency Study," (1) the workers' output is tabulated; (2) the organizational structure is decentralized; (3) the workers' output is once again tabulated; and (4) the conclusion is reached. This kind of design operates *without a control group*. As a result, there are a number of alternative causal sequences that might have produced the same result.

For example, a plausible alternative explanation for the increased productivity might be that the initial measurement of production, in which each worker kept track of output for a week, focused the workers' attention on productivity in a way that had not been done before, leading them to improve their productivity. In other words, it was not the decentralization of the agency, but the study itself, which caused productivity to rise.[4]

Had the study included a second agency as a control (see the next section), one in which output was measured at the same times as in the first agency but in which there was no decentralization, the alternative explanation would not have been plausible. That is, if the increased productivity in "Agency Study" had been due simply to the act of measuring, productivity in the control agency (in which the same measurements were taken as in the first agency) also should have increased. Accordingly, if we found that productivity increased more in the reorganized agency than in the control agency, we would know that this could not have been because of the act of measuring, for both agencies would have undergone the same measurements. That particular alternative interpretation would have been eliminated by the design of the study. In conducting the study without a control, the alternative interpretation can be eliminated only by assuming it away, which seems very risky.

The "Spock Revolution" provides an example of another sort of alternative explanation that may be plausible in studies without a control group. It is quite possible that other things that occurred between the two "measurements" of youth's radicalism (roughly, the early 1950s and the late 1960s) were the cause of the increased radicalism among young people rather than the changed patterns of child-rearing. The change in educational policies after Sputnik, the civil rights movement in the South, the Vietnam war, increased affluence—all might be proposed as alternative causes. If it were possible to construct a control group of American youths whose parents had not changed their child-rearing practices, these alternative explanations could be tested and perhaps eliminated. The control group would have experienced all the

---

[4]A famous example of this sort is the Hawthorne study, in which an attempt was made to measure how much productivity increased when factories were made brighter and more pleasant. As it turned out, the groups of workers who were placed in better surroundings did show major increases in productivity. But so did control groups whose surroundings had not been improved. The novelty of taking part in an experiment, the attention paid to the workers, and increased social cohesiveness among those groups chosen for the experiment—all these raised productivity irrespective of the experimental changes in physical working conditions that were made for some (but not all) of the groups. See Roethlisberger and Dickson (1939).

alternative causes in the same way as the original group. If it did not become as radical as the original, the alternative explanations of the shift would not be plausible.

The same general alternative explanation also might have applied to "Agency Study." If something else had happened between the two measurements of productivity—the weather improved, Christmas came, the president urged greater productivity, or whatever—this might have been the true cause of the increased production. Again, using a second agency as a control could eliminate such alternative explanations.

The Spock Revolution, incidentally, is an example of how difficult it may be to include a control group in a design. Where an event affects the entire population you wish to study, it may be impossible to build a control group. For example, the existence of the United Nations has affected the foreign policy of every country in the world since 1945. How can a student of international politics distinguish its effect on foreign policy from the effects of the Soviet–American rivalry, the development of atomic weapons, the liberation of former colonies, and so on, all of which have happened at the same time? One cannot, of course. It is simply not possible to provide a control group of contemporary countries for which the United Nations has not existed.

Studies without a control group pop up all the time. On January 4, 2004, the *Minneapolis Star Tribune* headlined a front-page story: "State Sex Ed Not Working, Study Finds." The story reported a study by the Minnesota Department of Health, which in 2001 had asked students in grades 7 and 8 of three schools that had adopted an abstinence-only sex education curriculum (not teaching contraception or safe sex, but rather providing materials to encourage students to abstain), whether "at any time in your life have you ever had sex (intercourse)?" They then came back in 2002 and repeated the question for the same group of students, now in grades 8 and 9. From 2001 to 2002 the number saying that they had ever had sexual intercourse rose from 5.8 percent to 12.4 percent. The conclusion of the article was that the abstinence-only curriculum had failed.

It could or could not be that an abstinence-only curriculum fails to reduce sexual intercourse, but this study cannot tell us whether that is so. Students of that age, as they grow a year older, are in any case probably more likely to have sexual intercourse than when they were younger. Without a control group of students of the same age who had had a different curriculum for sex education, we have no idea whether the students with the abstinence-only curriculum initiated sexual activity at a greater rate than they would have done without the curriculum, at a lesser rate, or at the same rate. We simply cannot tell whether the abstinence-only curriculum resulted in reduced sexual intercourse.

(The problem of interpreting results was also exacerbated in this case by the question, which asked students whether at any time in their life they had ever had sexual intercourse. The 5.8 percent who answered affirmatively in 2001 must have answered affirmatively again in 2002, so the percent responding "yes" in 2002 could have only risen or stayed the same; it was not possible for the percentage to decline. So, apparent failure of the program was baked into the study from the start. A better question wording, which would have been more sensitive to the impact of the new program, would have been: "During the past year, have you had sex [intercourse]?")

Use of a Control Group

The natural experiment.   "Organizing the Poor" is an example of a design in which a control group has been added to handle the sorts of problems we just encountered. It is a *natural experiment*, a design in which a test group (that is, a group exposed to the independent variable) and a control group (a group *not* exposed to the independent variable) are used, but in which the investigator has no control over who falls into the test group and who falls into the control group. In "Organizing the Poor," the matter of who was contacted by the campaign workers was decided by the workers' own choice of whom to contact and by the extent to which different people made themselves available for contact by the campaign workers. The natural experiment design is of the form:

1. Measure the dependent variable for a specific population before it is exposed to the independent variable.
2. Wait until some among the population have been exposed to the independent variable.
3. Measure the dependent variable again.
4. If between measurings the group that was exposed (called the *test group*) has changed relative to the control group, ascribe this to the effect of the independent variable on the dependent variable.

Thus, in "Organizing the Poor," (1) a number of poor people were surveyed as to their interest in politics; (2) the campaign occurred; (3) the same poor people were surveyed again; and (4) those who had been contacted by the campaign were compared with those who had not. This design eliminates many of the alternative explanations that can crop up in working without a control group. For instance, it could not have been the initial measurement that changed the group that had been contacted, compared with the control group, because both groups had been measured in the same way.

   Nevertheless, the natural experiment still allows alternative explanations. Because the researcher does not have control over who is exposed to the independent variable, it may be that the exposed group has a different predisposition to change than the control group. In "Organizing the Poor," for instance, the campaign workers are likely to approached those poor whom they thought they could most easily get interested in politics. Also, those among the poor who were most resistant to change might not have let the campaign workers in the door or might have been chronically absent when the campaign workers tried to contact them. Accordingly, a plausible alternative explanation in "Organizing the Poor" is that the poor who were contacted by the campaign increased their interest in politics more than those who were not contacted *simply because they were the ones who showed more potential to become more interested in politics at that time, regardless of the campaign.* This alternative must be either assumed away or controlled by using a design in which the researcher can determine who falls into the test group and who falls into the control group. A design that accomplishes this is a *true experiment;* but before going on to discuss this, let me discuss a poor cousin of the natural experiment.

The natural experiment without premeasurement.   This is a design in which no measurements are made before subjects are exposed to the independent variable.

This design follows the form:

1. Measure the dependent variable for subjects, some of whom have been exposed to the independent variable (the test group) and some of whom have not (the control group).
2. If the dependent variable differs between the groups, ascribe this to the effect of the independent variable.

The "Tax-Reform Mail" example is of this sort. In this design, (1) senators' votes on a tax-reform bill were noted, and (2) the votes of senators who had received favorable mail were compared with the votes of those who had not. The same kind of alternative explanation that has to be dealt with in natural experiments has to be dealt with in this design also. As in "Organizing the Poor," it may be that heavier pro-tax-reform mail went to senators who already were moving into a tax-reform position even without the mail. Such senators, about whom there might have been a great deal of speculation in the press, could have attracted more mail than did other senators.

Moreover, this design permits many additional alternative explanations beyond those that apply to a natural experiment. In the tax-reform example, it is probable that people were more likely to write letters favoring reform to senators they thought would agree with them. In other words, it might be that senators' mail did not cause their votes, but that their likely vote caused them to get certain kinds of mail. Hence, the relationship between a senator's vote on the bill and the mail she received might not be a causative relationship at all—merely a coincidence between pro-reform and pro-mail and anti-reform and anti-mail. This alternative could not apply to a natural experiment. In a natural experiment it would have been clear from the initial measurement whether or not those who fell into the test group had initially been different from those falling into the control group. In fact, what is compared in the natural experiment is not the measured variables themselves, but how the two groups change between measurements.

To sum up, the natural experiment without premeasurement is a design in which the test group and the control group are compared with respect to a dependent variable only after they have been exposed to the independent variable. It involves the same sorts of alternative explanations as the natural experiment does, plus some others that result from the fact that the investigator does not know what the test group and the control group looked like before the whole thing started.

True Experiment

In neither of the two versions of the natural experiment just outlined did the investigator have any control over who fell into the test group and who fell into the control group. If the investigator does have such control, she can perform a *true experiment.* A true experiment includes the following steps:

1. *Assign at random* some subjects to the test group and some to the control group.
2. Measure the dependent variable for both groups.
3. Administer the independent variable to the test group.

4. Measure the dependent variable again for both groups.
5. If the test group has changed between the first and second measurements in a way that is different from the control group, ascribe this difference to the presence of the independent variable.

Because investigators can control who falls into which group, they can set up theoretically equivalent groups. (The best, and simplest, way to do this is to assign subjects randomly to one group or the other.) The advantage of making the groups equivalent is that researchers can thereby eliminate almost all of the alternative causal interpretations that had to be assumed away in the various natural experiment designs. If the groups are equivalent to start with, for example, a difference in how the groups change cannot be due to the fact that the individuals in the test group were more prone to change in certain ways than were those in the control group. Thus the problem that the investigators faced in "Organizing the Poor" is eliminated.

"Presidential Lobbying" is an example of the true experiment. Here (1) the president chose half of the House randomly to be the test group, leaving the other half as the control; (2) he took a straw vote to measure the dependent variable (vote) for both groups; (3) he lobbied the test group; (4) the bill was voted on; and (5) he compared the voting of the two groups to see whether his lobbying had made a difference. Working with this design, the president would be pretty certain that a disproportionately favorable change among those he lobbied was due to his efforts. If he had not been able to control who was lobbied, he would have been faced with plausible alternative causal interpretations.

Table 6–1 summarizes the various research designs discussed in this chapter and some of the alternative explanations applicable in each case. Each design is presented there in a symbolic shorthand that is explained in the footnote to the table. In the last column of the table, one or two of the alternative interpretations left open by each design are highlighted.

DESIGNS FOR POLITICAL RESEARCH

The natural experiment without premeasurement is the single most commonly used design in political research. A few examples will indicate the broad use of the design: (1) any voting study that shows that persons of a certain type (working-class, educated, male, or what have you—the test group) vote differently from those who are not of this type (the control group); (2) any of the large number of studies estimating how much better incumbent presidents do in seeking reelection when the economy has improved in the preceding year (test group) compared with those for whom the economy has not been improving (control group); (3) most "policy output" studies, such as one by Fry and Winters (1970), which showed that states with high electoral participation (test group) tended to have governmental policies that were more helpful to the poor than those of states with low electoral participation (control group); and (4) studies of discrimination, such as Uhlaner and Schlozman (1986), who tested whether women candidates for office were less well financed

TABLE 6–1   Selected Research Designs

Type	Graphic Presentation[a]	Example from This Chapter	Selected Alternative Causal Interpretations
Observation with no control group	Test group: M * M	"Agency Study"	The first measurement itself may have caused the change observed in the second measurement;
			or
		"Spock Revolution"	something else that happened at the same time as * may have caused the change.
Natural experiment without pre-measurement	Test group: * M Control group: M	"Tax-reform Mail"	Those who made their way into the test group may have been more likely to change than those who made their way into the control group;
			or
			those who made their way into the test group may have been different from those in the control group even before they experienced *.
Natural experiment	Test group: M * M Control group: M M	"Organizing the Poor"	Those who made their way into the test group may have been more likely to change than those who made their way into the control group.
True experiment	Test group: R M * M Control group: R M M	"Presidential Lobbying"	None of the alternatives discussed in this chapter applies. This design permits only a very few alternative explanations. Consult Cook and Campbell (1979), cited at the end of this chapter.

[a]Notation adapted from Donald T. Campbell and Julian C. Stanley, *Experimental and Quasi-experimental Designs for Research* (Chicago: Rand McNally, 1963). In presenting the designs graphically, an asterisk (*) indicates that a group has been exposed to a stimulus or is distinguished in some other way so as to constitute a "test group"; M indicates that the dependent variable has been measured for the group; and R (used to describe the "true experiment") indicates that individuals have been assigned randomly to the groups.

than men because of experiential attributes such as seniority, or because of direct discrimination.

In short, any research is an example of the natural experiment without premeasurement if it (1) takes two or more types of subjects and compares their values on a dependent variable; and (2) infers that the difference on the dependent variable is the result of their difference on whatever it is that distinguishes them as "types."[5] This really describes the bulk of political research.

As we saw in earlier sections, this design is far from satisfactory. It permits relatively many alternative causal interpretations, which are difficult to handle. Nevertheless, this remains the most widely used design in political science. Other designs that have the advantage of control groups are to be preferred because they require less difficult assumptions, but these designs can be used only when the researcher has more control over the test variables than most political scientists can usually achieve.

In order to use a natural experiment design, for instance, researchers must be able to anticipate the occurrence of the test factor. They also must go to the expense in time and money of making two measurements of the subjects. Even then, the attempt may misfire; for example, it may be that the test factor (especially if it is one that affects only a small part of the population) will apply to only a few of the people included in the study. That is, the investigator may be left with a control group but no test group.

Many important variables in the social sciences are not at all susceptible to study by natural experiments. Some lie in the past: people's experiences during the Depression, the colonial histories of nations, the educational backgrounds and past professions of members of Congress, and so on. Others, such as assassinations, riots, and changes in the business cycle, are unpredictable. Such variables are difficult to fit into a natural experiment design. On the other hand, some events are more easily anticipated: the introduction of a poverty program in a town, high school graduates' entrance into college, regularly scheduled political events such as elections, and so on. These lend themselves readily to a natural experimental design.

A true experiment requires even greater control over the subjects of the study than does a natural experiment. The latter requires only that the investigator be able to anticipate events, but the true experiment requires that the researcher be able to manipulate those events—she must decide who is to fall into the control group and who is to fall into the experimental group. To do this in a field situation requires power over people in their normal lives. Thus it is no accident that the example I used of a true experiment, "Presidential Lobbying," was carried out by the president.

---

[5]It is apparent here and in the examples directly preceding this that I am taking some liberty with the notion of "control group." Where rates of participation in the middle class and working class are compared, for instance, it is not at all clear which class is the "test" group and which is the "control." The distinction is even muddier when one compares several groups simultaneously, such as voters from several age groups. But the logic of what is done here is the same as in the strict test/control situation, where the dependent variable is compared among groups of subjects distinguished by their values on the independent variable. It is convenient and revealing to treat this sort of analysis in terms of the analogy to experiments.

It is rare in real political situations that a researcher can exercise this kind of control over events. However, the experiment is so much more powerful than other designs—rejects alternative interpretations so decisively—that we should use it whenever possible, and probably should use it a good deal more than is now done.[6]

Achen (1986, p. 6), citing Gilbert, Light, and Mosteller (1975), points out that apparently *only* randomization provides a clear enough causal interpretation to settle issues of social-scientific research conclusively:

> Without it, even the cleverest statistical analysis meets strong resistance from other scholars, whose professional skepticism is quite natural. When the forces that determine the experimental and control groups are unknown, the imagination has full play to create alternative explanations for the data. Inventing hypotheses of this sort is enjoyable, unstrenuous labor that is rarely resisted.

It may be that in a small organization, such as a local political caucus or a portion of a campus, the investigator can carry out a true experimental design. For instance, students might conduct a political campaign among a randomly selected portion of the campus community and compare that portion over time with a randomly selected control.

It is sometimes possible to carry out true experiments on a larger scale than this, but only if the experimenter can control significant policies and manipulate them for the purposes of investigation. A good example of this sort of experiment is Gerber and Green (2000), in which 30,000 registered voters in New Haven, Connecticut, were each randomly assigned one of three different approaches in a nonpartisan get-out-the-vote program. It turned out that personal visits were effective in getting people to vote, direct mail appeals helped slightly, and telephone calls made no difference at all.

Another interesting example of a natural situation that produced something approximating a true experiment is the study by Howell, Wolf, Peterson, and Campbell (2000) of the effects of a private education on poor children. Programs were initiated in Dayton, Ohio; Washington, D.C.; and New York City that offered children in public schools partial scholarship vouchers to attend private schools. Since there were more applicants than could be funded, children were chosen by lottery to receive the vouchers. This selection process approximated a true experiment; the scholarships were assigned randomly, and there was a control group of children who applied for scholarships but did not receive them. Thus, the two groups should have been equivalent in all respects other than the experimental treatment. The result of the study was that African-American students who received the scholarships did significantly better on standardized tests two years later than African-American students who did not receive the scholarships. No other ethnic group appeared to benefit in the same way.

---

[6]Kinder and Palfrey (1993, especially the Introduction) argue persuasively that we in political science have overrated the problems and barriers to true experimentation in our field.

This study comes very close to a true experiment, and therefore offers very convincing results on an important policy issue. One remaining alternative explanation is that something akin to the problem we saw in "Agency Study" was operating. The children who received scholarships knew they had won something special. Also, they knew that their parents were paying extra money beyond the partial scholarship to further their education. This may have left them more highly motivated than the students who had not won in the lottery. (In an ideal experiment, people do not know whether they are in the experimental group or in the control; the New Haven study by Gerber and Green is an example.) This worry might be lessened, however, by the fact that it was only African-Americans who appeared to benefit from the vouchers; if the benefit were an artifact of children's knowing they had won in the lottery, one would think that would affect all ethnic groups in the same way.

When it is possible to construct true (or nearly true) experiments in real field situations like this, the results can be compelling. More often, true experimentation is useful for studying general aspects of small-group interactions or individual thought processes relevant to politics. For example, a group of subjects may be placed together and told to reach a decision on some question. The investigator then manipulates the way individuals in the group may communicate with each other, to see how this influences the result. In such studies, of course, true experiments are the most appropriate design, inasmuch as the investigator generally can control all the relevant variables. A good example of this sort of experiment is that of Iyengar and Kinder (1987), in which the investigators tested experimentally the effects of variations in the format of TV news reporting on subjects' political perceptions.

Special Design Problem for Policy Analysis: Regression to the Mean

I have introduced you above to some simple sources of alternative causal interpretations and some simple designs to control for them. A slightly more complex problem, while it has many applications in general explanation, is especially important in evaluating the impact of policy initiatives. This is a problem most public officials and journalists do not appear to understand at all, but it is well within your range of understanding at this point.

The problem is called *regression to the mean*. If we assume that essentially everything we observe has some element of randomness to it—that is, in addition to its true core value it varies somewhat from time to time—regression to the mean will always be present. Consider a student in a course, for example. When she is tested, her measured level of knowledge is generally about right, but if she has had a bad day (isn't feeling good, has bad luck in the instructor's choice of questions, and so on), she will score somewhat below her usual level; on a good day, she will score somewhat higher. Note that this sort of random variation in a measure is closely related to what we referred to as unreliability in Chapter 4.

For our purposes here, the important thing about this is that if we observe cases at two points in time, we can expect high values to drop somewhat from one time to the next, and low values to rise somewhat. Not all of them will do this; some of the high scores no doubt are genuinely high and may even rise by the next time they are observed. But a disproportionate number of the high cases are probably cases for whom things had lined up unusually well the first time; that is, the random part of their measure is likely to have been positive. We should expect that it is unlikely they would be so lucky twice in a row, so on the average they are likely to go down the next time they are observed. Similarly, the lowest scores probably include a disproportionate number of cases that were unusually low because of a negative random factor; on the average, we should see them rise.

We should therefore be a little suspicious of a statement like: "Team learning strategies are good in that the weakest students improve, but they are bad in that the strongest students appear to be dragged down by working with the weaker ones." This could be true. But an alternative explanation could be that this is simply regression to the mean. It might be that the stronger students' scores declined because when they were measured at the beginning of the experiment with team learning, a number of them had done unusually well and then just drifted back to their normal level of performance over time. Similarly, some of the poorer students might have drifted up to their normal levels. In other words, the scores of the weaker students might have improved, and the scores of the stronger students might have declined, even if the students had never been involved in team learning. The two alternative causal interpretations can only be sorted out by using an appropriate research design. (One is given on page 90.)

One variant of this problem shows up time and again in assessing the impact of new governmental policies. How often have you seen a statement of the sort: "After foot patrols were introduced in the entertainment district, our city's murder rate declined by a full 18 percent"? What is often missed in such statements is that this effect might also be due to regression to the mean. When do cities typically institute new policies? When the problem they are concerned about has flared up! But cities' problems, like students taking tests, probably have some element of randomness to their measures. If the murder rate has shot up in one year, it is more likely to go down the next year than to go still higher, whether or not the city institutes foot patrols in the entertainment district. In other words, governments are likely to pick a time when a problem is at a high point (which may or may not include some random element) to initiate a policy to solve the problem. Thus, in the case of the murder rates, on the basis of the information in the statement, we cannot tell whether or not foot patrols really curbed the murders, because regression to the mean provides a plausible alternative explanation.

Does this mean that we cannot assess the impact of changes in policies? Of course not. But it does mean that we must find a research design that allows us to distinguish between the two alternative explanations. The design in the statement about foot patrols and murder rates is our old friend:

$$M * M$$

Our problem is that we suspect that the first M may have been unusually high, making it likely that the second measurement would show a decrease whether or not the intervention between the two measures has had any impact.

A design that allows us to sort this out is an *interrupted time series,* that is, a series of measurements over time that is interrupted by the policy intervention:

MMMMM * MMMMM

If the measurement that came just before the intervention was unusually high, the measurements preceding it should tend to be lower than it is. The test for whether the intervention has had an effect in this design is whether the *average* of the several measurements preceding the intervention differs from the *average* of the measurements following the intervention.[7]

The interrupted time series is graphically illustrated in Figure 6–1. Graph A illustrates an interrupted time series in which the intervention appears to have caused a change. Graph B illustrates one in which it did not. Note that in graph B, if we had looked only at the adjacent "intervention and after" measures, regression to the mean would have led us to think the intervention had had an impact.

USE OF VARIED DESIGNS AND MEASURES

I suppose that the easiest conclusion to draw from our discussion thus far is that any kind of research in political science is difficult and that the results of political research are, in the last analysis, unreliable. But this would be far too sour. I did not discuss these selected research designs to convince you not to do political research but to show you some of the problems you must deal with.

Even if you are forced to rely solely on one of the weaker designs (operating without a control group, or using a control group with no premeasurement), you are better off if you set out your design formally and measure those variables that can be measured, acknowledge alternative causal interpretations, and try to assess just how likely it is that each alternative is true. The choice is between doing this or giving up and relying on your intuition and impressions.

But there is a more hopeful side to this chapter. The various weaknesses of different designs should suggest a solution: *Wherever possible, try to work simultaneously with a variety of designs, which can at least in part cancel out each other's weaknesses.* For example, in working solely with a contrived experiment, we may wonder whether the result we have obtained might be a result of something about the way the experiment was set up, rather than a "true" result. Relying totally on a natural experiment, we might wonder whether our results simply reflect a test group comprised of unusual people, rather than a "true" result. But if we could use both of these

---

[7]An even better design, where possible, would add a control to rule out the possibility that it was something else that happened at the same time as the intervention that caused the change:

MMMMM * MMMMM
MMMMM   MMMMM

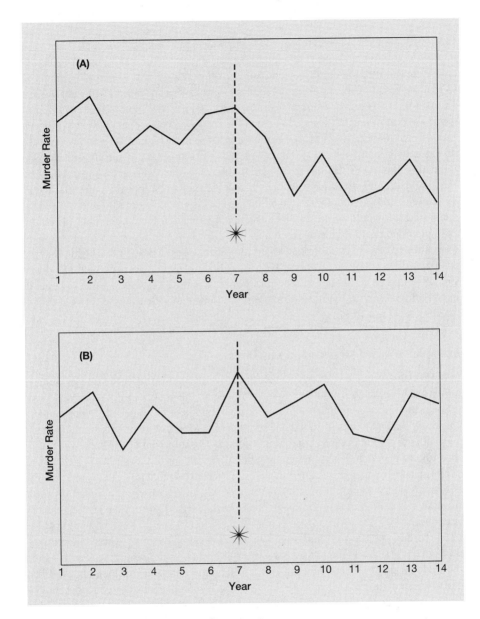

Figure 6–1 Examples of Interrupted Time Series

designs, employing either the same or closely related measures, each result would bolster the other. We could be more confident of the experimental result if we had gotten a similar result in a field situation. And we could be more confident of the result of the natural experiment if we had gotten a similar result in an artificial true experiment.

If we can mix research strategies in this way, the end result is more than the sum of its parts. The strengths of the various designs complement each other. The likelihood that the alternative explanations associated with each design are true decreases because of the confirmation from the other design. It will seem less likely to us that the result of the natural experiment is due to unusual people entering the test group, for example, if we obtain similar results in a true experiment, whose test group we controlled.

Note that the effect would not be the same if a single research design were repeated twice—if, say, a natural experiment were repeated in a different locality. Repeating the same design twice would increase our confidence somewhat, by showing us that the first result was not an accident or a result of the particular locality chosen. But the alternative causal interpretations associated with natural experimental design would in no way be suspended. Consider the "Organizing the Poor" example once again. If the campaign in one city tended to reach mainly those who were already becoming more interested in politics, thus creating the illusion that the campaign had gotten them interested in politics, there is no reason to think that a similar campaign would not do the same thing in a second city. Getting the same result in two different cities would not make it any less likely that the alternative causal interpretation was true.

Example of Varied Designs and Measures

In his *Making Democracy Work*, Robert Putnam (1993) uses the varied-design strategy rather well. His study sought to explain variation in the quality of governmental institutions; his theory was that traditions of civic cooperation, based on what he calls *social capital* (networks of social cooperation) are what lead to effective government.

First, in what is really a problem of valid measurement (see Chapter 4) rather than one of research design, he approached the problem of measuring "government performance" by using multiple measures. To the extent that he got the same results across a variety of methods of measurement, all with their own varied sources of invalidity, he could be more confident that he had measured governmental effectiveness accurately.

To this end, he first gathered a number of statistics about governmental performance in the 20 regions that he was studying, such as the promptness with which the regional governments developed their budget documents. He then checked and supplemented the official statistics by having research assistants call government agencies in each region with fictitious requests for help on such things as completing a claim for sickness benefits or applying for admission to vocational school. (Governments' response quality varied from response in under a week after a single letter, to responses that required numerous letters, numerous phone calls, and a personal visit over several weeks.) Finally, these objective measures of performance were supplemented by several opinion surveys in which people were asked how well they thought the regional government performed.

Once he had decided how to measure governmental performance, Putnam was faced with the question of research design. His basic design was the natural experiment with no premeasurement. The 20 regions were compared as to their level of civic engagement and the quality of their governments' performance, and those with high engagement proved to be those with a high quality of governmental performance.

To test the relationship more richly, he also added tests of *linking* relationships using the same design. For instance, he showed that the higher civic engagement was in communities, the less political leaders feared compromise. This makes sense as a component of the relationship between civic engagement and governmental effectiveness, since willingness to compromise should in turn lead to effective government. The fact that such linking relationships proved to be true under testing makes us more confident that the overall relationship was not a design fluke.

This design still suffered, though, from the possibility that the relationship was a matter of other contemporary things associated with civic engagement, such that those regions high in civic engagement were for some other reasons primed for governmental effectiveness. Putnam countered this, in part, by adding analyses over time of the form "observation with no control group." In these, he traced the development of civic involvement in regions over the past century and showed that high civic involvement in the latter part of the nineteenth century led to civic involvement and governmental effectiveness a century later. By combining the complementary strengths of varied measures and varied designs, Putnam was thus able to generate conclusions of which the reader is more confident than if they were based on a single measure or on a single design.

CONCLUSION

To pick up once again the refrain of this book, creativity and originality lie at the heart of elegant research. Anybody, or almost anybody, can take a research problem, carry out a fairly obvious test on it using one or two obvious measures, and either ignore or assume away the ever-present alternative causal interpretations. A creative researcher will not be satisfied with this but will try very hard to account for all plausible alternative interpretations. Such a student will muster logical arguments, will cite evidence from related studies, and may even vary the designs and measures in his own study. All of these techniques will help the investigator limit the number of alternative interpretations of his findings.

The suggestion made in the preceding section—to vary measures and designs—is, I think, a useful one, but it should not be thought of as the only answer. Varying designs is generally useful, but there are other ways to eliminate alternative interpretations, such as by logical argument or by indirect evidence of various sorts. No interpretation of a research result is cut and dried; interpreting a result and handling alternative interpretations of the result are difficult and challenging constituents of research.

HOLDING A VARIABLE CONSTANT

I have talked about holding a variable constant more than once in this chapter. If we want to know whether a relationship between two variables can be accounted for by a third variable that is related to both of them, we can hold the third variable constant to see whether the relationship between the first two continues to exist when the third variable is not free to vary. *Holding a variable constant* is often also called *controlling for the variable.*

The simplest way to do this is to divide the subjects into separate groups, each having a distinct value on the variable to be held constant, and then observe whether within each of these groups there is a relationship between the first two variables. If there is, it cannot be due to variation in the third variable, for within each of these groups the third variable literally is constant.

A good example of holding a variable constant is provided by the Przeworski et al. (2000) study of whether people live better in democracies than in dictatorships. They found that the life expectancy of people living in democracies was 69.3 years while that of people living in dictatorships was just 53.3 years. Those in democracies could expect to live 16 years longer, on the average, than those in dictatorships—a big difference.

However, an obvious alternative explanation offered itself. Dictatorships were much more likely than democracies to be poor, and poor countries in general have worse health and lower life expectancies than countries that are better off. Do the longer life expectancies in democracies indicate anything about what democracy does for people, or is it just that democracies are richer countries, and that is why people in democracies live longer?

As indicated in Table 6–2, if we divide countries into groups with approximately the same per capita incomes, there still remains an advantage for democracies, although it is nothing like sixteen years.[8] For countries with per capita incomes less than $1,001, life expectancy in both democracies and dictatorships is low, but the democracies have an advantage of eight-tenths of a year. At all levels of prosperity, democracies have some advantage, reaching as high as 5.2 years of life expectancy for countries with per capita income of $4,001 to $5,000, and 5.6 years for countries with per capita income greater than $6,000.

The number of countries falling into each type appears in parentheses, and from these we can see why the difference was so great before we controlled for the countries' per capita incomes.[9] The poorest group has 215 dictatorships, compared with only eleven democracies (countries such as India). At the other end are only eighteen dictatorships with per capita income over $6,000, but 239 democracies (mostly from North America and western Europe).

---

[8]Based on Przeworski et al. (2000), p. 229.

[9]The reason the number of countries is so high is that the authors counted each country at several different points in its history; some countries appear in the data set four or more times.

TABLE 6–2   Life Expectancy Under Dictatorships and Democracy

Per Capita Income, $	Life Expectancy, Democracies		Life Expectancy, Dictatorships		Difference
0–1,000	47.2	(11)	46.4	(215)	0.8
1,001–2,000	56.3	(39)	52.2	(144)	4.1
2,001–3,000	63.6	(34)	59.2	(59)	4.4
3,001–4,000	67.3	(30)	64.2	(44)	3.1
4,001–5,000	70.2	(19)	65.0	(25)	5.2
5,001–6,000	71.3	(23)	68.6	(18)	2.7
6,001–	73.2	(239)	67.6	(18)	5.6
Total	69.3	(395)	53.3	(521)	16.0

The conclusion we draw from holding per capita income constant is that although most of the difference in life expectancies was due to the difference in how well off democracies and dictatorships are, a substantial difference still exists between democracies and dictatorships even when per capita income is taken into account.

The technique demonstrated here of holding a variable constant—literally separating the subjects into new little groups and doing the same analysis within each of these groups—is the simplest technique one can use to eliminate a third variable. Statistical techniques such as multiple regression *artificially* hold variables constant, and their effect is approximately the same as the direct technique I used here.[10] The advantage of such statistical techniques is that they can conveniently hold several variables constant simultaneously. Doing this with the direct technique would not be easy. First, it would result in a horrendous number of tiny tables. More seriously, many of these would be based on rather small numbers of cases, and their meaning would thus be uncertain.

FURTHER DISCUSSION

I have presented here only a few examples of the more commonly used research designs, and my analysis of them has included only a sample of the possible alternative explanations for each design. A more complete treatment of research design, excellent and readable, is provided in Thomas D. Cook and Donald T. Campbell's *Quasi-experimentation: Design and Analysis Issues for Field Setting* (1979). I have relied heavily on their approach in this chapter. Christopher H. Achen's *The Statistical Analysis of Quasi-experiments* (1986) explores these issues with great wisdom; Chapters 1 and 2 are easily accessible to readers with limited technical preparation.

---

[10]See Chapter 9 for an elementary discussion of multiple regression.

A good treatment of the concept of "cause" in relation to research design is found in Blalock (1964, chaps. 1 and 2). Tingsten (1937) provides an example of unusually careful and creative interpretations, developed in the face of quite limited research designs. Several interesting examples of improvised research designs in field research on animal behavior can be found in Tinbergen (1968).

The literature on the use of true experiments in political science is burgeoning. Good examples are Kinder and Palfrey (1993); a special issue of the journal *Political Analysis* (volume 10, no. 4, Autumn 2002); and a special issue, edited by Donald Green and Alan Gerber, of *American Behavioral Scientist* (volume 48, no. 1, January 2004).

One question that you might consider in connection with this chapter is: Why should theory-oriented, empirical political research be based almost exclusively on causal relationships rather than on relationships in general?

Chapter 7

Selection of Observations for Study

So far in this book we have looked at how you can develop a research question, measure the variables involved, and look for relationships among them to provide answers to the research question. A further important factor underlies this whole process, however. You must select a set of observations to look at to do all this, and your selection of cases can sharply affect or even distort what you will find. Further, it is often the case that the "selection" occurs by subtle processes other than your own choice. In this chapter I want to alert you to the importance of case selection (whether it is done by you or by nature), and to show you some basic principles that will help you to select cases in ways that will allow you a clean examination of your research question.

A central theme in this book, which you saw especially in the two chapters on measurement and which you will see again in later chapters, is that we need to construct our research operations so that the relationships we observe among the variables we have measured mirror faithfully the theoretical relationships we are interested in. (This was the point of Figure 4–1, for instance.) It will not surprise you, then, that case selection is judged by how well it produces observed relationships that faithfully mirror the theoretical relationships we are trying to test.

Consider the following examples:

- I described earlier the strange case of the *Literary Digest*, which in 1936 predicted that Franklin Roosevelt would lose the election by a landslide on the basis of questionnaires sent to subscribers to their magazine, car owners, and those having telephone service (not a representative group of American voters) (see p. 50.) The cases they had chosen to look at did not faithfully mirror the American electorate.
- College students taking psychology tests are routinely used for experiments to measure psychological processes. For instance, an experiment using college students might study the effect of drinking coffee on one's ability to memorize long strings of

numbers. Researchers justify doing this by arguing that the processes they are studying are universal, so even though their test subjects are not at all representative of the human population, that does not matter. The relationship they are looking for would be expected to be the same in any kind of group of people, so their students are as good as any other for the test.

• Most graduate departments in political science admit students to their programs based in part on each student's scores on the Graduate Record Examination (GRE). From time to time, a department will consider dropping the exam, because when one looks at the performance of graduate students in the department, how they did on the GRE has little to do with how well they have done in the graduate program. Therefore, it is argued, the test is a nearly irrelevant predictor of success in the graduate program and should be dropped as a tool for assessment.

However, this argument relies on data from those admitted to the program to generalize to the population of all students who might apply to the program. Clearly, the students admitted into the program are an atypical sample from the population; they all did well enough on the GRE to get into the program. Would students who did badly on the GRE do well in the program? We cannot know, because no such students are in the group we are able to observe.

In this case, selection of a potentially biased sample did not result from a decision the researcher made, but inheres in the situation. Nature did it.

• John Zaller (1998), studying whether incumbent members of Congress had extra advantages in garnering votes, had to work with another selection problem dealt by nature. His theory predicted that incumbent members' safety from electoral defeat, as measured by their share of the vote, would increase with every term they served, but at a decreasing rate. So he examined the vote margins of incumbents running for reelection, at varying levels of seniority. However, a number of seats were uncontested, because the incumbent was so safe that no one wanted to take her on. So the available set of Congressional races consisted only of those districts in which someone felt it made sense to challenge the incumbent.

Zaller stated his problem:

> To set [these races] aside, as is sometimes done, would be to set aside those cases in which incumbents have been most successful in generating electoral security, thereby understating the amount of electoral security that develops. On the other hand, to regard victory in an uncontested race as evidence that the MC [member of congress] has captured 100 percent of the vote would probably exaggerate MCs' actual level of support (p. 136).

In other words, if he ignored the selection problem, he would understate the amount of safety that long-time incumbents accrue. But if instead he treated the unchallenged incumbents as having gotten 100 percent of the vote, he would be overstating their safety. (His approximated solution was to estimate from other factors the vote that the unchallenged incumbents would have gotten if they *had been* challenged, and then to insert those simulated estimates as the observations for the unchallenged incumbents—not a perfect solution, but the one that made the best approximation.)

• The general understanding of the new democracies of eastern Europe has been that unless they are culturally homogeneous as Poland is, they are "ethnic powderkegs" that had been held in check only by Soviet repression, and are now prone to explode in ethnic violence. As Mihaela Mihaelescu (2004) has pointed out, however, this general impression has come about because almost all scholars who have looked at ethnic conflict in new eastern European democracies have been drawn to the dramatic outbreaks of violence in the former Yugoslavia. In fact, of fourteen new states in eastern Europe with significant ethnic minorities, only four experienced violent ethnic conflict, and three of these were various parts of former Yugoslavia.

In this case, scholars' attraction to the dramatic cases led to a strangely "selected" body of scholarship, in which the full range of possibilities did not get examined.

SAMPLING FROM A POPULATION OF POTENTIAL OBSERVATIONS

Both the *Literary Digest* example and the discussion of using college students to generalize to all adults are examples of the problem of sampling. We usually cannot study all possible observations to which our theory applies. We cannot, for example, ask every American adult how he or she expects to vote in an election. And, though it would be (barely) possible to do detailed analysis and fieldwork in each country of the world, limitations of time and resources usually bar us from doing so. As a result, we usually work with a sample drawn from the universe of all possible observations to which a theory applies. As noted earlier, the guiding rule in choosing observations for study is that the relationships we are looking for in the full universe of possible cases should be mirrored faithfully among the observations we are using.

Random Sampling

When we are able to draw a fairly large number of observations, the "Cadillac" method is to draw a random sample from the full population of possible cases. In random sampling it is purely a matter of chance which cases from the full population end up in the sample for observation. It is as if we had flipped coins for each possible case and, say, admitted into the sample any case that got heads ten times in a row. (In reality, scholars use computer-generated random numbers to identify which members of the full population should join the sample for observation.)

If a sample has been drawn randomly, we are assured that any relationship in which we are interested should be mirrored faithfully in the sample, at least in the sense that, across repeated samplings of this sort, *on the average* the relationships we would see would be the same as the relationship in the full population. Even random samples will diverge by accident from the full population. For instance, although there is a "gender gap" in American voting, with men favoring the Republican party more than women do, it would not be unusual for a sample of ten Americans to include a group of women who were more Republican than the men in the sample. Since in fact men are more likely to be Republicans than women are, most samples of ten Americans would show men to be the more Republican, but it would still happen fairly often, by chance, that the ten people you drew for a sample would show the reverse of that. If you took a large number of such samples, however, and averaged them, the average expression of the gender gap would almost surely mirror faithfully the gender gap in the full population.

The principle here is the same as that in randomized experiments, which we looked at in Chapter 6. In randomized experiments, two groups are randomly chosen, so they cannot be expected to differ in any significant way that could interfere with a causal interpretation from the experiment. In other words, randomization ensures that any two groups chosen are essentially alike. But if that is true in experiments, it must also be true when trying to generalize to a population from a sample. If any group chosen randomly from the population can be expected to be essentially the same as any other, then they must all be essentially the same as the full population.

How much variation there is from one random sample to another is hugely influenced by the size of the sample. The larger the sample, the less variation there will be from one time to another when we draw samples and look at a relationship. If you drew samples of a thousand Americans, for instance, it would happen only rarely that you could have come up with a group among whom the women were more Republican than the men. (Review the discussion of the Law of Large Numbers, p. 61. We saw there that variation in anything we are observing becomes less variable as we use larger and larger samples to examine it.)

One nice thing about random samples is that there is a very precisely worked out mathematical system to ascertain, for a sample of any given size, exactly how likely it is that the sample result is any given distance from what you would have seen in the population. It is this mathematical system that allows pollsters to say of a national poll, for example, that it shows support of 48 percent for George Bush, within an error of plus or minus three percentage points.

It always seems surprising that samples do not really need to be all that large to give an accurate rendition of a population. Typically, surveys of American citizens are considered to have sufficient cases for accurately mirroring the population of 290,000,000 if they have questioned a sample of two or three thousand people. It is kind of amazing that just a few thousand out of hundreds of millions would be sufficient to estimate the population to within a couple of percentage points.

Now, while the true random sample is the Cadillac of sampling, it is rarely used, at least for large populations. For relatively small populations, such as the population of a city, true random sampling is often feasible, and is then, of course, the method of choice. But you can imagine what it would cost to sample the U.S. population in a truly random way—sending an interviewer to interview a single person in Menominee, Wisconsin, another to interview a person in San Diego, and so on.

Quasi-random Sampling

When a large population is involved, various methods exist to draw "quasi-random" approximations to a random sample. The National Election Study at the University of Michigan uses what is called a "cluster sample": About 100 localities are first selected, and then, within each of these, a certain number of individuals are randomly chosen for the sample. This allows the survey to use approximately 100 interviewers, one based in each of the localities chosen. Then, instead of having interviewers fly or drive hundreds of miles for a single interview, each interviewer can readily reach the 20 or 30 subjects randomly selected from her cluster. The end result approximates a random sample closely. And statistical adjustments can be made to take into account the clustered structure of the sample, so that it operates almost exactly like a random sample.

An alternative system is to draw a truly random sample of telephones by having a computer dial telephones randomly ("random digit dialing," or RDD sampling). This allows access to a random sample without the difficulty or expense of getting an interviewer to the person's door, but it is increasingly difficult to draw a sample in this way that represents the broad population accurately. In 1932, at the time of the *Literary Digest* poll described earlier, the problem with telephone lists was that only the middle class had telephones. Today almost everyone has a telephone, so in principle RDD sampling could work well. But in practice, people's use of their phones varies enough so that the group that can actually be reached by phone at a given time is problematic as a sample. Some people are at work all day, so their telephones will ring at any daytime hour but not be answered unless by a machine. Others are always gone in the evenings. Some telephones have devices to block unsolicited calls. Some families have two phone lines, and therefore would be twice as likely to end up in the sample. RDD samples are rather problematic as approximations of a random sample of the population.

Looking back now at the first two examples stated, we can see from our consideration of random sampling how they might (or might not) be questionable as samples. The *Literary Digest* poll was drawn before sampling was well understood. Its sample of telephone owners, subscribers to the magazine, and those appearing on state lists of registered automobiles was simply a terrible sample, very much skewed toward the middle class, and would have produced an erroneous prediction any time the middle class voted differently than the population as a whole. The sample of college students, on the other hand, might provide a reasonable basis for drawing psychological conclusions about people in general, even though they are clearly not a random sample of the full population *if* we are confident that their psychological processes are the same as psychological processes among the full population. In this case, even though the sample is not random, it is much cheaper than trying to draw a random sample of all people, and can serve as a satisfactory quasi-random sample if processes are the same as for the full population.

Purposive Sampling

Sometimes we deliberately want to sample in a nonrandom way, not just for reasons of efficiency or cost, but because a deliberately constructed, nonrandom sample serves a purpose for our research. If we wanted to compare the political choices of African-Americans and whites, for instance, a purely random sample (or good approximation, such as a national cluster sample) would probably not yield enough African-American citizens for a good comparison. If it faithfully mirrored the population, it should have about one-eighth of the sample African-American, too small a group for reliable comparisons in a sample of the usual size. One solution would be to draw a monstrously large sample, but that would, of course, be very expensive. Another solution, if the purpose of the study is to look at the politics of race, is to draw what is called a "purposive" sample.

A purposive sample does not attempt to replicate the full population. Rather, it draws subjects to maximize variation in the independent variable of interest, so that the relationships we are looking for will be very clear.[1] In the preceding example, we could sample African-Americans randomly and sample whites randomly, combining them to construct a sample that is half white and half African-American. Like all purposive samples, this would not work as a general reflection of the full population. If African-Americans were more likely to vote Democratic than whites, for instance, the sample would give an unreasonably high estimate of the Democratic vote. But the one thing for which the sample is going to be used, estimating a relationship or set of relationships based on race, is fine. Since both African-Americans and whites have been randomly (or quasi-randomly) selected, an estimate of, say, the news-watching habits of the two races should reflect accurately the difference in news-watching habits in the full population.

One reason that most sampling is random or quasi-random, rather than purposive, is that usually when we draw a sample, it is intended to serve multiple purposes. And we should probably also anticipate that as we proceed with analysis, we might want to look at things in the data other than what we had anticipated when we were first drawing up the sample. A purposive sample works only for the particular independent variable or variables on which we have based the sample. So it is usually safer and more useful to draw up a more general sample, random or quasi-random, rather than one focused just on the single task we start with.

Selection of Cases for Case Studies

Another kind of purposive sampling comes into play when we are dealing with such small numbers of cases that random sampling would not be very helpful in any case. A case study is an intensive study of one or a few cases. It might be a study of a particular president's administrative style, an intensive study of the attitudes and ideologies of a few people, or, as it is most frequently seen, a study of some aspect of politics in one or a few countries. In principle, even if we are looking at only two or three cases, random selection of the case or cases would reflect the full population in the long run. But in practice, the Law of Large Numbers is working so weakly when we study only a few cases that the divergence of any case from the full population, though it

---

[1] We will see (pp. 106–108) why we do not draw the sample to maximize variation in the *dependent* variable.

will be "only random," will still be huge.[2] Under these circumstances there is much more to be gained by intelligently choosing the case or cases to pick up the relationship of interest, rather than by randomly drawing the case(s). If we want to study the effect of authoritarian government on economic growth, for instance, it makes sense to seek a couple of authoritarian states and a couple of nonauthoritarian ones for comparison, rather than just taking four randomly chosen states.

CENSORED DATA

The last three of the five examples in the introduction to this chapter were examples of "censored data," instances in which part of the range of cases to which a theory applies are cut off and unavailable to the researcher, either by the researcher's choice or by circumstances. In the case of GRE scores, any generalization about the importance of test scores is obviously meant to apply to all students who could apply for admission, but the researcher can see the performance only of students who were admitted to the program. John Zaller's theory of Congressional elections was obviously meant to apply to all members of Congress, but he could observe election outcomes only for those members who were challenged by an opponent. In the case of ethnic violence in eastern Europe, the theory that ancient hatreds would flare up after Soviet repression was lifted from the region obviously was meant to apply to all eastern European democracies with large ethnic minorities, but scholars had chosen to look only at the dramatic cases in which conflict had actually occured.

The problem of censored data is always severe, because it requires researchers and their readers to make strong assumptions about what "might have been" in the range of data that are not available. Sometimes there are reasonable ways to fill in the spaces. Zaller, for instance, estimated on the basis of other variables what vote unchallenged members could have been expected to receive had they been challenged, and inserted those estimates into his study as imputed data. And sometimes the answer is easy: If investigators have ignored some of the range but can study it, that just makes a neat and interesting study for another investigator to conduct, filling in for their short-sightedness. Mihaelescu was able to do a useful and rewarding study, just picking up on what others had not noticed: that most east European states with ethnic minorities had not exploded when the Soviets left.

When Scholars Pick the Cases They're Interested In

Often, as in this example of ethnic conflict in eastern Europe, investigators doing case studies gravitate to the outcomes in which they are interested, and pick cases for

---

[2]This is a situation that seems to fit Keynes' well-known comment that in the long run we shall all be dead. In principle and in the long run, a randomly selected sample of even just a couple of cases will mirror the full population. But any given couple of cases—for instance, the ones you plan to study—are likely to diverge sharply from the full population.

which the outcome was strong or dramatic. They then look at those cases to see what caused the thing in which they are interested. Scholars of revolution are prone to look at the Soviet Union or Cuba. Scholars of economic growth are prone to look at countries such as Korea, Taiwan, or Brazil, which have grown rapidly. Scholars of the presidency are likely to look at the administrations of dramatically successful presidents such as Franklin Roosevelt or Ronald Reagan, rather than less showy presidents such as Calvin Coolidge.

I will argue later that choosing cases to maximize variation in the dependent variable distorts relationships, and that one should instead select to maximize variation in the independent variable or variables. But another result of choosing cases that exhibit most strongly the thing we are interested in is that it often also results in a censored data set. Barbara Geddes (2003) gives a nice example of this. She points out that a strong argument arose in the 1980s, based on case studies of rapidly developing countries, that it was important for developing countries' governments to repress organized labor to let industry develop rapidly. Most case studies of economic growth at the time focused on Mexico, Brazil, and the "Asian Tigers": Singapore, South Korea, and Taiwan. As Geddes points out, the focus on these several cases of rapid development led to a very wrong-headed conclusion.

Geddes developed a measure for how much labor organization was repressed by governments, and then placed the five frequently studied countries on a graph of labor repression, related to growth in per capita GDP from 1970 to 1981. As you can see in her graph, reproduced in Figure 7–1, all five cases fall in the upper-right hand of the graph (b: high labor repression, rapid economic growth); and the lowest growth (Mexico's) also happens to coincide with a lower repression of labor.

Figure 7–1 Labor repression and growth in the most frequently studied cases, 1970–81. (GDP percapita from Penn World Tables.) Source: Geddes (2003), p. 101.

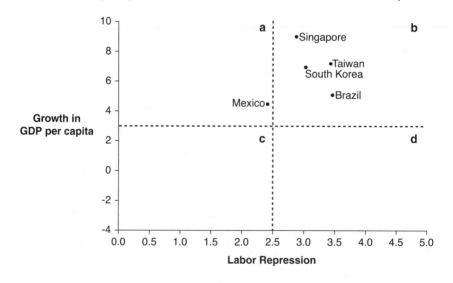

As Geddes showed in work adapted here in Figure 7–2, however, if we had all of the developing countries of the 1970s before us, we would see that there was little or no advantage for the countries that repressed labor. Looking at the full range of labor repression and the full range of economic outcomes, we find about as many low-growth countries with low levels of labor repression as with high labor repression. There is very little pattern in the figure, indicating little relationship between the two variables. There may be a slight relationship; the upper left-hand part of the figure is a little less thickly filled with cases, indicating that there were somewhat fewer low-repression countries with high growth. But overall, there is nothing like the kind of relationship that appeared from the censored data in Figure 7–1.

When Nature Censors Data

What can one do about censored data? If the data have been censored because of decisions of researchers, the problem is easy to solve, and can in fact offer a nice chance to another researcher to make a significant contribution. This is what Mihaelescu or Geddes did, for example. All one has to do in this case is to seek out a broader range of information, and bring it into the analysis.

But if the data have been censored by nature, as in the example of GRE scores, or Zaller's work on Congressional elections, there are no easy solutions. The missing cases are gone and are not going to reappear. One cannot under ordinary circumstances admit to graduate school a group of students who have done badly on the GRE test, to see how they perform. And one cannot decree that all Congressional incumbents will be challenged for reelection.

Figure 7–2   Labor repression and growth in the full universe of developing countries, 1970–81. (GDP per capita from Penn World Tables.) Adapted from Geddes (2003) p. 103.

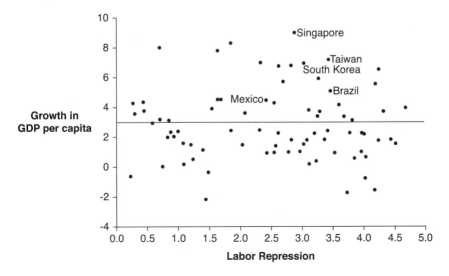

In such cases, we are forced to draw conclusions of what might have been had the data not been censored. This means we must make some assumptions, and justify them, for drawing "what if?" conclusions. We might, for example, seek out those graduate departments that for whatever reasons do not use the GRE as a criterion, find the GRE scores of students who attended there, and see how they did. This would not be a perfect solution; it would require the assumption that departments that did not require the GRE were like other departments in every other way, which is, of course, unlikely. And it would ignore the fact that the low-GRE students admitted to those departments would be atypical as well; since they would have been rejected by other departments but ended up being accepted into the non-GRE departments, they are probably unusually high achievers in other ways. Nonetheless, despite the fact that assumptions are required, this would be better than ignoring the initial problem of censored data.

Similarly, Zaller had to make a number of assumptions to predict what vote unchallenged members would have gotten had they been challenged.

A good deal of artfulness is required to analyze data that have been censored by nature, but a creative imagination will be rewarded by substantially improved estimation. And it's a nice challenge.

SELECTION ALONG THE DEPENDENT VARIABLE: DON'T DO IT!

When we looked at selection of samples, we noted that you might usefully draw a purposive sample to get sufficient variation in the variables of interest. A very important rule, however, is that this can work well when you select cases to maximize variation on the independent variable, but that you should never select to maximize variation on the dependent variable. If you maximize variation in the independent variable, the relationship you observe will mirror nicely the true relationship, at least if you have enough cases so that the Law of Large Numbers can work for you. But if you maximize variation in the dependent variable, you will distort the true relationship. And it does not matter in this case whether you have a large or a small sample.

Let us illustrate this with a hypothetical city with significant racial polarization. In Figure 7–3 we see the breakdown of support for the mayor, by race. These are the true population figures. Taking percentages, we find that 80 percent of whites support the mayor, but only 45 percent of nonwhites support the mayor.

In Figure 7–4 I have drawn two samples of 400 from this population, one a purposive sample to maximize variation in race, and the other a purposive sample to maximize variation in support or opposition to the mayor. Figure 7–4 (a) shows the results of drawing 200 nonwhites randomly from the pool of nonwhites shown in Figure 7–3, and similarly drawing 200 whites from the pool of whites. While this sample is on the small side, it draws enough nonwhites to make fairly reliable comparisons with whites; and since it is drawn along the independent variable, it replicates

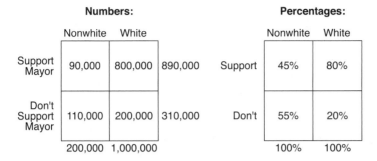

Figure 7–3 Race and support for the Mayor: hypothetical polarized city.

(a) Selection Along Independent Variable

	Numbers: Nonwhite	White				Percentages: Nonwhite	White
Support	86	171	262	Support		43%	85%
Don't	114	29	138	Don't		57%	15%
	200	200					

(b) Selection Along Dependent Variable

	Numbers: Nonwhite	White				Percentages: Nonwhite	White
Support	39	161	200	Support		38%	54%
Don't	64	136	200	Don't		62%	46%
	103	297					

Figure 7–4 Selection along independent, dependent variables.

faithfully the relationship in the full population. In the sample, 43 percent of nonwhites support the mayor (compared with 45 percent in the full population), as do 85 percent of whites (compared with 80 percent in the full population). The numbers diverge by about the amount we would normally expect in drawing a random sample of 400 cases, but the relationship is recognizably the same.[3] In fact, it is more accurate than what we would have gotten from a purely random sample of the population, since that would have produced only a small number of nonwhites, with a widely variable estimate of nonwhites' support for the mayor.

Figure 7–4 (b) shows the results of a purposive sample of the same size that maximizes variation in the dependent variable, support for the mayor. As we see, drawing this sort of sample does not produce a faithful reflection of the relationship in the full population. In the full population, 80 percent of whites support the mayor, compared with 45 percent of nonwhites, a relationship of sharp polarization. But the sample maximizing variation in support appears to indicate a considerably weaker relationship, with 54 percent of whites supporting the mayor, compared with 38 percent of nonwhites. This does not present the same picture of sharp polarization.

Why is it that sampling along the independent variable produces accurate estimates of the relationship, but sampling along the dependent variable does not? It makes sense, because the purpose of the analysis is to compare nonwhites' and whites' support for the mayor. Drawing groups from the two and comparing them fits this very well. But drawing groups of supporters and opponents of the mayor and then comparing whites' and nonwhites' support does not parallel the research question in the same way. And operationally, changing the relative numbers of supporters and opponents from what one sees in the full population changes the percent of supporters in both racial groups, in ways that distort the percentages in both groups. (Note that sampling on the independent variable distorts the proportions of whites and nonwhites in the population, but that this is actually helpful; it increases the number of nonwhites available for analysis. It leaves unaffected the percentages in which we are interested.)

SELECTION OF CASES FOR CASE STUDIES (AGAIN)

The preceding example clarifies why one should not sample on the dependent variable, but it may puzzle the reader a bit. It looks a little artificial—why would anyone do this in the first place? Actually, this does not come up often with regard to large-scale sampling. It does come up time and again, however, with regard to intensive studies of one or a few cases (so-called case studies), and the logic there is just the same as the logic of the preceding example. I chose to introduce the idea through a large-scale survey example because the problem is easier to see there, but the real importance of the argument is with regard to case studies.

It is so easy when studying a political outcome to choose a case in which the outcome occurred, and see whether the things you expected to have been the causes

---

[3]This sample, by the way, offers a good tangible example of about how much variability one gets with random sampling of this size.

were present. Or, if you properly wanted to avoid the problem of censored data, you might choose two cases, one in which the outcome had occurred and another in which it had not, and see whether the things you expected to have been the causes were present. In fact, doing something like this is the most obvious and intuitive thing to do; see where the thing you're trying to explain has occurred, and try to account for it.

It is intuitive, but it is wrong, for the same reason we saw in the earlier example—namely, that it distorts the likelihood that the outcome occurs or does not occur. Choosing instead cases that represent varying instances of your explanatory variable allows you to examine the full range over which your explanation is meant to apply, but it does not fiddle at all with the likelihood that the outcome occurs, and so allows you to examine straightforwardly where the chips fall under varying circumstances.

CONCLUSION

I have reviewed in this chapter a set of issues having to do with the selection of cases: the question of sampling from a larger population; the problem of censored data; and the question of whether to select cases on the basis of what you are trying to explain or on the basis of your independent variable. The selection of cases affects profoundly what results you see. It forms the foundation for all of your examination of evidence, and will work well as long as your procedures fulfill the basic principle enunciated in this chapter: The relationship to be observed among the cases you have selected must mirror faithfully the true relationship among all potential cases.

FURTHER DISCUSSION

Geddes (2003) has a very nice chapter, "How the Cases You Choose Affect the Answers You Get." A good, though fairly technical, treatment of censored data is presented in Przeworski, Alvarez, Cheibub, and Longi (2000) in an appendix, "Selection Models." Another good treatment of case selection is King, Keohane, and Verba (1994), Chapter 4.

Chapter 8

Introduction to Statistics

Measuring Relationships for Interval Data

In Chapter 6 we were concerned generally with "relationships" between independent and dependent variables. That is, we wanted to see whether the presence or absence of a test factor affected the value of the dependent variable. This was too simple, for two reasons.

First, as noted in footnote 5 in that chapter, the test factor in field research is frequently not something that is simply present or absent; rather, it takes on a variety of values. Our task then is not just to see whether the *presence or absence* of a test factor affects the value of the dependent variable, but instead, to see whether and how the *value* of the independent variable affects the value of the dependent variable. For example, in relating education to income, we do not treat people simply as "educated" or "not educated." They have varying amounts of education, and our task is to see whether the amount of education a person has affects his or her income.

Second, "relationship" cannot be dichotomized, although I treated it as a dichotomy in Chapter 6, to ease the presentation there. Two variables are not simply related or not related. Relationships vary in two ways: first, in how *strongly* the independent variable affects the dependent variable. For instance, education might have only a minor effect on income. The average income of college graduates might be $33,000 and the average income of high school dropouts might be $30,000. Or, it might have a major effect. College graduates might average $50,000 while high school dropouts average $15,000.

Relationships also vary in how *completely* the independent variable determines scores on the dependent variable. College graduates might average $50,000 income and high school dropouts $15,000, for instance, yet there might still be much variation in incomes that could not be attributed to variation in people's education. Some college graduates might make only $10,000 a year and some high school dropouts might make $80,000 or $90,000 a year, even though the *average* income of the college graduates was higher than the *average* income of the dropouts. This would indicate that although education affected incomes sharply, it was relatively incomplete as an explanation of people's incomes. Because income still varied a good deal within each level of the independent variable, there must be other things affecting income in important ways, and we often would guess incorrectly if we tried to predict a person's income solely on the basis of education. This is what it means to say that education is not a very "complete" explanation of income.

Thus variables are not simply "related" or "not related." Their relationship may be such that the independent variable has a *greater or lesser effect* on the dependent variable; and it may be such that the independent variable determines the dependent variable *more or less completely*. Generally speaking, political research is not so much concerned with whether or not two variables are related but with whether or not they have a "strong" relationship (in one or both of the senses used earlier). This can be seen in our examples of research design in the preceding chapter. Although for the sake of simplicity these were presented as if we were interested only in whether or not a relationship existed, it is clear that what was of interest to the investigators in each case was finding out how *strong* a relationship existed. In "Presidential Lobbying," for instance, the president was not simply concerned with whether or not he was able to influence voting for the bill, but with *how many* votes he could swing.

Our task in evaluating the results of research, then, is to measure how strong a relationship exists between the independent variable(s) and the dependent variable. The tools we need to accomplish this task are found in the field of statistics.

STATISTICS

Although modern political scientists have begun to use statistics extensively only in the past several decades, it was actually political scientists of a sort who first developed the field, for statistics originally grew out of the need to keep records for the state. The name *statistics* derives from the Latin *statisticus*, "of state affairs."

Statistics includes two main activities: statistical inference and statistical measurement (including the measurement of relationships, with which we are concerned in this chapter). Statistical inference consists of estimating how likely it is that a particular result could be due to chance; it tells us how reliable the results of our research are. I discuss inference in Chapter 10. In this chapter and in Chapter 9, I introduce some statistical techniques for measuring the strength of relationships.

IMPORTANCE OF LEVELS OF MEASUREMENT

In Chapter 5 we saw that we have more information about a relationship between variables if we work at a higher level of measurement than if we work at a lower level of measurement. It should not be too surprising that methods of measuring relationships between variables are different depending on the level at which the variables were measured. If we know more about a relationship, we should be able to measure a greater variety of things about it. Just as higher levels of measurement yield relatively richer information about a variable, so techniques for measuring relationships at high levels of measurement give relatively richer information about those relationships.

Basically, there are two major types of techniques: those appropriate for data measured at the interval and those suited for lower-level measurements. Recall that we mentioned two ways to measure the "strength" of a relationship between two variables: (1) by how great a difference the independent variable makes in the dependent variable, that is, how greatly values of the dependent variable differ, given varying scores on the independent variable; or (2) by how completely the independent variable determines the dependent variable, that is, how *complete* an explanation of the independent variable dependent variable is provided by the independent variable. I shall call the first way of measuring a relationship *effect-descriptive*, and the second *correlational*. The critical difference between working with interval-measured data and working with data measured at a lower level is that effect-descriptive measurement can apply only to interval-scale data. Correlational measurement of one sort or another can apply to data measured at any level.

Ordinal and nominal measurement techniques do not tell us how great a difference in the dependent variable is produced by a given difference in the independent variable, although this is precisely what is required to measure the relationship in an effect-descriptive way. The whole point of nominal and ordinal measurement is that in neither do we have available a unit by which to measure the difference between two values of a variable. This means that we cannot measure how great a difference is induced in the dependent variable by a change in the independent variable. If we are using an ordinal-scale variable, we know whether one value is higher than another, but we do not know how much higher it is. If we are using a nominal-scale variable, of course, all we know is whether the two values are distinct.

This becomes a particularly important distinction in political research, because under most circumstances, effect-descriptive ways of measuring the strength of a relationship are more useful than correlational ways. I demonstrate this in the next few sections.

WORKING WITH INTERVAL DATA

Regression Analysis

A convenient way to summarize data on two interval-scale variables so that we can easily see what is going on in the relationship between them is to plot all the observations on a *scattergram*, as in Figure 8–1. Each dot in the scattergram represents one observation (a person, state, or country, for example), placed on the graph according to its scores on the two variables. For instance, dot A represents an observation that

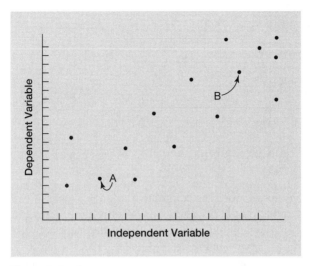

Figure 8–1   Scattergram

combines scores of 3.5 on the independent variable and 5 on the dependent variable. Dot B represents an observation with scores of 12 on the independent variable and 17 on the dependent variable.

By looking at the pattern formed by the dots, we can tell a good deal about the relationship between the two variables. For instance, in Figure 8–1, we note that there are few dots in the lower-right and upper-left corners of the graph. This means that high scores on the dependent variable tend to coincide with high scores on the independent variable, and low scores on the dependent variable tend to coincide with low scores on the independent variable. Thus we know that the two variables are positively related. Furthermore, this relationship appears to be approximately linear. (See the discussion of "linear relationships" in the box on page 70.)

We have done two things so far. We have observed which way the dependent variable moves with changes in the independent variable, and we have observed that it moves at a steady rate at all values of the independent variable (a linear relationship) rather than at changing rates (a nonlinear relationship). These are both part of an effect-descriptive measurement of the relationship.

The scattergrams in Figure 8–2 illustrate various other patterns we might have observed. Graph A shows a nonlinear relationship (the dependent variable increases faster with increases in the independent variable if the independent variable has a high value). Graph B shows a linear relationship in which the dependent variable increases more gradually than in the graph in Figure 8–1. Graph C shows a negative linear relationship in which the dependent variable decreases as the independent variable increases. Graph D shows a pattern in which there is no relationship.

Although the scattergram tells us a good deal about a relationship, it can be unwieldy to work with. It is not uncommon in a research report to discuss 30 or 40

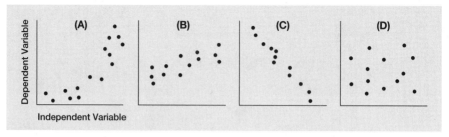

Figure 8–2   Assorted Scattergrams

separate relationships. It would be painful to read such a paper if each relationship were presented in the form of a scattergram. What is more, comparing two scattergrams gives us only an approximate idea of the differences between two relationships. Comparing the graphs in Figures 8–1 and 8–2(B), we can say that in the first graph the independent variable causes greater shifts in the dependent variable than in the second, but we cannot say precisely how much greater the shifts are. If the differences were more subtle, or if we were comparing several relationships, the job would become well-nigh impossible.

Finally and most important, we often measure the strength of a relationship between two variables while holding a third variable constant. (See the discussion of this topic on pages 94–95.) To do this using scattergrams may be extremely cumbersome.

For all of these reasons, it is useful to devise a precise numerical measure to summarize the relevant characteristics of a relationship shown in a scattergram. The measure commonly used to summarize the effect-descriptive characteristics of a scattergram is the *regression coefficient.*

The linear regression coefficient is derived in the following way. First, the pattern in the dots of a scattergram is summed up by the single line that best approximates it. For a linear relationship, the mathematically best procedure is to choose the unique line that minimizes the squared differences between observed values of the dependent variable and its idealized values as given by the simplifying line. This is illustrated in Figure 8–3, where a simplifying line has been drawn through a scattergram with observations on seven hypothetical countries to summarize the pattern across the countries. It has been drawn to minimize the squared differences between each of the observed points, such as A, and the point B at which a country having A's score on the independent variable would be expected to fall on the idealized simplifying line.

The simplifying line may be thought of as a rule for predicting scores on the dependent variable from scores on the independent variables. Its usefulness as a predictor depends on keeping the average squared value of "deviant" scores on the dependent variable as low as possible. A single summarizing line can be described more easily than a pattern of dots. In particular, a straight line such as this can be fully described by the equation

$$y = a + bx$$

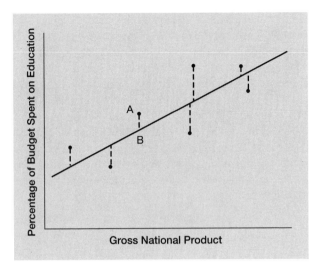

Figure 8–3   The Regression Line

where y is the predicted value of the dependent variable, x is the value of the independent variable, and a and b are numbers relating y to x. The number a, the expected value of y when x equals zero, is called the *intercept* of the regression equation; it is the value of y where the regression line crosses the y axis, that is, where x equals zero (see Figure 8–4). The number b, or the *slope* of the regression equation, shows

Figure 8–4   The Regression Equation

The equation of this line is $y = 6 + 3x$. The predicted value of y when x is 4, for instance, is $6 + (4 \times 3)$, or 18.

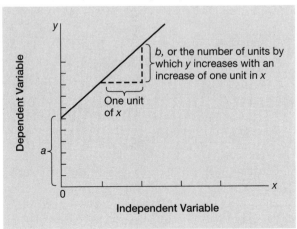

by how many units *y* increases as *x* increases one unit. (If *b* is negative, *y* decreases as *x* increases; there is a negative relationship between the variables.) In other words, to find the predicted value of the dependent variable for any specified value of the independent variable, you must add *a* (the predicted value of *y* when *x* equals zero) to *b* times the number of units by which *x* exceeds zero.

The slope, often simply called the *regression coefficient*, is the most valuable part of this equation for most purposes in the social sciences. By telling how great a shift we can expect in the dependent variable if the independent variable shifts by one unit, the slope provides a single, precise summary measure of how great an impact the independent variable has on the dependent variable. Let's assume, for instance, that the relationship between income and electoral participation is linear and can be summarized by the regression equation

$$\text{percent voting} = 50.5 + {}^1/_2\,(\text{income in thousands of dollars})$$

This means that with every additional thousand dollars of income, $^1/_2$ percent more potential voters vote. For example, if income is $2,000, the predicted percent voting equals $50.5 + ({}^1/_2 \times 2)$, or 51.5. If income is $3,000, the predicted percent voting equals $50.5 + ({}^1/_2 \times 3)$, or 52.0.

Remember, however, that even though we work with neat, impersonal numbers, we do not escape the scholar's obligation to think. If we have guessed the direction of causation between *x* and *y* incorrectly, plugging in our data and getting numbers out will not make the results valid. If *y* causes *x* rather than vice versa, the formulas will still give us an *a* and a *b*, but the shift of one unit in *x* in the real world will *not* be followed by a shift of *b* units in *y*. Thus the arguments made in Chapter 6 apply even when we work with simple numbers like these.

The problem of comparing units. It may be seen from an examination of the concept *slope* (the number of units by which *y* changes with a change of one unit in *x*) that the slope has meaning only with regard to the units in which *x* and *y* are measured. For example, if there is a regression coefficient of -10.5 for nations' diplomatic involvement with the United States (measured by the number or magnitude of exchanges per year) predicted from their distance from the United States measured in thousands of miles, there would be a regression coefficient of -0.0105 for the same dependent variable if distance were measured in miles. That is, if diplomatic involvement could be expected to decrease by 10.5 with every thousand miles of distance from the United States, it would be expected to decrease by 0.0105 with every mile of distance.

If we are working with just two variables, this poses no real difficulty. But often we may be interested in comparing the effects of two or more independent variables on a particular dependent variable. If the two independent variables are measured in different sorts of units, this can be difficult. Continuing with our example, we might want to know which variable—nations' distance from the United States or the volume of their trade with the United States—has a greater impact on their diplomatic interaction with the United States. If the regression coefficient for volume of trade, measured in millions of dollars, is +0.024, how can we tell whether it has a greater impact on diplomatic interaction than does geographic distance, with its slope of −10.5? The units—thousands of miles and millions of dollars—are not comparable; therefore, the coefficients based on those units are not comparable either.

The technique of *standardized regression coefficients*, or *beta weights*, has been developed to wash out the effect of varying units in regression analysis. To present it is beyond the technical level of this book, but you should at least be aware of its existence. It is no cure-all; essentially it transforms regression coefficients into a form of correlation coefficient (see pp. 121–128), which are independent of unit but involve problems of their own. Personally, I do not recommend the technique of standardized regression for most purposes, but it has its adherents. A good presentation is that of Blalock (1979, pp. 477–482).

Checking for linearity.   We must be careful to make certain in using linear regression analysis that the data do fit a more or less linear pattern. Otherwise, the regression equation will not summarize the pattern in the data, but will distort it. Figure 8–5 shows a linear regression equation passed through the scattergram of a nonlinear relationship. This regression line fits the data very badly and is not a useful summary of the relationship. You should always check your data before using linear regression analysis. The best way to do this is simply to draw a scattergram (or better yet, let the computer do it for you) and see whether it looks linear.

Many relationships in political science do turn out to be linear. But if the relationship you are investigating turns out to be nonlinear, that is no reason to give up analyzing it. It merely means that the relationship is more complex than you anticipated—and probably more interesting. A nonlinear regression equation may be found to fit the pattern fairly well.

Figure 8–5   Linear Regression on a Nonlinear Relationship

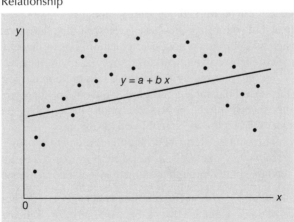

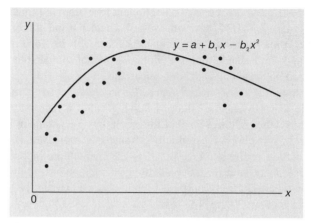

Figure 8–6   Nonlinear Regression Equation

In Figure 8–6, a nonlinear regression equation $y = a + b_1x - b_2x^2$ has been passed through the scattergram from Figure 8–5. It summarizes the pattern in the data more accurately. In this case, two coefficients, b_1 and b_2, are required to express the impact that a change in x will have on y, since that change is not the same at all values of x. We can see that y increases with x but decreases with the square of x. The regression equation provides a handy summary description of the effect, now a bit more complicated, that x has on y.

Formulas are available to calculate equations for regression lines satisfying the least-squares criteria. This is particularly true for linear regression; the formulas for a and b are found in every standard statistics text, including the ones cited at the end of this chapter. But there are no set "formulas" for nonlinear regression equations, for there is an infinite variety of nonlinear equations that you might fit to any set of data. It usually is necessary to play around with alternative nonlinear equations for a while. But these, too, can be worked out readily enough.

To the extent that your research is based on a well-thought-out theory, this will help you to design an appropriate nonlinear equation. For instance, if your theory predicts that the dependent variable will always increase with increases in the independent variable, but at a constantly diminishing rate (a "diminishing marginal returns" model), the equation depicted in Figure 8–6 would be inappropriate because it must inevitably reverse direction at some point. An equation such as $y = a + b \log x$, as depicted in Figure 8–7, would be appropriate.

One important warning: Remember that the presentation I have made here is only a broad, introductory overview. Competence in using measures like those presented here requires more thorough training than is within the scope of this book.

Examining the residuals.   Any regression line is actually a reflection of the stage that we have reached in developing a theory. Because our theory anticipates a relationship between two variables, we measure the relationship between them by calculating

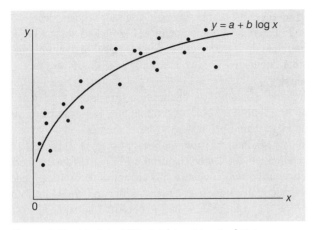

Figure 8–7   Model of Diminishing Marginal Returns

the regression equation for the line that best summarizes the pattern of the relationship. In this sense, regression analysis is an expression of what we already think about the subject. It may surprise us; where we expected a relationship there may be none, or it may be nonlinear, and so on. But it is an expression of what we already have been thinking about the subject.

However, the regression line can serve a further important function; by pointing out important independent variables that had not yet occurred to us, it can help refine our theory. Looking back at Figure 8–3, note that the regression line does not provide perfect prediction of the values on the dependent variable for the cases in the scattergram. This means that there is still unexplained variation in the values of the dependent variable. Some of the observations are higher on the dependent variable than we would expect from their value on the independent variable, and some are lower. *Something else, beyond the independent variable, is also affecting the dependent variable.*

This difference between the observed value and the predicted value is called the *residual*. Examining these residuals points out to us those cases in which the "something else" has the effect of raising (or, conversely, lowering) the dependent variable. In Figure 8–3, for instance, a case such as A is one in which the effect of the "something else" is to raise the value of the dependent variable; the actual value for case A is higher than the value B, which would have been predicted from the regression line.

Now, once the cases have been sorted out in this way, we may notice that cases with similar residuals have some additional characteristic in common; this may then suggest an additional variable that may be brought into our theory. Consider Figure 8–3. On examining the residuals in that figure, you might notice that all of the countries for which educational spending was higher than predicted were not democracies, and all of the countries for which it was unexpectedly low were democracies. In this way you might have discovered the identity of the "something else," beyond GNP, that acts as an independent variable. Notice also that it would have been difficult to identify the presence of another factor if you had not first regressed educational spending on GNP. The richest democracies in Figure 8–3 show a higher rate of educational spending than do the poorest nondemocracies, so that it might not have been at all obvious that "democracy" was a variable you should use to explain levels of educational spending.

The technique of examining residuals is illustrated in Figure 8–8, adapted from V. O. Key, Jr.'s *Southern Politics* (1950, p. 48). Key wanted to measure the impact of factions in Alabama primaries, so he related counties' votes for Folsom, a progressive candidate in the 1946 gubernatorial primary, to their votes for Sparkman, a progressive candidate in the 1946 senatorial primary. He found a moderately strong relationship between the two. Because this meant that counties tended to lean the same way in both elections, it indicated the presence of conservative and progressive factions structuring the vote, as Key had expected. Had such factions not existed,

Figure 8–8   Example of Residual Analysis

Source: V. O. Key, Jr., *Southern Politics* (New York: Alfred A. Knopf, 1950), p. 48.

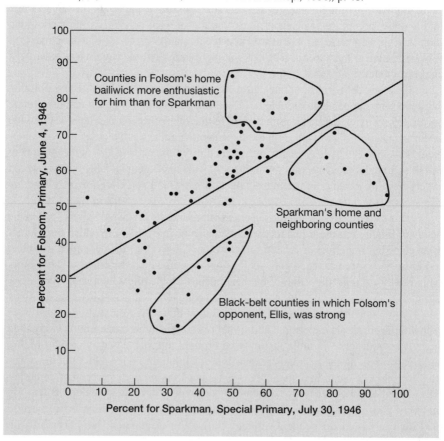

there would have been no particular reason to expect a county to vote in much the same way in the two primaries. But the relationship was not very tight. Many counties, such as the one that gave 90 percent of its vote to Folsom but only 45 percent to Sparkman, voted far differently from what one would have expected simply on the basis of conservative and progressive factions. This indicated the presence of other variables, which were causing additional variations in the vote.

By examining the residuals around the regression line, Key got some idea of what those variables might be. In this case it turned out that the residuals could be explained in part by the effect of "friends and neighbors." Counties in Folsom's home part of the state voted for him more enthusiastically than would have been expected on the basis of their vote for Sparkman. Counties in Sparkman's home part of the state voted less enthusiastically for Folsom than would have been expected from their vote for Sparkman (which presumably was high because he was a local boy). Similarly, the "home" counties of Folsom's opponent went less heavily for Folsom than would have been expected on the basis of their vote for Sparkman. This pointed out to Key the importance of local solidarity, one of the major forces retarding the development of stable statewide factions in Alabama politics at that time. Much of the looseness in the relationship between the votes for two candidates of the same faction was shown to be a result of people's tendency to vote for a candidate on the basis of where he came from in the state rather than the faction with which he was identified.

Users of regression analysis in political science far too rarely go on to the creative and exploratory labor of examining the residuals to see what additional variables affect the dependent variable. Usually, the spread of dots around the regression line is treated as an act of God, or as a measure of the basic uncertainty of human affairs. On the contrary, it is a trove in which new variables lie waiting to be discovered. I suspect the reason most of us do not go on to examine this trove is that we have developed a proprietorial sense toward our theories before we ever get to the point of testing them. There is a certain completeness about one's own theory, and it does not occur to us to use our theory as a "mere" starting point in the search for explanations.

Correlation Analysis

At the beginning of this chapter I pointed out that there are two ways to measure the strength of a relationship: by measuring how much difference the independent variable makes in the dependent variable, and by measuring how completely the independent variable determines the dependent variable. For interval-scale data, the regression coefficient accomplishes the first of these; the correlation coefficient accomplishes the second.

Consider the graphs in Figure 8–9. Both relationships can be summarized by the same regression line, but the value of the dependent variable in graph B is less closely determined by the independent variable than in graph A. A change in the independent variable tends to produce the same change in the dependent variable, on the average, in both graphs. But this tendency is weaker, and more likely to be disturbed

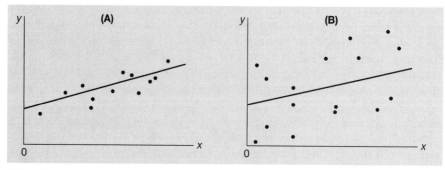

Figure 8–9   Two Correlations

by "other factors," in graph B; in other words, the residuals tend to be larger in graph B than in graph A. In one sense, then, the relationship in graph B is weaker than that in graph A. The dependent variable is less a result of the independent variable, compared to "other factors" (the unknown things that cause the residuals to exist), in B than in A.

The *correlation coefficient, r,* measures how widely such a body of data spreads around a regression line. This coefficient compares a set of data with ideal models of a perfect relationship and a perfect lack of relationship, and assigns to the relationship a score ranging in absolute value from zero to 1, depending on how closely the data approximate a perfect relationship. The two extreme models are illustrated in Figure 8–10.

In graph A of Figure 8–10, the data all fall on a straight line through the scattergram. A regression line passed through them would leave no residual variation at all in

Figure 8–10   Extreme Models of Correlation

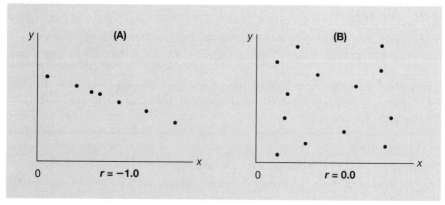

the dependent variable. Thus the independent variable determines the dependent variable completely. The correlation coefficient for this type has an absolute value of 1.

In graph B, on the other hand, values of the dependent variable are combined randomly with values of the independent variable, so that any given value of the dependent variable is as likely to coincide with a low value on the independent variable as with a high one. Thus there is no pattern to the relationship. This indicates that the independent variable has no effect on the dependent variable. The correlation coefficient for this type has absolute value of zero.

Most relationships, of course, fall somewhere between these two extremes; the closer a relationship approaches the situation in graph A, the higher its correlation coefficient will be in absolute value. Thus the correlation coefficient provides a measure by which the strengths of various relationships can be compared, in the *correlational* sense of "strength of relationship."

I have referred here only to the absolute value of the correlation coefficient. In addition to showing how closely a relationship approaches the situation in graph A, the correlation coefficient indicates by its sign whether the relationship is positive or negative. The coefficient ranges from -1.0 (a perfect negative relationship, such as the one in graph A of Figure 8–10) through 0.0 (graph B) to $+1.0$ (a perfect positive relationship, similar to the one in graph A but tilted up). In a positive relationship, increases in the dependent variable produce increases in the independent variable; in a negative relationship, increases in the independent variable produce decreases in the dependent variable.

Interpreting the correlation coefficient.   Although it is clear enough what correlation coefficients of $-1, 0$, or $+1$ mean, there is no easy way of interpreting what coefficients between these values mean. It is true that the higher the absolute value of the coefficient, the closer it approaches the model in graph A of Figure 8–10, so that if we wish to compare two different relationships, we can say which is stronger. But it is not easy to see what the difference between them means. It is *not* true, for instance, that the difference between $r = .8$ and $r = .6$ is the same as the difference between $r = .4$ and $r = .2$. And it is also not true that $r = -.6$ is twice as strong as $r = -.3$. This is reminiscent of the difference between ordinal and interval measurement: We know that the higher the absolute value of r, the stronger the relationship; but we do not know *how much* stronger one relationship is than another.

Fortunately, the square of the correlation coefficient (sometimes called the *coefficient of determination*, but more often just r^2) does have a usable interpretation at all values of r. Before we can consider this, however, I must first introduce the concept of *variance*.

Variance.   The variance of a variable is the average squared deviation of values of that variable from their own mean.[1] For instance, if there are just three cases,

---

[1]The mean of any variable is its arithmetic mean, or average: the sum of all the values divided by the number of cases.

with scores of $-1, 4$, and 5 for a variable, their mean is $(-1 + 4 + 5)/3 = 8/3$, and their variance is

$$\frac{\left(-1 - \frac{8}{3}\right)^2 + \left(4 - \frac{8}{3}\right)^2 + \left(5 - \frac{8}{3}\right)^2}{3}$$

$$= \frac{\left(-\frac{11}{3}\right)^2 + \left(\frac{4}{3}\right)^2 + \left(\frac{7}{3}\right)^2}{3}$$

$$= \frac{\frac{121}{9} + \frac{16}{9} + \frac{49}{9}}{3} = 6.89$$

The formula for the variance of any variable x is

$$\text{variance}_x = \frac{\Sigma(x - \bar{x})^2}{N}$$

where $\bar{x}$ is the mean of x and N is the number of observations we wish to average. The Σ sign simply means that for all the observations, we are to calculate $(x - \bar{x})^2$ and then add these results together. The expression $\Sigma(x - \bar{x})^2$ is equivalent to writing $(x_1 - \bar{x})^2 + (x_2 - \bar{x})^2 + \cdots + (x_N - \bar{x})^2$, where x_1 is the observation for the first case, x_2 the observation for the second case, and so on.

The variance is a measure of how widely the observed values of a variable vary among themselves. If they do not vary at all but each has the same value, the variance will be zero. This is true because each value will equal the mean, and thus the sum of the squared deviations from the mean will equal zero. The more the values vary among themselves, the further each will be from the mean of them all, and consequently, the greater the sum of squared deviations from the mean. Thus, the more that values vary among themselves, the higher their variance will be.

The variance of the dependent variable y can be depicted in a scattergram by drawing a horizontal line at $y = \bar{y}$, and drawing in the residuals from this line, as in Figure 8–11. The average squared value of the residuals, because it is the average squared deviation of the values of y from their own mean, is the variance of y.

One way to view our goal in theoretical social science research is to note that our task is usually to account for the variance in a dependent variable. It is the variance in something that puzzles us and challenges us to produce an explanation. Why is it that some people make more money than other people? That some nations are frequently involved in wars and others are not? That some members of Congress vote for a bill and others oppose it? That some people are more politically alienated than others? All of these questions simply ask: To what can the variance in this variable be attributed—*why does this variable vary?*

Comparing Figures 8–3 and 8–11, we should see at least a superficial similarity between the residuals around the least-squares line and the variance of the dependent variable. The least-squares line is a line passed through the scattergram in any direction such that the squared deviations of values of the dependent variable from that

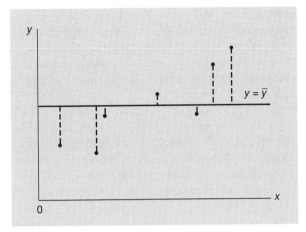

Figure 8–11 The Variance of y

line are minimized. The line $y = \bar{y}$ is a *horizontal* line passed through the data in the scattergram, and inspection will suggest what is, in fact, mathematically true: This line is the one *horizontal* line that minimizes the squared deviations of values of the dependent variable from itself (see Blalock, 1979, p. 58). That is, any other horizontal line passed through the data would yield a greater sum of squared deviations in the dependent variable.

This similarity suggests that the squared deviations around the regression line may be treated as the variance of the dependent variable around the values predicted for it by the regression equation. As already noted, this is the variance in the dependent variable that is still left unaccounted for after the effect of the independent variable has been estimated.

Thus we have two variances for the dependent variable: its variance around its own mean (the "total variance") and its variance around the regression line ("variance left unexplained by the independent variable"). To the extent that the dependent variable is determined by the independent variable, this unexplained variance will be small compared to the total variance. If the dependent variable can be predicted perfectly from the independent variable, as in Figure 8–10(A), the unexplained variance will be zero. If the dependent variable is unrelated to the independent variable, as in Figure 8–10(B), the regression line will be horizontal, indicating that the same value of the dependent variable is predicted at all values of the independent variable; inasmuch as the line $y = \bar{y}$ is the horizontal line that minimizes squared deviations around itself, the regression line will equal the line $y = \bar{y}$ in this case. Thus the unexplained variance will equal the total variance.

Dividing the unexplained variance by the total variance tells us what proportion of the total variance is left after we have allowed the independent variable to explain as much as it can explain. As it happens, r^2 equals 1 minus this proportion, or

$$1 - \frac{\text{unexplained variance}}{\text{total variance}}$$

that is, the proportion of the total variance in the dependent variable that can be ascribed to the independent variable.[2] The explained variance, therefore, gives us a useful interpretation of r at all values. If you read that an author has found a correlation of $-.30$ between two variables, you should mentally square the correlation and interpret that statement: "The two variables are negatively related, and 9 percent of the variance in one is due to the other."

Another helpful way to look at this interpretation is to think in terms of prediction. Operating without any knowledge of the independent variable, our best strategy in trying to predict values of the dependent variable for particular cases would be to guess that the value in any given case is the mean. We would be less wrong more of the time than with any other guess we could make.[3] If we now add knowledge of the independent variable, our best guess becomes the value predicted from the regression equation. The magnitude of the mistakes in each case is now represented by squared deviations around the predictions. The value r^2 measures the proportion by which we have reduced our mistakes in predicting the dependent variable by introducing knowledge of the independent variable.

Correlation and Regression Compared

Our discussion so far leaves us with the question, "Is correlation or regression analysis the better way to measure the strength of a relationship?" Obviously, the answer must be, "Sometimes one is, sometimes the other." The key to deciding when to use each measure lies in the fact that the correlation coefficient reflects the variability of the independent variable directly, whereas the regression coefficient does not.

Consider the two scattergrams in Figure 8–12. The scattergram from graph A has been reproduced in graph B, except that all observations for which the independent variable is less than 2 or greater than 4 have been eliminated. The effect is to reduce the variability of the independent variable while leaving the basic relationship between the independent and dependent variables unchanged. *Under these circumstances, the regression coefficient in B will be approximately the same as that in A, but the correlation coefficient will be sharply lowered in B.*

Let us see why this should be so. The regression line that minimized squared deviations in the full set of data in graph A should continue to minimize squared deviations in the partial set of data in graph B. Therefore, we would expect the regression coefficient to be about the same in both graphs. On the other hand, because the variability of the independent variable has been reduced in graph B, the extent of its possible effects on the dependent variable are reduced. Relative to other causes of

---

[2]For a good presentation of this interpretation, including the proof that

$$r^2 = 1 - \frac{\text{unexplained variance}}{\text{total variance}}$$

see Blalock (1979, pp. 405–409).

[3]At least this is true if we think of "mistakes" as squared deviations from the true value.

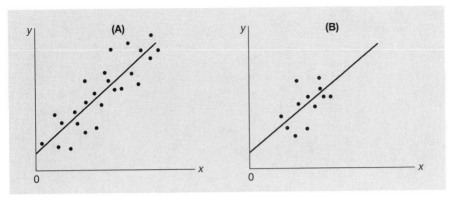

Figure 8–12   Regression and Correlation, with the Independent Variable Attenuated

the dependent variable, which are just as free to operate as they were in graph A, the importance of the independent variable as a cause of the dependent variable must decline. But this is simply to say that the proportion of the total variance that is attributable to the independent variable declines. In other words, r^2 is reduced.

This becomes a matter of considerable importance in field research, because generally the variability of independent variables is beyond the investigator's control. For instance, a researcher might be interested in knowing whether sex or race had more to do with whether a person voted. The researcher might use census tract data on a large city, correlating percent black with percent voting and percent male with percent voting. But the distribution of people in most cities is such that the percent black would vary greatly while the percent male would not. (Blacks are concentrated highly in some tracts and almost absent in others; men are spread more or less evenly across all the tracts.)

The fact that percent male scarcely varies from one census tract to another guarantees that this researcher would find practically no correlation between percent male and percent voting. As indicated in the hypothetical scattergram in Figure 8–13, there is near zero variance in percent male; hence very little of the variance in percent voting can be due to it. On the other hand, if residential patterns were such that percent male could vary as much as percent black does, it might be that gender would show up as a major determinant of voter turnout.[4] There is limited usefulness to a measure that would have us conclude from this that race is a more important cause of participation than sex.[5]

---

[4]This example also incorporates a major statistical problem in some correlation and regression analyses, the *ecological fallacy*. This can occur when data on aggregate units (such as percent black, median income, and so on, for census tracts, counties, or states) are used to infer how variables are related among individuals living in those aggregate units. See Robinson (1950), Stokes (1969), and Achen and Shively (1995).

[5]Problems such as this are a result of censored data. (See above, pp. 103–106.)

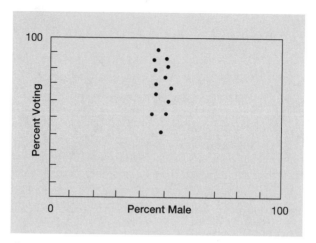

Figure 8–13   Predicting Percent Voting from Percent Male

The problem with using correlation coefficients in both of these cases is that while the coefficient is affected by the particular variance of the independent variable in the data at hand, the investigator clearly intends to extrapolate from these particular data to a more general case. In the census tract study, the researcher wants to make a statement about the impact of race or sex on voting, regardless of how people are located in the city. In the GRE study, the researcher wants to make a judgment about how to treat new applicants (among whom the variability of GRE scores would be higher) on the basis of the relationship between GRE scores and grades among the students currently in the department.

A good rule is that in any situation in which you wish to extrapolate from a particular set of data to a more general case, you should use regression coefficients. Because theoretical research almost always is interested in generalizing, regression analysis usually will be superior to correlation analysis. (This advice holds despite the fact, which I mentioned earlier, that in regression analysis there is always some difficulty in handling varying units.)

There are circumstances, however, in which you may not intend to generalize, but only to describe a particular situation. For instance, someone might want to describe how a particular Congress, say the 80th or the 92nd, operated. It would then be appropriate to note that in that particular Congress, there was a negligible correlation between members' race and their votes on various bills. This would help establish what were the important factors influencing outcomes *in that Congress*. However, this would not deny the possibility of a relationship between race and voting record for Congresses in general.

Problem of Measurement Error

Our understanding of relationships between variables is intimately bound up with the extent to which we have been able to measure the variables validly. To the extent that there is *nonrandom error* in our variables, we are simply unable to state accurately what the relationship between those variables is. This should be clear from our earlier discussion of measurement error in Chapter 4.

Random measurement error also distorts the relationship between variables. Refer back to Table 4–1 (pp. 52–53). The relationship between the two variables is increasingly attenuated from left to right, as it might appear under conditions of increasing levels of random measurement error. The scattergrams for the three sets of data drawn from Table 4–1 are presented in Figure 8–14. As progressively greater amounts of random measurement error are present in two variables, the true form of the relationship between the variables is more and more lost to us. Not only is it lost to us, but it is systematically distorted. To the extent that there is random error in two variables, they will appear to us to be unrelated. Thus there is a real danger that the only relationships we will be able to perceive are those between variables that are easy to measure accurately, a possibility that bodes ill for social science.

Figure 8–14   Relationship Under Varying Degrees of Random Measurement Error

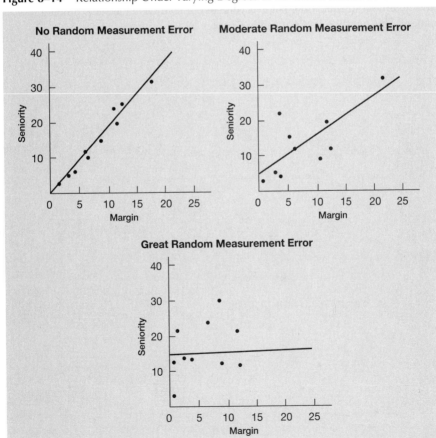

If we are willing to make some assumptions regarding the nature of the random error, it is possible to correct for it, and thus reconstruct the true relationship between two variables. A good example of this technique is seen in Bartels (1993). (Unfortunately, this article and most other discussions of measurement error are difficult for the untrained reader.)

FURTHER DISCUSSION

In this chapter I have drawn only the broad outlines of correlation and regression analysis for interval data. In fact, I have purposely refrained from giving formulas for calculating these measures, so that anyone wishing to put these techniques to use would be forced to seek out more detailed training. David Knoke, George W. Bohrnstedt, and Alissa Potter Mee's *Statistics for Social Data Analysis* (2002) is a good, standard text in statistics—one of many—for social scientists.

One question you might consider is this: What would happen in a regression analysis if the independent variable did not vary at all—if, say, we wanted to relate voting turnout to education, but everyone in our study had the same amount of education? This question looks ahead to Chapter 10.

Chapter 9

Introduction
to Statistics

Further Topics on Measurement
of Relationships

In this chapter I build on the introduction in Chapter 8 to discuss in brief how to measure three types of relationships: (1) those among ordinal and nominal variables; (2) those that involve dichotomous variables; and (3) those that involve several variables simultaneously.[1]

MEASURES OF RELATIONSHIP FOR ORDINAL DATA

As we saw at the beginning of Chapter 8, there are two main ways in which we can measure the strength of a relationship. We can measure how much change is produced in the dependent variable by a change in the independent variable, or we can measure how strongly the dependent variable is determined by the independent variable relative to other things that also help determine it.

Only for the second of these is it possible to develop a standard measure for use with ordinal-scale data. To measure how much change is produced in the dependent variable, it is necessary to have some sort of unit by which to measure that change. But this is not available under ordinal measurement. Accordingly, the most we can hope for from ordinal variables is some form of correlational analysis.

A cross-tabulation is to the analysis of ordinal variables what a scattergram is to the analysis of interval variables. Consider Table 9–1, in which voters' willingness to have the United States use military force to solve problems abroad is related to their willingness to have the United States give financial aid to countries in economic

---

[1]This chapter presents advanced material that can be skipped over without any loss in comprehension of the remaining material covered in this book.

TABLE 9–1   Relationship Between Support for Military Intervention and Support for Economic Aid

Willingness to Have United States Use Military Force to Solve Problems	Willingness to Have United States Give Financial Aid to Countries in Crisis			
	Not Willing	*Somewhat Willing*	*Very Willing*	*Extremely Willing*
Extremely willing	18	66	33	29
Very willing	47	152	75	14
Somewhat willing	120	355	112	34
Not willing	48	119	38	5

Source: 1998 Congressional Election Survey, National Election Study, University of Michigan.

crisis. This is an interesting question. There might be a negative relationship, in which voters who favored the use of military force did not want to see more "soft" involvement, and voters who favored helping those in economic crises did not want to see other sorts of involvement. Or there might be a positive relationship if both questions were tapping an "internationalist" dimension such that those favoring one sort of involvement would favor other sorts as well, and those opposing U.S. involvement abroad in one form opposed it in all other ways as well.

Like a scattergram, the table shows how frequently the various combinations of the two variables occur. And just as in a scattergram that shows the relationship between two intervally measured variables, a positive relationship would mean that relatively few cases should fall in the upper left corner of the table (not many cases willing to intervene militarily but unwilling to send aid) or the lower right corner (not many cases willing to send aid but unwilling to intervene militarily). A negative relationship would imply the opposite: relatively few cases in the lower left or upper right. And no relationship at all would, of course, imply an even spread across the table. Each number in the table gives the number of people in the 1998 study who exhibited a given combination of attitudes toward the two sorts of international intervention. These are actual numbers of cases, not percentages. The table reveals a pattern between these variables, just as a scattergram does for interval-scale data.

In general, we can say that there is a modest positive relationship in the table, with willingness to use military force increasing somewhat as voters are more willing to give financial aid. For instance, of the 82 voters who are extremely willing to give financial aid, 29 are extremely willing to have the United States use military force, while of the 233 who are not willing to give aid, only 18 are extremely willing to have the United States use military force. There are two differences between a table such as this and a scattergram, however:

1. Because there is a limited number of values available for each variable (four for the independent variable and four for the dependent variable), it is not necessary to use the infinite space of a plane to locate the observations. Instead, the observations are located

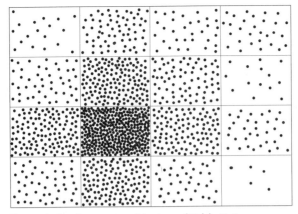

Figure 9–1   Scattergram Version of Table 9–1

in one or another of the cells of a table. Because so many observations are tied on each value, their presence is indicated by counting the number of observations falling in each cell and printing the number there rather than by printing a dot for each observation. If the observations are indicated by dots, as in Figure 9–1, the similarity to a scattergram becomes more obvious.

2. Because there are no units by which to measure the difference between two values of a variable, however, the *precise* pattern in the table is meaningless. How great a change there is in attitudes as we move from "Very willing" to "Extremely willing" tells us nothing specific, because for all we know, "Very willing" might represent only slightly less support than "Extremely willing."

Thus it is not possible to measure the strength of relationships in a way analogous to regression. On the other hand, it *is* possible to develop measures analogous to the correlation coefficient. To do this, we must develop models of the perfect relationship and of perfect independence, as was done with the correlation coefficient, and also develop a measure to indicate how close the data in our table come to these two models.[2]

One such measure for use with ordinal variables is Goodman and Kruskal's gamma.[3] It takes as its model of perfect independence a table in which the data are distributed uniformly throughout the table; that is, the same percent of each category of the dependent variable occurs at each category of the independent variable, and vice versa. Under such "perfect independence," the data in Table 9–1 would appear as in Table 9–2. The numbers in Table 9–2 are printed in italics to emphasize that they are base-line counterparts for comparison with the observed numbers in Table 9–1.

---

[2]Even though there is not a precise regression line to define residuals, however, it might still be useful to look at the "residuals" in Table 9–1—the cases that do not fit the generally positive relationship. Is there anything special, for instance, about those who buck the general trend by favoring the use of military force but opposing financial aid, or vice versa?

[3]This measure was described in Goodman and Kruskal (1954).

TABLE 9–2   Independent Version of Table 9–1

Willingness to Have United States Use Military Force to Solve Problems	Willingness to Have United States Give Financial Aid to Countries in Crisis			
	Not Willing	*Somewhat Willing*	*Very Willing*	*Extremely Willing*
Extremely willing	*27*	*80*	*30*	*9*
Very willing	*53*	*157*	*59*	*19*
Somewhat willing	*114*	*340*	*127*	*40*
Not willing	*39*	*115*	*42*	*14*

Measures like the Goodman–Kruskal gamma are designed to compare the distributions in Tables 9–1 and 9–2 to see how different they are in a positive or negative direction. For instance, there are fewer cases in the upper-left corner (8 vs. *27*) and lower-right corner (5 vs. *14*) than one would expect if there were no relationship; and there are more in the lower left (48 vs. *39*) and upper right (29 vs. *9*) than expected. This indicates a pattern consistent with a mildly positive relationship. A measure like Goodman–Kruskal's will use *all* cells of the table, not just the corners, but this is the general principle of how they work.

From a measure based on cell-by-cell comparisons like this, we can develop a measure of correlation. But none of the measures that have been developed is all that satisfactory, and often two rather different patterns will produce the same result. Accordingly, relationships between ordinal variables are often accounted for by some form of regression analysis, with the ordinal variables forced into interval assumptions. Sometimes, this lapses into real abuse of the data, as investigators bludgeon a model assuming interval measurement onto data that depart badly from that assumption.

MEASURES OF RELATIONSHIP FOR NOMINAL DATA

In relating two nominally measured variables, cross-tabulation again approximates the function of a scattergram—that is, it shows which values of one variable tend to coincide with which values of the other. However, in contrast to a table relating ordinal variables, the *position* of a cell in the table no longer tells us anything, for the order of values of a nominal variable means nothing. Consider the example in Table 9–3, in which versions A and B are equivalent. The table could not be rearranged in this way if the variables were measured ordinally.

As with ordinally measured data, all we can do in measuring the strength of a relationship between two nominally measured variables is to assess the degree to which one variable is determined by the other. Various measures have been developed to do this, just as has been done with ordinal variables. But the problem is really better dealt with by adaptations of regression analysis to nominal variable analysis. Unlike the case of relationships between ordinal variables, these adaptations do not require

TABLE 9–3　Interchangeable Order in Nominal Data

Candidate Preferred	(A) Religion			Candidate Preferred	(B) Religion		
	Cath.	*Prot.*	*Other*		*Prot.*	*Cath.*	*Other*
X	20	0	0	X	0	20	0
Z	5	30	4	Y	0	0	26
Y	0	0	26	Z	30	5	4

distorting the measurement of the variables to force them into interval assumptions. Regression adaptations for analyzing nominal variables are dealt with in the next two sections.

Dichotomies and Regression Analysis

Dichotomies are classifications that involve only two categories: for example, gender (male or female), referendum vote (yes or no), or participation (voter or nonvoter). Such classifications have a useful property, which at first glance appears to be a bit mysterious: Although dichotomies are nominal scales, they can quite properly be treated as interval scales and can be analyzed using measures appropriate for such scales. This greatly expands the value and applicability of regression analysis, for obvious reasons. It means that not only intervally measured variables, but also dichotomous nominal scale variables—and mixtures of the two—can be analyzed using regression analysis.

The trick is that because a dichotomous variable can take on only one of two values, there is by definition a common unit in which differences between values of the variable can be measured, namely the difference between the two categories. Let us call the categories A and B. Then the distance between two observations falling into category A is zero units, and the distance between two observations, one of which is in A and the other in B, is one unit. Because there usually is no natural ordering to the dichotomy, the decision of whether A is one unit greater than B, or one unit less, must be arbitrary.

An alternative way to look at this situation is to think of a dichotomy as measuring the degree to which an observation *embodies* one of its categories. The category is either present or not present for each observation. For instance, the dichotomy "gender: male or female" can also be viewed as a variable "femaleness" (or alternatively, "maleness"). Each subject is either totally "female" or totally "not female." If the difference between totally female and totally not female is taken to be one unit, women have values of $+1.0$ for the variable "femaleness" and men have values of 0.0. Because this is a true interval measure, it can be used together with other interval measures, such as income or age, in regression and correlation analysis.

(The same interpretation cannot be placed on nominal-scale variables with more than two categories. We would have no common unit, for example, in which to place Catholics relative to Protestants or Jews in the variable "religion." As you will see on page 137, however, there is yet another trick we can use in this case that will allow us to work with multiple-category variables.)

For example, we might regress income at a low-paying factory on gender, with gender equal to 0 for men and 1 for women. The best-fitting regression line might be

income = 14,000 − 2,000 gender

This would mean that the expected income of men at the factory was $14,000, since the value of "gender" for men is zero. Similarly, the expected income for women would be $14,000 − ($2,000 × 1) = $12,000. Since the independent variable can take on only two values, the scattergram for this analysis will look odd, with a set of data arrayed vertically above "gender = 0" and another set arrayed vertically above "gender = 1." A scattergram that would be consistent with these hypothetical regression results is shown in Figure 9–2.

The regression line will actually pass directly through the mean income at gender = 0 and the mean income at gender = 1. Since a regression line serves as a convenient way of summarizing the central pattern in a set of means, there is no particular advantage to using regression analysis in cases like these, in which we are interested in the relationship between an interval-scaled variable and a *single* dichotomous variable. (Exactly the same result could be presented, somewhat more simply, by noting that the average income of men at the factory is $14,000, while the average income of women is $12,000.) Where this technique of treating dichotomous variables does become valuable is when we wish to combine a dichotomous variable

Figure 9–2   Hypothetical Regression of Income on Gender

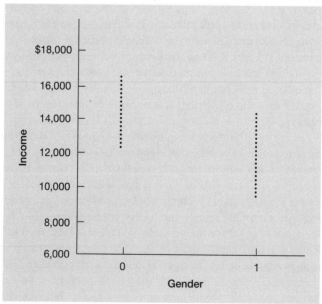

with other independent variables in an analysis. This would be the case if we wished to look at the simultaneous effects of sex and education on income. There is a well-developed technique described in the section "Multivariate Analysis" on pp. 140–145 that allows us to use interval-level measures simultaneously in this way, but there is no such technique for nominal measures. The ability to include dichotomous nominal variables in such analyses is extraordinarily valuable.

When faced with the difficulties of working with ordinal-scaled variables, or nominal-scaled variables with multiple categories, it might be tempting to cut the Gordian knot by collapsing all of these variables into dichotomies and treating them as interval variables. "Religion," for instance, might be collapsed into "Protestant/non-Protestant." This backward analog of the "enrichment" technique I advocated in Chapter 5 is only very rarely either useful or necessary, however. It should be intuitively clear that its effects generally would be pernicious, simply because it involves throwing away information. Fortunately, it is hardly ever necessary. In multivariate analysis (a subject too complex for me to deal with in detail here but which I touch on briefly in the section after next), a variable with several categories can be treated as a series of dichotomies and can thus be included in regression or correlation analysis. For instance, "religion" can be translated into a *group* of dichotomous variables: "Presbyterian/non-Presbyterian," "Methodist/non-Methodist," "Catholic/non-Catholic," and so on. Each person presumably would have a score of 1 on one of these and scores of zero on the others. This entire group of dichotomous variables can then be included together in a multivariate regression analysis. Variables such as these generally are known as *dummy variables* or *binary variables*.

(Ordinal variables cannot be handled in this manner, because the notion of order would be lost. However, regression analysis is so superior to methods that have been developed specifically for ordinal variables that most analysts end up forcing ordinal variables into regression analysis either by "enriching" them into interval measures [see pp. 68–70] or by breaking them into a cluster of dichotomous variables in the manner described above for multiple-category nominal scale variables. However, doing the latter sacrifices the ordinal information because it turns the ordinal scale variable into a cluster of nominal scale variables.)

The value of this trick, whereby we can include nominal scale dichotomies in the powerful technique of regression analysis, cannot be stated too strongly. However, this works only for dichotomous nominal measures used as independent variables. We cannot appropriately use them as *dependent* variables in ordinary regression. One indication that this would be problematic is that it would be impossible to construct a meaningful correlation coefficient for such an analysis. Consider the scattergram in Figure 9–3. In any reasonable sense, there is a perfect relationship here. Above levels of $x = 10$, y is always 1; and when x is less than 10, y is always zero. But there is still "error" around the regression line. Since the regression line cannot bend, it cannot follow the jump from $y = 0$ to $y = 1$ at the point at which x equals 10 and thus cannot register the full extent to which values of y are determined by x. It is therefore incapable of serving as the "best summarizing line" to describe the relationship between x and y.

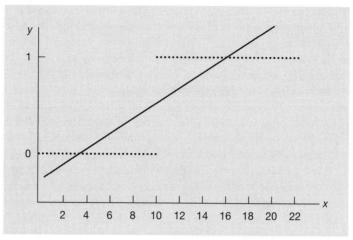

Figure 9–3   Dichotomous Dependent Variable

LOGIT AND PROBIT ANALYSIS

To handle the problem of describing the relationship between a continuous independent variable and a dichotomous dependent variable, statisticians have developed an alternative model that is found in two very similar variations, called *logit analysis* and *probit analysis*. I describe logit analysis here, but the general explanation holds for both.

The regression line, as you will recall, can be interpreted as the path of expected values of the dependent variable across varying values of the independent variable. From the regression line in Figure 8–4, for instance, we would predict that y would equal 9 when x equaled 1, that y would equal 18 when x equaled 4, and so on. This does not make sense for a dichotomous variable, since it can take on values of only zero or 1. It would not make sense in Figure 9–3, for instance, to predict that the dependent variable would have a value of 0.3 when the independent variable equaled 8; this would be nonsensical.

An analogy to the expected value of a dependent variable, however, would be the probability that the dependent variable equals 1. Such a model would portray, across the variation in an independent variable, the varying probability that a dichotomous variable equals 1. It would need to be S-shaped and bounded vertically by zero and 1, since a probability must be positive and less than or equal to 1. Figure 9–4 provides an example. The model would predict, for example, that at $x = 5$, about 70 percent of the cases would have $y = 1$. That is, $P(y = 1)$, the probability that y equals 1, is about 0.7.

We do not have any way to work directly with such a model, but the logit model allows us to derive estimates of the sort such a model would yield. Letting $p = P(y = 1)$, the logit is the logarithm to base e, that is the natural logarithm, of

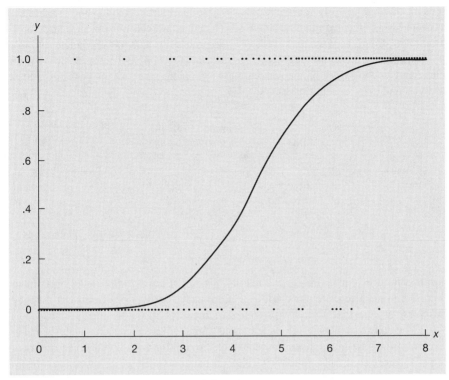

Figure 9–4   Path-of-Probabilities Model

$\frac{p}{(1 - p)}$. This is a difficult quantity to conceive! But it does embody the probability in which we are interested; and most important, the logit model allows us to use regular regression analysis to analyze a dichotomous dependent variable. It turns out that the logit can appropriately be taken as a linear function of a continuous independent variable, in the standard form

logit of $y = a + bx$

Mechanically, the way this works is that the dependent variable has values of either zero or 1. The computer calculates from the number of zeroes and 1s at given values of the independent variable what the expected logit of the dependent variable is across the range of the independent variable. Because the analysis is so indirect, the a and b in the logit equation are not intuitively interpretable. Remember, it is not y, or even the probability of y, that is predicted from x in this equation; rather, it is the natural logarithm of $\frac{p}{(1 - p)}$. The best way to interpret logit analysis, and the way it is usually presented in studies, is to calculate by a series of transformations on the logit coefficients what the expected probability of y is at various values of x and to present those discretely. This is done by first calculating from a and b what the expected logit [the natural logarithm of $\frac{p}{(1 - p)}$] is at each of several values of x. Then, it is straightforward to solve for p (the probability that the dependent variable is 1 rather than zero), from the natural logarithm of $\frac{p}{(1 - p)}$. For instance, if we were interested in the effect of age on voting participation, we might perform a logit analysis and then present the results:

Age	Estimated Probability of Voting
25	0.37
35	0.58
45	0.68
55	0.70
65	0.71
75	0.71

A table like this approximates the results one might have gotten from a nonlinear regression line. There are also various analogs to the correlation coefficient for logit analyses but none that is readily presented at this level.

The ability to incorporate dichotomous variables into regression analysis, either directly if they are independent variables, or through the logit and probit variants of regression analysis if the dichotomy is a dependent variable, has made regression analysis a powerful statistical tool and the dominant tool for data analysis in political science.

MULTIVARIATE ANALYSIS

In Chapter 6 we saw that frequently it is important to hold one variable constant while measuring the relationship between two other variables. The easiest way to do this is literally to "hold the variable constant," as in the example on pages 94–95, by separating the subjects into groups along the control variable (a group of Democrats, a group of Republicans, and a group of independents, for example, if registration is the variable to be held constant). The relationship between the other two variables is then measured for each group.

This technique has serious disadvantages, though. First, if we want to control for an intervally measured variable, the number of "groups" we set up might be too large. For instance, in controlling for income, we might have a group of all those with an income of $18,243, another of all those with an income of $43,402, and so on; in this case there probably would be as many groups as there were subjects in the study. This problem can be averted by lumping subjects into a few broad categories of the independent variable, but doing so throws away a great deal of the precision in the measure—something one may not want to do.

A second and more serious problem in literally holding a variable constant is that the process quite rapidly leaves the researcher with only small numbers of subjects among whom to measure a relationship. Suppose that someone wanted to examine the relationship between occupation and voting, holding constant race and age. The investigator might divide the population into groups such as blacks aged 20 to 30, whites aged 20 to 30, blacks aged 31 to 40, and so on, and then look at the occupation/vote relationship for each of these groups. But the typical national survey, with about 2,000 respondents, might include no more than five or six whites aged 20 to 30, blacks aged 51 to 60, or whatever. Such small groups would give very unreliable estimates of the relationship between occupation and vote.[4]

A final disadvantage of literal controlling is that it produces a series of measures of the relationship (one measure for each group) that is unwieldy and difficult to absorb. Particularly if we wanted to control simultaneously for more than one variable, as in our example of race and age, this might leave us with as many as 20 or 30 separate measures to consider. Especially, as noted above, any multicategory nominal variables included in the analysis will show up as a set of several dichotomous variables.

Fortunately, there is an easier way to control for a variable—at least if we are using interval-scale variables (including dichotomies that are taken as independent variables). The technique of multivariate regression allows us to look at the pattern in several variables among all of our observations (without breaking these down into separate subgroups) and to estimate what the relationship between the dependent variable and any particular independent variable would be if none of the other variables varied—that is, if each of the other variables were "held constant."

To sketch the technique in a general way, I will use as an example the case of two independent variables (w and x) and a dependent variable (y). You will recall that the relationship between two variables can be plotted in a flat space of two dimensions (represented by a scattergram). Similarly, the relationship among three variables

Figure 9–5   Three-Dimensional Scattergram

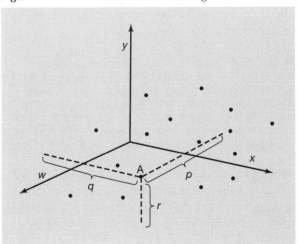

---

[4]Refer again to the box "Law of Large Numbers" on page 61.

can be plotted in a three-dimensional space, as seen in Figure 9–5. The vertical dimension is the dependent variable, and each of the horizontal dimensions is one of the independent variables. Each observation is a dot floating in three-dimensional space, located according to its values on each of the three variables. Dot A has had coordinates drawn to show how it is located in the three-dimensional space by its values on *w*, *x*, and *y*, where these values are *p, q,* and *r*, respectively.

Just as a one-dimensional line through the two-dimensional scattergram could summarize the pattern in a two-variable relationship, so a two-dimensional plane through the three-dimensional scattergram can summarize the pattern in its three-variable relationship. The plane is picked on the basis of the same criterion by which the regression line was chosen. It must be the plane that minimizes the sum of squared deviations of actual *y* values from the *y* values predicted from the plane.

This regression plane would look like a flat piece of cardboard set at some tilt in the middle of the three-dimensional space over a grid containing all possible combinations of values of *w* and *x*. By counting out a certain distance along *x* and then a certain distance along *w*, we can locate a particular combination of *w* and *x* on this grid. The height of the cardboard plane above the grid at this point is the value of *y* predicted from the given values of *w* and *x* by the regression plane. The regression equation associated with the plane is of the form

$$y = a + b_1 w + b_2 x$$

As in the two-variable case, *a* is the intercept—the predicted value of *y* when both *x* and *w* equal zero. Similarly, b_1 tells by how many units *y* can be expected to increase if *w* increases by one unit *and x does not change*; and b_2 tells by how many units *y* can be expected to increase if *x* increases by one unit *and w does not change*. Here b_1 and b_2 are the regression coefficients of the equation.

To calculate from the multivariate regression the *y* value you would expect from a particular combination of *w* and *x:*

1. Start with *a*, the expected value of *y* when both *x* and *w* equal zero.
2. Add to this b_1 times *w*, or the amount by which *y* could be expected to change if the value of *w* shifted from zero to the particular value you are using. At this point, you have the expected value of *y* when *x* equals zero and *w* equals the particular value.
3. To this sum, add b_2 times *x*, the amount by which *y* could be expected to change if *x* shifted from zero to the particular value you are using and *w* remained unchanged. You now have the expected value of *y*, given these particular values of *w* and *x*.

Notice in this that b_1 describes the relationship between *w* and *y* if *x* does not vary, and that b_2 describes the relationship between *x* and *y* if *w* does not vary. In this way, without requiring us to break our observations into separate small and awkward groups, multivariate regression allows us to examine relationships with certain other variables controlled.

For example, if we had data for U.S. counties giving the percentages of African-American students attending all-black schools, the median income of each county, and the percentage of African-Americans in each county's population, we might find the following situation:

Let I be the percentage of African-American students attending all-black schools.
Let M be the county's median income (in thousands of dollars).
Let B be the percentage of African-Americans in the county's population.

On examining just the relationship between I and M, we might find that the regression equation was

$$I = 68.2 - 2.1M$$

This would indicate that school integration is more widespread in richer counties. The percentage of African-Americans attending all-black schools decreases by 2.1 percent as the median income of the county increases by 1,000 dollars.

Obviously, however, we need to control for percent African-American in assessing this relationship. It might be that the apparent integration of the well-heeled counties is simply a result of the fact that in the richer counties there are so few African-Americans that there are not likely to be any all-black schools. We could test for this by adding the variable "percent African-American" as an additional independent variable. The regression equation

$$I = 49.5 - 0.1M + 0.6B$$

would indicate that this is true. With the control for "percent African-American" added, the relationship between median income and percent of African-American students attending all-black schools largely disappears. In the multiple regression equation, a decrease of only 0.1 percent can be expected from an increase of 1,000 dollars in median income.[5]

This freedom from the need to "hold variables constant" physically is an important advantage of multivariate regression analysis. This is especially true when working with several variables simultaneously.[6] Because there is no satisfactory analog to this technique for use with ordinal data, we can add this to our list of arguments for trying to measure variables intervally as often as possible. Nominal variables may be included in multiple regression equations by treating them as dichotomies (refer to p. 136).

As in simple linear regression, it is important in multiple linear regression that the data actually fit a model in which all the relationships between the dependent variable and the independent variables are linear. Otherwise, the regression plane described by the equation we come up with will be an inaccurate representation of the relationships.

---

[5]This little analysis is wholly fictitious. For a multiple regression analysis of black voting registration, using county data for southern states in the 1950s, see Matthews and Prothro (1963).

[6]Although I have used the case of three variables in this section because that case can be represented by perspective drawings, the general multivariate regression technique applies to any number of variables. The same logic would apply to a four-variable case, with the equation $y = a + b_1w + b_2x + b_3z$, although no scattergram can be drawn in these four dimensions.

Interaction in Research and Theory

Although interaction among variables is a nuisance from the standpoint of multivariate regression analysis, in itself it is an interesting phenomenon. It is exciting to think that a relationship itself may depend on a further variable. Because such interaction occurs frequently in the social sciences, it is important that you be alert to it in your research. Because "common sense" rarely gets so complicated as to suggest this sort of thing, interaction is almost always unexpected, and discovering it is fun and dramatic. As one example, Philip Converse was able to argue very neatly for the importance of a measure of ideological sophistication by showing that the relationship between social class and voting was strongly affected by it (1964, esp. pp. 231–234). [7] Among those who scored lowest in ideological sophistication, there was no relationship between social class and voting. As the score on ideological sophistication increased, however, a relationship appeared, reaching its apex among those with the highest sophistication score.

There is also an additional requirement in *multiple* linear regression. It is important that the data best fit a model in which the relationship between the dependent variable and each independent variable is the same no matter what value the other independent variable(s) takes on. In our three-variable example of w, x, and y, we had to assume that an increase of one unit in x produced the same change in y, no matter what the value of w was. Otherwise, we could not have calculated the expected value of y simply by adding a plus b_1 times w plus b_2 times x. We would have had to pick a value for b_1 that was appropriate for whatever value of x we were using, and a value of b_2 that was appropriate for whatever value of w we were using. It is obvious that this would be a complicated procedure. In fact, it is often impossible to operate under these conditions.

When this happens—when the relationship between variables A and B differs, depending on the value of a variable C—there is said to be "interaction" among the variables. A concrete example may make more clear what interaction is and how it might arise. Consider the relationship between party affiliation and how members of Congress vote on a bill. This relationship could be strong (all Democrats vote one way, all Republicans the other), or weak (less clear-cut party differences). Now, the strength of the relationship might be related to a member's seniority. New members, who are rather dependent on party leadership for favors, might vote obediently along straight party lines. Those with more seniority, who had built up respect among fellow members, might vote more independently.

Thus, there would be interaction among the variables. The relationship between party and vote would change as the third variable, seniority, changed. Under these circumstances, a regression equation of the form

$$\text{vote} = a + b_1 \cdot \text{party} + b_2 \cdot \text{seniority}$$

[7]This example is a particularly interesting one because Converse demonstrated yet a second level of interaction (the interaction itself varies with gender) that I have chosen to ignore here.

TABLE 9–4   Example of Results from a Multivariate
                      Logit Analysis

Age	Gender	
	Male	*Female*
25	.52*	.62
35	.48	.58
45	.46	.55
55	.45	.53
65	.44	.51
75	.44	.50

*Estimated probability of voting Democratic, for various combinations of age and gender.

would not be appropriate. It would not be true that "vote" always increased by the same amount with a given change in "party." How much "vote" changed with a given change in "party" would depend on the value of "seniority."[8]

Like ordinary regression analysis, logit and probit analyses may readily incorporate a number of independent variables. The coefficients for the variables are difficult to interpret, since they are predicting not directly to the variable or its probability but (in the case of the logit) to the natural logarithm of $\frac{p}{(1 - p)}$, where p is the probability that $y = 1$. As in logit analysis with a single independent variable, the results are usually made understandable by calculating from transformations of the coefficients what the probability of y is estimated to be, given varying combinations of the independent variables. For instance, if we were predicting voting for the Democratic party from age and gender, we might present the results as in Table 9–4.

CONCLUSION

You might expect me to conclude, "Go out and use these measures." However, I am more interested in cautioning you against using them unwisely. All of these techniques simplify what is going on in a set of data by screening out certain aspects of relationships. This is their great virtue, and it *is* a virtue. Still, it is your responsibility to delve a bit deeper and see just what is being screened out. For instance, each of the scattergrams in Figure 9–6 would give approximately the same regression equation, but the relationships depicted mean quite different things. It is critical that you examine as carefully as possible each scattergram on which you base a regression equation, checking for nonlinearity, noting which observations are mavericks in the relationship, and so on.

[8]It is possible to add "interaction terms" to the regression equation to take into account certain types of interaction, but that goes beyond the scope of this presentation. See, for example, Blalock (1969, Appendix A, "Theory Building and the Statistical Concept of Interaction").

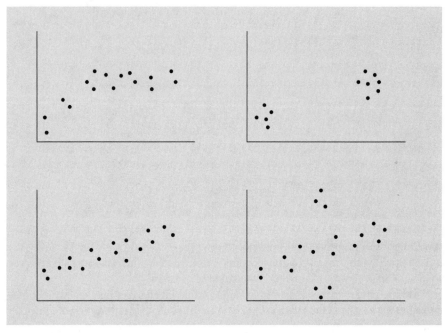

Figure 9–6   Four Alternative Scattergrams with the Same Regression Equation

A computer can chug out hundreds of regression equations in a few seconds. It is tempting simply to call for a mound of results, especially given the uncertainty involved in working with most social science theories. Usually, however, you will be better served if you first think carefully about what you want to do, pick a limited number of relationships of interest to you, and examine each of these relationships in detail. Your measures will then be useful summarizing tools, not substitutes for a full look at what is going on.

The important thing is that you stay in charge. Use your measures and computer analyses as tools rather than ends in themselves, and keep your eye on the question you want to answer. Data will talk to you, but you must let them speak softly.

Chapter 10

Introduction to Statistics

Inference, or How to Gamble on Your Research

As I pointed out in Chapter 8, there are two main areas of statistics: (1) measuring things, especially measuring relationships between variables; and (2) estimating how likely it is that the measure you have gotten could have occurred by chance. In Chapters 8 and 9 we looked at the first of these aspects, and now we examine the second. (I must note parenthetically that, as in preceding chapters, I do not intend to teach you *how to use* statistical tests. Instead I present the general logic of such tests to help you understand what they mean when you see them. This approach might also serve as a useful supplement to a statistics course, which sometimes teaches students how to use the tests without putting the tests in a broader perspective.)

It is quite possible to get a particular result by chance, even though the result is not true in general. If you chose ten U.S. senators at random, for instance, it would be possible to come up with a group consisting largely of conservative Democrats and liberal Republicans. From that you might conclude—erroneously—that there was a relationship between party and ideology in the Senate, with Republicans the more liberal group.

However, if you repeatedly drew groups of ten senators, selecting the ten at random from the whole Senate, *most* of the time you would find that the Democrats in your group were more liberal than the Republicans, simply because Democratic senators do tend to be more liberal than Republican senators. But some of the time you would find that the Republicans in your sample were more liberal than the Democrats, or that the two parties did not differ at all. The problem in drawing a single group and describing the Senate from it is that you cannot know whether your group is of the first type (the relationship between the variables is the same in your subset as in the Senate as a whole) or of the second (the relationship between the variables is different in the subset from that in the Senate as a whole). If it is of the first type, your conclusion will be true; if it is of the second (a distorted sample), your conclusion will be false.

This is a common problem that must be dealt with whenever anyone tries to describe a whole population of cases by looking only at a sample drawn out of the population. It comes up in conducting social science research, opinion polling, assigning television ratings, conducting market analyses, administering quality control in manufacturing, and in performing numerous other activities.

Fortunately, there are ways to determine just how likely it is that a particular result could have occurred by chance even if its opposite were generally true. By means of these techniques we can calculate how much stock to put in our findings. It is a very close analogy to say that we can gamble intelligently on the results of our study by calculating the odds that the results are false. When we do this, we are said to measure (or "test") the *statistical significance* of our results.

In looking at how to measure relationships in Chapter 9, we found that there were qualitatively different ways to go about it, depending on the level at which the variables were measured. In measuring the statistical significance of a relationship, one broad procedure holds for all levels of data, although there are differences in specific techniques.

LOGIC OF MEASURING SIGNIFICANCE

The general procedure by which we calculate the probability that a given result could have occurred by chance, even though the true state of affairs was something other than what is indicated by the result, is the same procedure that we use in calculating the odds of any event happening.

As usual when talking about probability, let us start with a deck of cards. Given an honest deck of cards, thoroughly shuffled, you are instructed to draw a card. You know that the probability that you will draw the king of hearts is 1/52, for there are 52 cards and only one of them is the king of hearts. Next, you are instructed to do this two times, replacing the card and reshuffling after the first draw. You know that the probability of drawing a king of hearts *both times* is $1/52 \times 1/52 = 1/2,704$, or .00037, and so on.[1]

You were able to calculate these probabilities because, given a sufficient set of assumptions, the probability that any particular result would occur could be determined. These assumptions had to account for all of the factors that could influence the outcome of the drawing. With such a set of assumptions, it was possible to calculate exactly how likely any particular result was. The set of assumptions in this case was as follows:

1. The deck has 52 cards, of which only one is the king of hearts.
2. The deck is thoroughly and honestly shuffled before each drawing.
3. The drawing is blind, so that each card is equally likely to be drawn (you don't peek, none of the cards stick together, and so on).

---

[1]The logic of this is as follows: In order to draw two kings of hearts in two draws, you must accomplish two things. First, you must draw the king of hearts on the first round. This can be expected to happen only one fifty-second of the time. Now, assuming that you have succeeded in the first round, you still can expect success in the second round only one fifty-second of the time. In other words, in the full two-draw process, you can expect to proceed to final success only one fifty-second of one fifty-second of the time.

If any of these assumptions were not true, your calculation of probabilities would be incorrect. For instance, if there were two kings of hearts (that is, assumption 1 above was wrong), the probability of drawing one in a single draw would have been 2/52, not 1/52. Or if the deck had been stacked so as to make drawing the king of hearts likely (that is, assumption 2 above was false), the probability of drawing one would have been greater than 1/52.

This is the way in which we normally use odds and probability. We have a set of assumptions of which we are confident. Those assumptions determine the probability that any particular event will happen. From this we know with how much confidence we can predict that the event will occur, that is, at what odds we should bet that it will occur.

Statistical inference uses this same logical structure, but turns it on its head. An example may be the best way to demonstrate this.

EXAMPLE OF STATISTICAL INFERENCE

Let us return to our previous example, taking a sample of ten senators to see whether there is a difference in how liberal the two senatorial parties are. Let us say that you have drawn such a sample and that your results are shown in Table 10–1. Of the ten senators in the sample, 75 percent of the Democrats, but only 33 percent of the Republicans, are liberal. How safe would you be to conclude from this limited sample that senatorial Democrats are on the whole more liberal?

To find out, you must proceed just as you did in our card-drawing example, by setting a list of assumptions that would be sufficient to let you calculate the probability of drawing ten senators that look like those you have, if in fact Democratic and Republican senators do *not* differ in the degree to which they are liberal. These assumptions would be:

1. The ten senators have been drawn at random.
2. There is *no relationship* between party and ideology in the "full" Senate from which these have been drawn.

Just from these two assumptions, using probability theory, it is possible for you to calculate how likely it is that you would have gotten any particular result in your sample. In this particular case, using a "chi square" test (which I introduce later in the chapter), you can calculate that the probability of having gotten at least as

TABLE 10–1   Sample Result

	Democrats	Republicans
Liberal	3	2
Conservative	1	4

great a difference as you found between the parties, given the assumptions, is .264.[2] Thus there is a good chance that you could have gotten a relationship as strong as this in a sample of ten even if the assumptions that you set up were true—that is, even if there were no difference between Democrats and Republicans.

How you would then treat your research results depends on whether you are a long-shot gambler at heart, what kind of risks ride on your decision, and so on. Approximately three times out of four you would not have gotten as strong a relationship as you did if the assumptions you wish to test were true. Will you reject that set of assumptions on the basis of your sample result, accepting the one chance in four that you are wrong in doing so? If you are willing to reject the assumptions, notice that the truth is questionable with regard to only one of the assumptions in the set; you purposely have set up the test this way. You know whether or not you have drawn the ten senators at random. Therefore, in rejecting the set of assumptions, you really are rejecting only one assumption, the assumption that there is no relationship between party and ideology in the Senate. What you are saying is: "By rejecting its opposite, I am making the statement, 'There is an ideological difference between the senatorial parties.' I know that given the amount of evidence I have gathered, I am running considerable risk in making the statement. There is a probability of .264 that I am wrong."

HYPOTHESIS TESTING

The example we have used is a typical problem in statistical inference: We have a particular result in hand, and we wish to calculate the probability that this event could have occurred given some set of assumptions. We cannot be confident of one of these assumptions, for it involves the very thing we are trying to infer. If there is a sufficiently small probability that the event we have in mind could have occurred, given the set of assumptions, we decide to treat the set of assumptions as false. (This usually is referred to as "rejecting the hypothesis" that the assumptions are true.) And since we are confident of all but one of the assumptions (the thing we want to test), rejecting the set of assumptions really means that we are rejecting that one assumption.

We run some risk of being wrong in treating the assumptions as false. After all, the result we have observed could have occurred even if the assumptions were true. The probability we have calculated tells us precisely how likely it is that we are wrong. It tells us the probability that the result we have observed could have occurred if the assumptions we are rejecting were in fact true—that is, the probability that we are making a mistake in rejecting the assumptions. We normally will reject a set of

---

[2]There is a great variety of statistical tests available to fit different circumstances of research. Statistical tests vary in the level of measurement that they require and in the particular set of assumptions that they embody. The chi-square test used here is particularly designed for testing the significance of a relationship between two nominal-scale variables. See the discussion on pages 152–157.

assumptions only when the probability that they could have produced the result we have observed is comfortably low.[3]

You can see now why I said that statistical inference uses the same logic as setting odds, but turns it on its head. Normally, in setting odds, we select a set of assumptions from which we can confidently predict how likely it is that certain things will happen in the future. In statistical inference, we calculate how likely it is that an *observed* result could have occurred if some hypothetical and contrary assumption were true. If the probability is sufficiently low, we use the result to reject the assumption. Just as in everyday setting of odds, the probability shows us how likely it is that we are making a mistake.

Null Hypothesis

It is clear from our description of statistical inference that we do not test directly the statement we wish to make about a relationship. Instead, we insert its opposite—which is called the *null hypothesis*, the hypothesis we should like to reject—into the set of assumptions from which we calculate the probability. Because it is the only questionable member of the set of assumptions, if we decide to reject the set, we really are rejecting only the null hypothesis. By rejecting the null hypothesis we in effect assert its opposite, which is the statement we wished to make in the first place.

The twisted and convoluted way one must think to understand this process is discouraging to most people when they see it for the first time. "Why," they ask, "can't we just test our hypothesis directly instead of having to turn it inside out?"

But think about how you might go about doing this. First of all, you could never test the hypothesis that your sample result was exactly the same as the true value in the population from which you had drawn the sample. Taken to a sufficient number of decimal places, it would virtually always *not* be the same as the true population value. For instance, 47.871698 percent of voters in the United States voted for George W. Bush in 2000; no sample would have produced exactly this figure. But because your sample was not that precise a reflection of reality, you would not want automatically to reject it. Accordingly, you would pick some range of values around the true value and test whether or not the sample result was in that range. However, because you do not know what the true value is, this is a test that is impossible to set up.

In using the null hypothesis, on the other hand, a single alternative is chosen, which negates *all* possible true values that would be consistent with the statement you wish to make. For instance, in the Senate example, if you wanted to assert that your sample result was sufficiently close to the true relationship for you to accept the sample result as valid, you would have to choose among an infinite variety of

---

[3]Whether the probability is "comfortably low," of course, is a difficult thing to judge. In setting odds, one usually has objective outside criteria to "help" in making the decision—an amount of money to be lost if the person is wrong, for instance. In much *engineering* research, there also will be such criteria available. In *theory-oriented* research, however, there usually are no fixed criteria, because the result is supposed to hold not just for some particular occasion, but in general. It is supposed to apply to occasions as yet unforeseen. Therefore, because objective criteria are lacking, a convention usually is followed of rejecting a set of assumptions only if the probability is less than 0.05.

possible true relationships (80 percent of Democrats liberal, 75 percent of Republicans liberal; 100 percent of Democrats liberal, 51 percent of Republicans liberal; 100 percent of Democrats liberal, 1 percent of Republicans liberal; and so on). By using a null hypothesis ("there is no difference between the parties"), you can deal with a single statement that negates all possible versions of the statement you want to make. It is simply easier to disprove a specific hypothesis than to prove an open-ended hypothesis.

Example: χ^2

One popular significance test is χ^2 (*chi-square*), which we used in our liberal–conservative example. It is designed for use with a table relating two nominal-scale variables. Given the strength of the relationship between the variables in the table, χ^2 allows us to estimate the probability that there is no relationship between the variables in the full population from which the sample has been drawn.

In Table 10–2, a hypothetical relationship between ethnicity and policy priorities has been drawn, based on a sample of 200 respondents to a survey. We want to know whether it is safe to assert, on the evidence of this sample, that there is a relationship between the two variables.

To calculate χ^2, this table must be compared with a construct designed to show a *lack* of relationship between the variables. Such a construct is shown in Table 10–3. The entries in Table 10–3 are arrived at by calculating how many WASPs, say, would give first priority to employment and welfare if exactly the same proportion of WASPs as of African-Americans and "other ethnics" favored the employment/welfare priority. Thus, because there are 70 WASPs in the sample, and 110/200 of the sample favor the employment/welfare priority, we would expect to find that the sample contained 110/200 × 70 = 38.5 WASPs who chose employment/welfare. Similarly, we would expect to find that 110/200 of the 40 African-Americans, or 22.0, chose employment/welfare; and so on, cell by cell, until the hypothetical table was filled. Notice that to construct a table in which the variables are completely unrelated, it was necessary to maintain the fiction that there could have been one-half of a WASP in favor of the employment/welfare priority.

TABLE 10–2   Ethnicity and Preferred Government Action Priorities

Preferred Priority	Ethnicity			
	WASP	*African-American*	*Other*	*Total*
Employment and welfare	30	27	53	110
Foreign affairs	11	5	14	30
Environment	29	8	23	60
Total	70	40	90	200

TABLE 10–3   Table of Nonrelationship

Preferred Priority	Ethnicity			
	WASP	*African-American*	*Other*	*Total*
Employment and welfare	38.5	22.0	49.5	110
Foreign affairs	10.5	6.0	13.5	30
Environment	21.0	12.0	27.0	60
Total	70	40	90	200

Table 10–3 embodies the null hypothesis that we want to test—that there is no relationship between the variables. Each cell in the table has the characteristic (1) that its entry is the same proportion of its row frequency as its column frequency is of the total sample, and (2) that its entry is the same proportion of its column frequency as its row frequency is of the total sample. That is, the members of each row are equally likely to fall into any given column, and vice versa. This is what we should expect if the two variables were unrelated.

The question we want to ask is: Are the two tables sufficiently different that we can say, on the basis of what we found when we looked at the sample, that the full population does not look like the distribution in the hypothetical table? Chi-square is a measure of how different the two tables are. It is calculated from the formula

$$\chi^2 = \Sigma \frac{(F_o - F_h)^2}{F_h}$$

where for each cell in the table, F_o is the observed frequency and F_h is the frequency predicted for the hypothetical table. Thus for each cell in the table, (1) the prediction from the hypothetical table is subtracted from the actual figure, (2) this figure is squared, and (3) the squared difference is then divided by the prediction from the hypothetical table. The results of this, from all the cells of the table, are added together (you will recall that this is what the sign "Σ" means) to give us the χ^2. The more the tables differ, the greater χ^2 will be. If the tables are exactly the same, χ^2 will equal zero, inasmuch as each cell's result will be

$$\frac{(F_o - F_h)^2}{F_h} = \frac{0^2}{F_h} = 0$$

In Table 10–4, χ^2 is calculated for the present example. Cell a is the upper-left cell of Table 10–2 or 10–3 (the cell in which WASPs choosing employment/welfare fall), cell b is the next cell to the right, cell c is the upper-right cell, cell d is the middle left cell, cell e falls at the exact center of the table, and so on.

TABLE 10–4   Calculations for χ^2

Cell	F_h	$(F_o - F_h)$	$(F_o - F_h)^2$	$(F_o - F_h)^2/F_h$
a	38.5	−8.5	72.25	1.877
b	22.0	+5.0	25.00	1.136
c	49.5	+3.5	12.25	0.247
d	10.5	+0.5	0.25	0.024
e	6.0	−1.0	1.00	0.167
f	13.5	+0.5	0.25	0.019
g	21.0	+8.0	64.00	3.048
h	12.0	−4.0	16.00	1.333
i	27.0	−4.0	16.00	0.593
			$\chi^2 = $ total $= $	8.444

Sampling Distribution

Before I can show how we go from measuring the difference between the observed and null hypothesis tables to calculating the probability that the null hypothesis is true, I must first introduce the idea of a *sampling distribution*.

For any particular set of assumptions, a sampling distribution shows what proportion of the time each particular result could be expected to occur if the sampling technique chosen were repeated a very large number of times and the set of assumptions (including the null hypothesis) were true. That is, it gives the *probability* of getting a particular result if you applied the techniques you are using to a population for which the null hypothesis is true.

A sampling distribution embodies all the assumptions you make in a test, including the null hypothesis. It represents the application of probability theory to those assumptions, to calculate the probability that each possible result would occur. Some simple sampling distributions can be calculated easily. For instance, in the card-drawing example on page 148, the sampling distribution states that the probability of drawing the ace of hearts is 1/52, the probability of drawing the king of hearts is 1/52, and so on, through all the cards of the deck. Of course, this sampling distribution depends on the set of assumptions you made in that example. The sampling distribution for a different set of assumptions would look different.

In another simple case, suppose that you had to predict the probability of getting just one head in two flips of a coin. Assume that (1) the coin is honest, (2) the flipper is honest, and (3) the coin will not stand on its edge. You can now calculate that the probability of getting a head followed by a tail is 0.25, the probability of getting a head followed by a head is 0.25, the probability of getting a tail followed by a head is 0.25, and the probability of getting a tail followed by a tail is 0.25. Because two of the possibilities involve getting just one head in the two throws, the probability of getting just one head in either of the two ways is 0.50, the probability of getting no heads is 0.25, and the probability of getting two heads is 0.25. This sampling distribution is presented graphically in Figure 10–1.

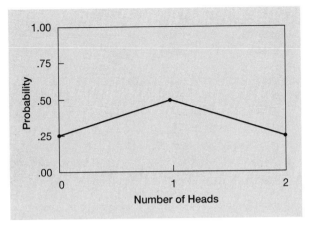

Figure 10–1   Sampling Distribution for Two Flips of a Coin

The same sampling distribution could be presented in a cumulative graph, showing the probability of getting *at least* no heads, at least one head, or at least two heads. Figure 10–2 charts the sampling distribution in this way. We always will get at least zero heads (we cannot get a negative number), so the probability of that outcome is 1.0; we could get at least one head either by getting no heads (probability of .25) or by getting one head (probability of .50), so the probability of at least one head is .75; we could only get at least two heads by getting exactly two heads, so the probability of at least two heads is .25.

These sampling distributions are simple. The sampling distributions for most statistical tests are more complex, and we must use tables developed by statisticians to visualize them. The cumulative sampling distribution of χ^2 for a three-by-three

Figure 10–2   Cumulative Sampling Distribution for Two Flips of a Coin

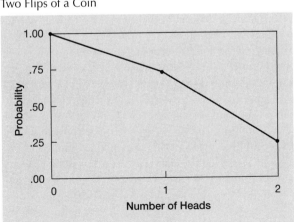

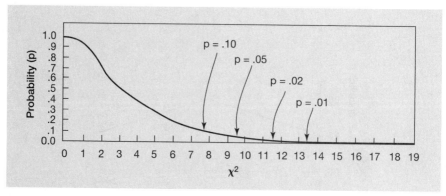

Figure 10–3   Sampling Distribution of χ^2, for Three-by-Three Tables

table (a table with three categories in the rows and three categories in the columns, such as Tables 10–2 and 10–3) is presented in Figure 10–3.

Chi-square sampling distributions vary depending on the number of categories in the rows and columns of the table used. The probabilities given are the probability that a χ^2 *at least as* high as the one observed would have been obtained if the sample were drawn by random selection from a parent population in which the variables were unrelated. (Note that this is a cumulative sampling distribution, like the one depicted in Figure 10–2.) Thus, if you had found a χ^2 of 4.9, you would know that the probability of getting χ^2 as high as this was 0.3 if the variables you were working with were, in fact, not related. (The sampling distribution is based on assumptions of [1] the null hypothesis you wish to test, and [2] random selection, which you know you have done.)

From this sampling distribution we see that there is a probability of between 0.05 and 0.10 that we would have found a χ^2 as high as 8.44 from a three-by-three table if there were really no relationship between ethnicity and choice of priority (that is, if the null hypothesis were true). This means that we would run a risk of between 1 chance in 10 and 1 chance in 20 of being wrong in asserting on the basis of Table 10–2 that the null hypothesis is false—that there *is* a relationship between ethnicity and the choice of priorities.

To summarize these sections: A sampling distribution is a list of the probabilities that each possible event (out of a set of events) will happen. The probabilities in a sampling distribution are based on a set of assumptions. If we choose our significance test appropriately, the set of assumptions on which its sampling distribution is based will consist of (1) a null hypothesis (the assumption that what we really want to say about the data is false), and (2) a group of other assumptions that we feel certain are true. If we find from the sampling distribution that it is very unlikely, given those assumptions, that the event we have observed (in our ethnicity/choice of priorities example above, finding a χ^2 of 8.44) could have occurred, we reject the assumptions on which the sampling distribution is based. Because we are sure that all but one of those assumptions (the null hypothesis) are true, this amounts to rejecting the null hypothesis and asserting its opposite, which is what we had originally wanted to say about the data. The probability that we could have gotten the observed result if all the assumptions underlying the sampling distribution were true tells us how likely it is that we are wrong to reject the null hypothesis. Thus a significance test furnishes a useful check on our research. It tells us how likely it is that we could have gotten our results by chance alone—the probability that in fact the opposite of what we are asserting is true.

Importance of *N*

N, the number of cases in a sample, is always a factor in significance tests. All other things being equal, the greater the number of cases on which a statement is based, the more certain you can be that the statement is true.[4] Every significance test, accordingly, takes the number of cases into account. If each number in Tables 10–2 and 10–3 were doubled, for example, the quantity $(F_o - F_h)^2/F_h$ would double for each cell. The χ^2 would thus be double 8.444, or 16.888. From Figure 10–3 we see that if the null hypothesis of no relationship were true, the probability of getting a χ^2 at least this high would be less than 0.01. Thus from a table showing exactly the same pattern as Table 10–2 but based on a sample of 400 cases instead of the 200 used in that table, we would run a risk of less than 1 chance in 100 of being wrong in asserting that there is a relationship between the variables.[5]

N is the most obvious factor affecting the statistical significance of findings. In many sorts of statistical tests, it is the only factor we need to worry about. But there may be others. For example, in regression analysis the amount of confidence we can have in our estimate of what the relationship looks like is a matter not only of how many cases we have used but also of how much the independent variable varies. In the extreme case of zero variance in the independent variable, depicted in the scattergram in Figure 10–4, we are simply unable to choose any regression line. Because all the data points fall above a single value of the independent variable, an infinite number of lines (a few of which are indicated on the graph) can be passed through the data, each of which has an equal sum of squared deviations about itself. In other words, it is impossible to choose a single "best" line by least-squares criteria.

This is the extreme case. In general, the greater the variation in the independent variable, the more firmly fixed the estimate of the regression line can be and, accordingly, the more stock we can put in our findings. One way to look at this is to think of the regression line as wobbling on a fulcrum. As it happens, every regression line must pass through point $\bar{x}, \bar{y}$ in the scattergram; this is determined mathematically by the formulas for *a* and *b*. (In other words, the expected value of *y* when *x* equals its own mean *must* be the mean of *y*.) If there is relatively little variation in the independent

---

[4]See the box "Law of Large Numbers" on page 61.

[5]The following five paragraphs present advanced material that can be skipped over without any loss in comprehension of other material covered in this book.

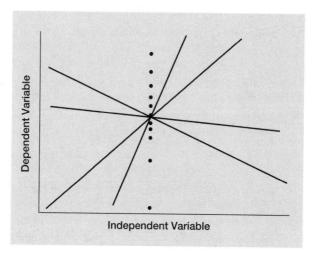

Figure 10–4   Regression Analysis with Zero Variance in the Independent Variable

variable, as in Figure 10–5, the line is free to wobble a good deal, using this point as a fulcrum. A considerable change in the angle at which the line passes through the point $\bar{x}, \bar{y}$ will not change the size of the squared deviations from the line by very much. This is due to the fact that for observations whose value on x is close to $\bar{x}$, wobble in the line does not change the expected value of y very greatly; thus the difference between the observed and expected values of y also is not greatly changed.

No one of the observations is able significantly to affect the regression line in Figure 10–5. The line is simply not held firmly in place by these observations, whose

Figure 10–5   Regression Analysis with Little Variance in the Independent Variable

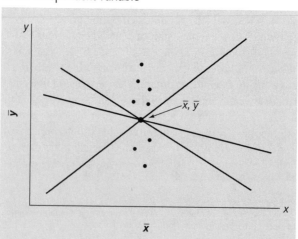

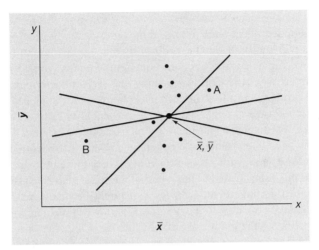

Figure 10–6   The Stabilizing Effect of Variance in the Independent Variable

values on *x* fall so close together. Observations with widely varying values on *x*, however, would hold a much firmer grip on the regression line. Two such observations have been added in Figure 10–6.

If the regression line were now to wobble through the same angles as in Figure 10–5, the size of the deviations of observations A and B (in Figure 10–6) from the line would increase dramatically. Remember, the regression line must be the line that minimizes the sum of squared deviations about itself. The regression line in Figure 10–6 cannot stray very far from points A and B without sharply increasing that sum.

Thus a few points whose *x* values are extreme have more impact in determining the slope of the line than do a larger number of points whose *x* values fall close to the mean. Accordingly, in calculating how likely it is that our estimate of a regression has been due to chance, we must take into account not only how many observations have been used in the analysis, but also how widely they are spread on the independent variable. Significance tests designed for use with regression analysis take into account *both* the number of cases and the amount of variation in the independent variable.[6]

Problem of Independent Observations

It often happens that a researcher draws a conclusion based on a set of observations that appear to be independent but are really not. Because there are in effect fewer observations in the study than the scholar believes, he or she may overestimate the strength of the evidence. The relationship in question might be due to chance, without the researcher realizing it. The difficulty here is that statistical tests will not be able to

---

[6]The general extension of this problem to multivariate regression is the problem of multicollinearity. For a good expository discussion of multicollinearity, see King, Keohane and Verba (1994, ch. 4, part 1).

alert us to the danger, because statistical tests already assume that the data to be analyzed consist of independent observations. If the observations are not independent, all statistical tests will underestimate the probability that a relationship might be due to chance. Thus we might be inappropriately confident of our assertions.

An example may help. Consider a study that seeks to determine the extent to which "police brutality" is a function of the explicitness of guidelines issued to police patrols, with close and explicit directions presumed to be associated with low "brutality." The investigator might measure the explicitness of guidelines to patrols in the 11 towns and 63 townships of a county and relate this measure by regression analysis to the roughness with which police in each of those units handle suspects. Statistical tests might be applied to the regression results, with N stated as 74.

Unknown to the investigator, however, it might be that some of these units shared a coordinated police force. For example, all township police forces might be under the direction of the county sheriff. In this case, although the 63 townships looked like separate units, they would all be separate parts of a single police administration, with one set of guidelines and one set of expectations with regard to roughness. Thus there would in fact be only 12 independent observations (each of the 11 town forces, plus the sheriff's office), which should raise a specter of doubt about the correctness of an assertion based on these data.

The problem of nonindependent observations does not often occur in a simple form such as this, and if it does arise, it can generally be avoided by simple common sense. However, the problem occurs frequently in a more subtle (and more technical) way under the guise of *autocorrelation.* Autocorrelation occurs when observations are related to some extent but are not (as in the study of police brutality) identical to each other. For example, if we look at the relationship between trends in the economy and trends in the U.S. president's popularity, month by month, we will probably have a problem of autocorrelation. February 1943 had much in common with May 1943, for instance. Though one would not go so far as to say that gathering information from these two months is simply equivalent to having information about a single month (as we could say about any two townships in the other example), neither can we say that we have as much information here as we would have with two widely separated months.

I mention the problem at this point only to alert you to it. Partial solutions are available, but they are beyond the scope of this book. Most texts in statistics or econometrics, such as the one by Knoke, Bohrnstedt, and Mee (2002) or Kmenta (1997), discuss the problem.

SIGNIFICANCE TEST: ALWAYS NECESSARY?

Even when we do not work with a limited sample drawn from a larger group of subjects, there is a sense in which all research involves "sampling" of a sort and in which misleading results can occur by chance. For instance, we might look at all 50 states and find that the generosity of their welfare budgets is related to the degree of party competition in the states' elections. In one sense, there is no question but that this is the "true" result. Because we have included all the states in our sample, anything we find out about them is by definition "true generally." But suppose we think of ourselves as trying to say something not just about the 50 states as they exist at this one point in time, but about "state politics." Then we must regard these 50 states as a sample drawn for us by chance and accident from a larger metaphysical population of "states"—all states as they might be in the future or as they might have been had their boundaries been drawn differently or had history proceeded differently.

The latter view seems to reflect more accurately what we try to do in developing political theories out of empirical research. There are times when we wish to describe a specific population as it exists at one point in time; this is particularly likely in what I have termed "engineering" research. In such research we frequently are interested in measuring some condition of a population so as to react to it or make adjustments in it, rather than to develop explanatory theories from it. For instance, a tax administrator may want to know how many states administer sales taxes, how great a portion of national income these states involve, and so on. What the administrator is concerned with is a description of the tax situation as it currently exists, not, by and large, with developing theories to *explain* why things are as they are.[7] In most theory-oriented research, however, we should seek a more inclusive sort of generality.

Sometimes an author claims that she need not be concerned about the possibility of chance results because her sample is synonymous with the total population of subjects (all the states, all the nations in the United Nations, all the U.S. senators, or what have you). This is a statement that should arouse suspicion. If the author is trying to draw general conclusions from the study, propositions that one would expect to be as true of states or nations or senators a decade from now as they are today, she *must* be concerned with the problem of chance results. With infrequent exceptions, then, this is a problem all of us must take seriously in our research.

POLLING AND SIGNIFICANCE TESTS

A ubiquitous activity in our society is *polling*, asking a sample of the population whom they will vote for, whether they support regulation of handguns, or whatever.[8] Typically, about 2,000 respondents are polled to describe a population such as that of the United States, and the results are reported as "accurate to within plus or minus 3 percent"—or 2 percent, or some other level of accuracy.

This operation is a variant of statistical significance testing. Based on a given number of cases, which of course can be set as desired by the person doing the polling,

---

[7]Note, by the way, that to the extent that an engineer sees her task as *changing* and *reforming* patterns rather than continuing ongoing administrative procedures, explanatory theory will be relatively more important. A tax administrator who wanted to change the extent to which states relied on sales taxes to generate income would first have to try to find out why states use sales taxes. Status quo administrators, on the other hand, can be more content with purely descriptive information, because their chief concern is with plugging established procedures into any given state of affairs, and what they need is simply to know what the "state of affairs" is.

[8]See the discussion of sampling on pp. 99–102.

and with knowledge of how the individuals have been chosen for the sample (usually some variant of random sampling), the pollster can conclude that according to the sampling distribution of percent approval that one would get using repeated samples of this sort and of this size, sample results would fall within plus or minus X percent of the true population value 95 percent of the time. Thus the pollster claims that the result is accurate to "within plus or minus X percent." Note that this does not mean that the result absolutely falls within plus or minus X percent of the true value; it means that 95 percent of the time it would fall within that range of the true value.

Note here, also, that changing N changes the width of the "plus or minus" range. If an N of about 2,000 respondents gave you plus or minus 3 percent, increasing N to 4,000 would give you a lower range, perhaps plus or minus 1 percent.

USES AND LIMITATIONS OF STATISTICAL TESTS

I have tried in this chapter to present a significance test for what it is—a useful check on research results. The real meat of research, however—the way we find out about politics—is by looking at data and seeking out relationships between variables, the sorts of things I discussed in Chapters 2 through 9.

Unfortunately, researchers often place undue emphasis on significance tests. It is a pity that looking at data requires less formal training (but more practice) than does calculating significance tests. Perhaps because they have spent so much time in courses learning to use significance tests, many researchers give the tests an undue emphasis in their research. The status of these tests should be strictly that of a secondary check on the *creative* work the researcher has done in looking at relationships.

A recent article illustrates the problem. In this study the authors reported that two variables were more strongly related among the working-class portion of their sample than among the middle-class portion. Their evidence for this was that among the working-class respondents, the relationship was more highly significant, with a probability of less than 0.01 that there was no relationship. Among the middle-class respondents, by contrast, the relationship was less highly significant, with probability between 0.01 and 0.05. Because previous theorists had said that one should expect a stronger relationship between these variables among the middle class than among the working class, these authors were understandably excited about their findings.

Unfortunately, they were using significance tests for something the tests were not meant to do. The significance test is not itself a measure of the strength of a relationship but rather, a check on how likely it is that a given measure is due to chance. In this example, as it happened, the middle-class portion of the authors' sample was only about half as large as the working-class portion. It was because of the smaller number of cases in the middle-class portion that its relationship showed up as less significant than the same relationship for the working-class portion. In fact, when the strength of the relationship was measured by an appropriate technique (the Goodman–Kruskal gamma, for instance), it turned out that there was a *stronger* relationship among the middle class. The authors' conclusion from their own data was wrong.

CONCLUSION

I have tried in this chapter to give you some idea of the general logic of inference, which is the common thread running through all statistical tests. These tests vary among themselves, however, in terms of their suitability for a given level of measurement and the particular mix of assumptions (other than the null hypothesis) they require the investigator to guarantee. This is why there are so many different tests. For a description of particular tests, the reader should consult a statistics text such as the one cited at the end of Chapter 8.

FURTHER DISCUSSION

A particularly good discussion of the misapplication of significance tests, along the lines of the example I used, is Duggan and Dean, "Common Misinterpretations of Significance Levels in Sociological Journals" (1968). See also Winch and Campbell, "Proof? No. Evidence? Yes. The Significance of Tests of Significance" (1969).

Anyone thinking of using these tests should first take a course in statistics; barring that, however, useful presentations of the techniques are given in the text cited at the end of Chapter 8. The second chapter of Siegel (1956) is a particularly useful review of the overall logic of significance tests. It aims at much the same presentation as I have attempted in this chapter, but in rather more technical detail. Another very good treatment is that of Simon (1985).

For further consideration, think about the two following situations. *What is wrong in each situation?*

1. A researcher studying Congress examines the vote on 100 or so bills. For two of these votes, she finds a statistically significant relationship (at the .05 level) between a representative's height and the way he voted on the bill. This strikes her as a surprising finding, and she uses it as the basis for a chapter and a half of her book.
2. A large number of scholars study committee systems to see whether democracy in committee decision making leads the members to be satisfied with their work on the committee. All but one of these scholars fail to find a statistically significant relationship between these two variables. Most of those who fail to find a relationship leave that question and start to work on other things. A few of them write up their results, but these are rejected by journal editors because they are negative, not positive, findings. The one scholar who did find a statistically significant result publishes it. Net result: one published article, reporting a statistically significant relationship between committee democracy and members' satisfaction.

Chapter 11

Where Do Theories Come From?

This has been a book about developing theories and trying them out on reality. In Chapter 2, I equated the research process with a search for elegant theories. In succeeding chapters, I have discussed various aspects of research: concept formation, measurement, data analysis. My criterion for the usefulness of any of these techniques has been the extent to which that technique aided in the creation of elegant theories. A high degree of "precision in measurement" is important, I have argued, because it allows us more flexibility in stating the *theory* we choose to work with. Measurement accuracy, whether it is a matter of reliability or validity, is important because without accurate measurement we cannot establish the connection between the data we are handling and the *theory* with which we are working. Regression analysis usually is more useful than correlation analysis, because the results of regression analysis applies generally to a *theory*, whereas the results of correlation analysis can serve only as a description of a particular situation; and so on.

In all of this, I have never dealt with the critical question: Just how does one find a theory on which to work? There is one deceptively simple answer to this question, which is to choose theories for study from the already existing body of work in political science. That is, take an existing theory and try it out on some data. I discussed some of the limitations of this procedure in Chapter 2, but the important point for my discussion here is that this answer begs the question of how the original theorist found the theory.

What makes a political scientist describe the relationship among a group of variables in a particular way? Probably it most frequently happens that the researcher observes a body of data and tries to see a pattern among them. This is the most obvious way to go about devising a theory; it follows quite naturally from the things a theory is supposed to achieve. The purpose of a theory is to provide a simplified pattern to describe a complicated jumble of observations. Would it not follow, then, that the most appropriate way to devise a theory is simply to look at the jumble of observations and pick out the most prominent pattern running through them?

Unfortunately, "observations" in political science are riddled with problems of accurate measurement; they are often measured imprecisely, and the nonexperimental circumstances under which we gather them make it difficult to isolate the effects of single variables. These are all problems I discussed earlier in the book. Their combined effect is to make it very difficult to look at a batch of observations and pick out the best simplifying pattern. There is so much going on in a group of observations, much of which is extraneous to what we want to do, that the pattern we ideally would hope to pick out is obscured.

This problem is not confined to the social sciences. An amusing example of the difficulty of choosing among potential explanations without the benefit of prior theory is offered by a discussion among Samuel Johnson, James Boswell, and some of their friends in 1769 about the mystery of why the residents of the Scottish island of St. Kilda caught cold whenever a ship arrived there.[1] There was at that time already speculation that illnesses were transmitted from one person to another, but Johnson regarded this as a "prejudice," and not "smart modern thought." Eventually the explanation favored by Boswell was offered in a letter from a Lady of Norfolk:

> Now for the explication of this seeming mystery, which is so very obvious as, for that reason, to have escaped the penetration of Dr. Johnson and his friend, as well as that of the author. Reading the book with my ingenious friend, the late Reverend Mr. Christian, of Docking—after ruminating a little, "The cause, (says he,) is a natural one. The situation of St. Kilda renders a North-East Wind indispensably necessary before a stranger can land. The wind, not the stranger, occasions an epidemic cold."[2]

In a similar vein, James S. Coleman described the way the theory of gravity might *not* have been devised had Galileo gone about his task in the way most data-analyzing social scientists do:

> A simple example will illustrate some of the difficulties which might arise by this kind of "brick-by-brick" approach to theory. Suppose that early mechanics had developed by the use of regression equations. Suppose, specifically, that an investigation had been carried out relating the length of time a body had fallen through the air and the velocity it attained. The relation in mechanics is that the velocity attained is equal to the acceleration due to gravity times the time the object has fallen, or
>
> $$v = gt$$
>
> where g is the acceleration due to gravity. Now if there had been numerous investigations involving different-sized bodies, different velocities, and bodies with differing densities, the investigators would have ended with numerous pairs of observations (v_i, t_i, which they would locate on a scatter diagram in order to find the line of best fit. But in every case, and especially for high velocities (i.e., objects which fell a great distance)

[1] G. Birkbeck Hill. *Boswell's Life of Johnson*, vol. 2 (London, 1887: Clarendon Press), pp. 51–52.
[2] Ibid., p.52.

and low-density objects (i.e., feathers), the observed velocity would fall considerably below that which the theoretical equation predicts. The resulting regression equation might have ended up including other variables, such as mass or density of the object; and there would have been indications that at high velocities the relation of velocity to time was not even linear. The reason, of course, would be air resistance, which has different effects as a function of the density of the object, its shape, its velocity, and other things. The regression equation would of course have been empirically correct, but it wouldn't have corresponded to the simple velocity-time relation which served as the basis for Galileo's remarkable contribution to the science of mechanics. They might even have served to confound the issue, by bringing in too soon a factor—i.e., air resistance—which was irrelevant to the fundamentals of mechanics.[3]

The moral of these stories is that we almost always are better off if we have some idea of what kind of pattern we want to look for before we start to look at data. If we have in mind a particular kind of pattern, it is easy to tell, among the jumble of things we find, what is relevant to that pattern and what is extraneous. Galileo was able to ignore the effects of air resistance because he knew that they were not the thing he should use to explain the speed of falling objects.

The distinction here is between "inductive" and "deductive" theory building. To build theory inductively, the researcher scans the observations looking for patterns. To build theory deductively, the researcher deduces (from something else, some prior expectations) what sort of a pattern to expect and then looks for it among the observations.

According to the argument I have presented so far in this chapter, deductive theory building is clearly the better of the two. The problem lies with that "something else" from which the student is supposed to deduce theories. There simply are not many well-established *premises* in the social sciences from which to deduce anything. One way of distinguishing an ongoing "science" from a "pre-science" is that the former includes a generally agreed-upon body of assumptions from which most of its theories can be deduced (Kuhn, 1962). Political science, sociology, and similar social sciences cannot be said to possess such a body of assumptions.

Lacking this base for deduction, it is hard to argue patly that theory building must be done deductively. On the other hand, it is important to bear in mind the advantages of deduction, where it is feasible. There are some tricks that may heighten your awareness of situations in which deduction is feasible. One of the best sources of deductive theory is a well-established theory from another field. Theories of epidemic growth and population dynamics, from such fields as epidemiology and ecology, may suggest theories to political scientists or sociologists. So may microeconomic theory; as noted in Chapter 1, rational choice theory drawn from microeconomic theory has been particularly fruitful for political science. A healthy awareness of major theories in fields such as these, some of which are not all that closely related to our field, can be a helpful source of theory.

---

[3]James S. Coleman, *Introduction to Mathematical Sociology* (New York: The Free Press 1964), pp. 100–101. Copyright 1964 by the Free Press.

The art of building a theory remains in flux in political science—partly deductive, but largely inductive. The resulting confusion can be both enjoyable and fruitful, because more than in most disciplines, it allows a place for every sort of imagination to work: literary imagination, scientific imagination, moral imagination, mathematical imagination. It is in this spirit that I have tried to stress the "craft" in the "craft of political research."

Selected Bibliography

ACHEN, CHRISTOPHER H. 1975. "Attitudes and the Survey Response," *American Political Science Review*, 69 (December), 1218–1231.

———. 1986. *The Statistical Analysis of Quasi-experiments*. Berkeley, Calif.: University of California Press.

———, and W. PHILLIPS SHIVELY. 1995. *Cross-Level Inference*. Chicago: University of Chicago Press.

ANSOLABEHERE, STEPHEN, ALAN GERBER, and JAMES M. SNYDER, JR. 2000. "Equal Votes, Equal Money: Court-Ordered Redistricting and the Distribution of Public Expenditures in the American States." Paper presented at the Midwest Political Science Association Meetings, Chicago, April 26–30, 2000.

ASHER, HERBERT B. 1974. "Some Consequences of Measurement Error in Survey Data," *American Journal of Political Science*, 18 (May), 469–485.

BACHRACH, PETER, and MORTON BARATZ. 1962. "The Two Faces of Power," *American Political Science Review*, 56 (December), 947–953.

BARBER, JAMES D. 1972. *The Presidential Character: Predicting Performance in the White House*. Upper Saddle River, N.J.: Prentice Hall.

BARTELS, LARRY M. 1993. "Messages Received: The Political Impact of Media Exposure," *American Political Science Review*, 87 (June), 267–285.

BARTON, ALLAN H. 1955. "The Concept of Property-Space in Social Research." In Paul F. Lazarsfeld and Morris Rosenberg, eds., *The Language of Social Research*, pp. 40–53. New York: Free Press.

BATALLA, JAVIER ORTIZ. 1993. "Essays on the Early History of Latin American Central Banking," Ph.D. dissertation in economics, University of California–Los Angeles.

BERNSTEIN, RICHARD J. 1978. *Restructuring of Social and Political Theory*. Philadelphia: University of Pennsylvania Press.

BLALOCK, HUBERT M. 1964. *Causal Inferences in Nonexperimental Research*. Chapel Hill, N.C.: University of North Carolina Press.

———. 1969. *Theory Construction: From Verbal to Mathematical Formulations*. Upper Saddle River, N.J.: Prentice Hall.

———. 1979. *Social Statistics*, rev. 2nd ed. New York: McGraw-Hill.

BRUNNER, RONALD D. 1977. "An 'Intentional' Alternative in Public Opinion Research," *American Journal of Political Science*, 21 (August), 435–464.

BUENO DE MESQUITA, BRUCE, JAMES D. MORROW, RANDOLPH M. SIVERSON, and ALASTAIR SMITH. 1999. "An Institutional Explanation of the Democratic Peace," *American Political Science Review*, 93 (December), 791–808.

BUTLER, DAVID, and DONALD STOKES. 1969. *Political Change in Britain*. New York: St. Martin's.

168

CAMPBELL, ANGUS, and others. 1960. *The American Voter*. New York: John Wiley & Sons.

CAMPBELL, DONALD T., and JULIAN C. STANLEY. 1963. *Experimental and Quasi-experimental Designs for Research*. Chicago: Rand McNally.

CARTER, LEWIS F. 1971. "Inadvertent Sociological Theory," *Social Forces*, 50, 12–25.

COLEMAN, JAMES S. 1964. *Introduction to Mathematical Sociology*. New York: Free Press.

CONVERSE, PHILIP E. 1964. "The Nature of Belief Systems in Mass Publics." In David Apter, ed., *Ideology and Discontent*, pp. 206–261. New York: Free Press.

———. 1969. "Of Time and Partisan Stability," *Comparative Political Studies*, 2, 139–171.

———, and GEORGES DUPEUX. 1962. "Politicization of the Electorate in France and the United States," *Public Opinion Quarterly*, 26 (Spring), 1–23.

———, and ROY PIERCE. 1985. "Measuring Partisanship," *Political Methodology*, 11, 143–166.

COOK, THOMAS D., and DONALD T. CAMPBELL. 1979. *Quasi-experimentation: Design and Analysis Issues for Field Setting*. Chicago: Rand McNally.

DAHL, ROBERT. 1961. *Who Governs?* New Haven, Conn.: Yale University Press.

———. 1966. *Political Oppositions in Western Democracies*. New Haven, Conn.: Yale University Press.

———. 1984. *Modern Political Analysis*, 4th ed. Upper Saddle River, N.J.: Prentice Hall.

DIEHL, PAUL F., and JEAN KINGSTON. 1987. "Messenger or Message? Military Buildups and the Initiation of Conflict," *Journal of Politics*, 49 (August), 801–813.

DIGESER, PETER. 1992. "The Fourth Face of Power," *Journal of Politics*, 54 (November), 977–1007.

DOWNS, ANTHONY. 1957. *An Economic Theory of Democracy*. New York: Harper & Row.

DRAPER, N. R., and H. SMITH. 1981. *Applied Regression Analysis*, 2nd ed. New York: John Wiley & Sons.

DUGGAN, THOMAS J., and CHARLES W. DEAN. 1968. "Common Misinterpretations of Significance Levels in Sociological Journals," *American Sociologist*, 3 (February), 45–46.

DUVERGER, MAURICE. 1963. *Political Parties*. New York: Science Editions.

ECKSTEIN, HARRY. 1960. *Pressure Group Politics*. London: George Allen & Unwin.

———. 1966. *Division and Cohesion in Democracy*. Princeton, N.J.: Princeton University Press.

EDWARDS, ALLEN L. 1973. *Statistical Methods*, 3rd ed. New York: Holt, Rinehart & Winston.

FELDMAN, STANLEY. 1983. "The Measurement and Meaning of Trust in Government," *Political Methodology*, 9, 341–354.

FRY, BRIAN R., and RICHARD F. WINTERS. 1970. "The Politics of Redistribution," *American Political Science Review*, 54 (June), 508–523.

GEDDES, BARBARA. 2003. *Paradigms and Sand Castles: Theory Building and Research Design in Comparative Politics*. Ann Arbor: University of Michigan Press.

GERBER, ALAN S., and DONALD P. GREEN. 2000. "The Effects of Personal Canvassing, Telephone Calls, and Direct Mail on Voter Turnout: A Field Experiment," *American Political Science Review*, 94 (September), 653–664.

GILBERT, JOHN P., RICHARD J. LIGHT, and FREDERICK MOSTELLER. 1975. "Assessing Social Innovations: An Empirical Basis for Policy." In Carl A. Bennett and Arthur A. Lumsdaine, eds., *Evaluation and Experiment*, pp. 39–193. New York: Academic Press.

GOLDSMITH, ARTHUR A. 1987. "Does Political Stability Hinder Economic Development?" *Comparative Politics*, 19, 471–480.

GOODMAN, LEO A., and WILLIAM H. KRUSKAL. 1954. "Measures of Association for Cross Classifications," *Journal of the American Statistical Association*, 49 (December), 747–754.

GREEN, DONALD, and ALAN GERBER, eds. 2004. *American Behavioral Scientists*, 48, 1, (January).

GREENSTEIN, FRED I. 2000. *The Presidential Difference: Leadership and Style from FDR to Clinton*. New York: Free Press.

HAMMOND, THOMAS H., and JANE M. FRASER. 1984. "Studying Presidential Performance in Congress," *Political Methodology*, 10, 211–244.

HILDEBRAND, DAVID K., JAMES D. LAING, and HOWARD ROSENTHAL. 1977. *Analysis of Nominal Data*. Beverly Hills, Calif.: Sage.

HOWELL, WILLIAM G., PATRICK J. WOLF, PAUL E. PETERSON, and DAVID E. CAMPBELL. 2000. "Test-Score Effects of School Vouchers in Dayton, Ohio, New York City, and Washington, D.C.: Evidence from Randomized Field Trials." Paper presented at the annual meetings of the American Political Science Association, Washington, D.C., September 2000.

INTERNATIONAL INSTITUTE FOR STRATEGIC STUDIES. 2003. *The Military Balance*. Oxford: Oxford University Press.

IYENGAR, SHANTO, and DONALD R. KINDER. 1987. *News That Matters*. Chicago: University of Chicago Press.

JACOB, PHILIP E. 1955. "A Multi-dimensional Classification of Atrocity Stories." In Paul F. Lazarsfeld and Morris Rosenberg, eds., *The Language of Social Research*, pp. 54–57. New York: Free Press.

KARSTEN, PETER, and others. 1971. "ROTC, Mylai and the Volunteer Army," *Foreign Policy*, 2 (Spring), 135–161.

KEY, V. O., JR. 1950. *Southern Politics*. New York: Alfred A. Knopf.

KINDER, DONALD R., and THOMAS R. PALFREY, eds. 1993. *Experimental Foundations of Political Science*. Ann Arbor, Mich.: University of Michigan Press.

KING, GARY, ROBERT O. KEOHANE, and SIDNEY VERBA. 1994. *Designing Social Inquiry: Scientific Inference in Qualitative Research*. Princeton, N.J.: Princeton University Press.

KIRK, JEROME, and MARC L. MILLER. 1985. *Reliability and Validity in Qualitative Research*. Beverly Hills, Calif.: Sage.

KMENTA, JAN. 1997. *Elements of Econometrics*, 2nd ed. Ann Arbor: University of Michigan Press.

KNOKE, DAVID, GEORGE W. BOHRNSTET, and ALISSA POTTER MEE. 2002. *Statistics for Social Data Analysis*, 4th ed. Belmont, Calif.: Wadsworth.

KOENIG, LOUIS W. 1968. *The Chief Executive*, rev. ed. New York: Harcourt Brace Jovanovich.

KOESTLER, ARTHUR. 1969. *The Act of Creation*. London: Hutchinson.

KROEBER, A. L., and CLYDE KLUCKHOHN. 1952. *Culture: A Critical Review of Concepts and Definitions*. Cambridge, Mass.: The Museum.

KUHN, THOMAS S. 1962. *The Structure of Scientific Revolutions*. Chicago: University of Chicago Press.

LAVE, CHARLES, and JAMES G. MARCH. 1975. *Introduction to Models in the Social Sciences*. New York: Harper & Row.

LUKES, STEVEN. 1974. *Power: A Radical View*. London: Macmillan.

MASSEY, DOUGLAS S., and KRISTIN E. ESPINOSA. 1997. "What's Driving Mexico–U.S. Migration? A Theoretical, Empirical, and Policy Analysis," *American Journal of Sociology*, 102 (January), 939–999.

MATTHEWS, DONALD R., and JAMES W. PROTHRO. 1963. "Social and Economic Factors and Voter Registration in the South," *American Political Science Review*, 57 (March), 24ff.

MIHAELESCU, MIHAELA. 2004. "*Interethnic Cooperation in Post-Communist Eastern Europe.*" Ph. D. dissertation in political science, University of Minnesota, expected completion 2005.

MOON, J. DONALD 1975. "The Logic of Political Inquiry: A Synthesis of Opposed Perspectives." In Fred Greenstein and Nelson Polsby, eds., *Handbook of Political Science*, Vol. 1, pp. 131–228. Reading, Mass.: Addison-Wesley.

MOSTELLER, FREDERICK. 1968. "Errors," *International Encyclopedia of the Social Sciences*. New York: Macmillan.

NEUSTADT, RICHARD E. 1991. *Presidential Power and the Modern Presidents*. New York: Free Press.

NIEMI, RICHARD G., and KEITH KREHBIEL. 1984. "The Quality of Surveying Responses About Parents and the Family: A Longitudinal Analysis," *Political Methodology*, 10, 193–210.

OLSON, MANCUR. 1965. *The Logic of Collective Action*. Cambridge, Mass.: Harvard University Press.

———. 1982. *The Rise and Decline of Nations*. New Haven, Conn.: Yale University Press.

OPPENHEIM, FELIX. 1975. "The Language of Political Inquiry: Problems of Clarification." In Fred Greenstein and Nelson Polsby, eds., *Handbook of Political Science*, Vol. 1, pp. 283–336. Reading, Mass.: Addison-Wesley.

PITKIN, HANNA. 1967. *The Concept of Representation*. Berkeley, Calif.: University of California Press.

———. 1969. *Representation*. New York: Atherton.

PROTHRO, JAMES W. 1956. "The Nonsense Fight over Scientific Method: A Plea for Peace," *Journal of Politics*, 18, 565–570.

PRZEWORSKI, ADAM. 1975. "Institutionalization of Voting Patterns, or Is Mobilization the Source of Decay?" *American Political Science Review*, 69 (March), 49–67.

———, Michael E. Alvarez, José Antonio Cheibub, and Fernando Longi. 2000. *Democracy and Development: Political Institutions and Well-Being in the World, 1950–1990*. New York: Cambridge University Press.

PUTNAM, ROBERT D. 1993. *Making Democracy Work*. Cambridge, Mass.: Harvard University Press.

REYNOLDS, H. T. 1977. *Analysis of Nominal Data*. Beverly Hills, Calif.: Sage.

ROBINSON, W. S. 1950. "Ecological Correlations and the Behavior of Individuals," *American Sociological Review*, 15 (June), 351–357.

ROETHLISBERGER, F. J., and W. J. DICKSON. 1939. *Management and the Worker*. Cambridge, Mass.: Harvard University Press.

SARTORI, GIOVANNI. 1976. *Parties and Party Systems*. London: Cambridge University Press.

SHIVELY, W. PHILLIPS. 1972. "Party Identification, Party Choice, and Voting Stability: The Weimar Case," *American Political Science Review*, 66 (December), 1203–1225.

SIEGEL, SIDNEY. 1956. *Nonparametric Statistics for the Behavioral Sciences*. New York: McGraw-Hill.

SIMON, JULIAN. 1985. *Basic Research Methods in Social Science*, 3rd ed. New York: Random House.

STOKES, DONALD E. 1969. "Cross-Level Inference as a Game Against Nature." In Joseph L. Bernd, ed., *Mathematical Applications in Political Science*, Vol. 4, pp. 62–83. Charlottesville, Va.: The University of Virginia Press.

STOUFFER, SAMUEL, and others. 1949. *The American Soldier*, Vol. 1. Princeton, N.J.: Princeton University Press.

TARROW, SIDNEY. 1996. "Making Social Science Work Across Space and Time: A Critical Reflection on Robert Putnam's *Making Democracy Work*," *American Political Science Review*, 90 (June), 389–398.

———. 1971. "The Urban–Rural Cleavage in Political Involvement: The Case of France," *American Political Science Review*, 65 (June), 341–357.

TINBERGEN, NIKO. 1968. *Curious Naturalists*. Garden City, N.Y.: Doubleday.

TINGSTEN, HERBERT. 1937. *Political Behavior*. London: Longmans.

TUFTE, EDWARD R. 1968–1969. "Improving Data Analysis in Political Science," *World Politics*, 21, 641–654.

———. 1983. *The Visual Display of Quantitative Information*. Cheshire, Conn.: Graphics Press.

UHLANER, CAROLE JEAN, and KAY LEHMAN SCHLOZMAN. 1986. Candidate Gender and Congressional Campaign Receipts," *Journal of Politics*, 48 (February), 30–50.

VAN DETH, JAN W. 2000. "Interesting but Irrelevant: Social Capital and the Saliency of Politics in Europe," *European Journal of Political Science*, 115–147.

WATSON, JAMES D. 1968. *The Double Helix*. New York: Atheneum.

WEBB, EUGENE J., DONALD T. CAMPBELL, RICHARD D. SCHWARTZ, and LEE SECHRIST. 1966. *Unobtrusive Measures*. Chicago: Rand McNally.

WILSON, THOMAS P. 1971. "Critique of Ordinal Variables." In Hubert M. Blalock, Jr., ed., *Causal Models in the Social Sciences*, pp. 415–431. Chicago: Aldine-Atherton.

WINCH, ROBERT F., and DONALD T. CAMPBELL. 1969. "Proof? No. Evidence? Yes. The Significance of Tests of Significance," *American Sociologist*, 4 (May), 140–143.

ZALLER, JOHN. 1998. "Politicians as Prize Fighters: Electoral Selection and Incumbency Advantage." In John Geer, ed., *Politicians and Party Politics*. Baltimore: Johns Hopkins University Press.

Index